Reading Wittgenstein's
Philosophical Investigations

Reading Wittgenstein's
Philosophical Investigations

A Beginner's Guide

John J. Ross

LEXINGTON BOOKS
A division of

ROWMAN & LITTLEFIELD PUBLISHERS, INC.
Lanham • Boulder • New York • Toronto • Plymouth, UK

Published by Lexington Books
A division of Rowman & Littlefield Publishers, Inc.
A wholly owned subsidary of The Rowman & Littlefield Publishing Group, Inc.
4501 Forbes Boulevard, Suite 200, Lanham, Maryland 20706
http://www.lexingtonbooks.com

Estover Road, Plymouth PL6 7PY, United Kingdom

British Library Cataloguing in Publication Information Available

Library of Congress Cataloging-in-Publication Data

Ross, John J., 1956-
    Reading Wittgenstein's Philosophical investigations : a beginner's guide / John J. Ross.
        p. cm.
    Includes bibliographical references.
    ISBN 978-0-7391-3674-4 (cloth : alk. paper) — ISBN 978-0-7391-3675-1 (pbk. : alk. paper) — ISBN 978-0-7391-3676-8 (ebook)
    1. Wittgenstein, Ludwig, 1889-1951. Philosophische Untersuchungen.
    2. Philosophy. 3. Language and languages—Philosophy. 4. Semantics (Philosophy) I. Title.
    B3376.W563P532715 2009
    192—dc22   2009033029

Printed in the United States of America

For Nina

Contents

Introduction

The Aim of the Present Work

This book is intended as a guide for anyone who faces the daunting task of reading Ludwig Wittgenstein's *Philosophical Investigations*. Hence, it is primarily aimed at philosophy students, but I think it might be used by anyone with an interest in reading the *Investigations*. The key word here is *used*. This book is intended to be a handbook, and so should be read in conjunction with the *Investigations*. It is not meant to be a summary or exposition of the *Investigations* that can be read independently. I will elaborate on this in what follows.

Attempting any sort of commentary on Wittgenstein's *Philosophical Investigations* is bound to be a difficult business. The chief difficulty is the obscurity of the work. Most of the "blame" for this rests with Wittgenstein himself, who took no pains to clarify his work or make understanding it any easier for the reader. A further tendency among commentators that adds greatly to the confusion surrounding the *Investigations* is the attempt at fitting Wittgenstein into a particular philosophical mold. There has been an inclination, particularly early on, but which still exists, to see Wittgenstein simply as an analytic philosopher or a positivist. Many commentators have tried to understand Wittgenstein through the lens of traditional philosophy—whether that tradition is classical, modern, analytic, or even phenomenological. He has also been linked to Freudianism, deconstruction, existentialism, skepticism—the list of "Wittgenstein and . . . " books is long. Clearly, there is an enormous amount of secondary literature on Wittgenstein, and it shows no sign of abating. It has been well said that for someone who generally disdained academic philosophy, Wittgenstein has certainly kept many of us in business.

It is not my purpose here to take issue with any of Wittgenstein's interpreters, but it should be noted that there are a variety of often-conflicting approaches to Wittgenstein and the study of his work. A beginning student trying to survey this secondary literature would understandably get confused, possibly dizzy (or maybe just bored silly).

Obviously, this scholarship on Wittgenstein contains a great deal that is commendable—his work would be impossible to understand without it. And there is undoubtedly a similarity between Wittgenstein and some other thinkers of the twentieth century, particularly those we would call "postmodern." It would be wrong to deny the connection between Wittgenstein and analytic philosophy or positivism. For a while Wittgenstein was certainly taken with Freud, and many have noted the "therapeutic" nature of Wittgenstein's later work. Wittgenstein's admiration for Kierkegaard is well documented, and so a connection with existentialism is certainly not beyond the pale.

Be that as it may, I think many of the approaches that connect Wittgenstein to various "isms" have suffered, in general, from trying to connect Wittgerstein to one or more philosophical theories. Typically, from Wittgenstein's remarks on psychology one thinker tries to see Wittgenstein as advancing or supporting some psychological hypothesis. Based on his remarks on language another makes a connection to a theory of meaning. But I hope I can demonstrate in what follows that this approach to the *Investigations* clouds rather than clarifies the work.

Wittgenstein expressly denies that he is advancing any philosophical theories in the *Investigations*, and I would say that he makes a similar denial in the *Tractatus*. Consider the following quote from the *Tractatus*.[1]

> 6.53 The correct method in philosophy would really be the following: to say nothing except what can be said, i.e., the propositions of natural science—i.e. something that has nothing to do with philosophy—and then, whenever someone else wanted to say something metaphysical, to demonstrate to him that he had failed to give a meaning to certain signs in his propositions. Although this would not be satisfying to the other person—he would not have the feeling that we were teaching him philosophy—this method would be the only correct one.

While reading *Philosophical Investigations* I have often felt like the would-be student of philosophy mentioned above. That the work contains a critique of various philosophical ideas becomes obvious after a while, but I have often wanted to say, "Well, if this is wrong, then tell me what is right. What is the correct theory of concepts, the mind, language, etc.?" Despite vehement protests from the work to the contrary, I kept thinking that there were theories or viewpoints to be found, that it must be a puzzle that I was supposed to figure out, as in one of Wittgenstein's much beloved detective magazines. After all, Wittgenstein said in his preface that he was not trying to "spare anyone the trouble of thinking." But the theories or philosophy that I was hoping to find eluded me, and I began to think that perhaps they always would.

However, once I let go of the notion that the *Investigations* contained certain theories or ideas that were cryptically presented, the work became clearer. Contrary to first impressions, I think Wittgenstein is being very straightforward in the *Investigations*. Wittgenstein maintains (and often corrects) many important themes of the *Tractatus*. In fact, although this statement will require a great deal of elaboration, I would say that the heart of both the *Tractatus* and the *Investigations* is logic. The *Investigations* identifies philosophy with the logical critique of language, and the whole project is aimed at showing the futility of trying to cross the boundaries of language. We invest in many pictures that we think will get us "there." It is only when we give up these pictures that the truth has a chance to emerge. But don't look to Wittgenstein for this truth. Wittgenstein's work is of a logical nature, and so is neither true nor false in that sense. In other words, a truth of logic such as a = b, b = c, therefore a = c does not represent an empirical or scientific truth. A logical truth cannot be proven by real-world facts or evidence in the way, for example, a scientific theory is proven true by an experiment or an observation. So, as we will see, Wittgenstein is not doing science, psychology, anthropology, or anything of the sort. His aim is to focus the lens through which we look at language so that we say clearly only what can be said.

Of course I am sure there are those who would disagree, at least in part, with the above paragraph. Again, it's not the purpose of this book to disagree with or analyze other interpretations of the *Investigations*. This would involve critiquing readings of readings of Wittgenstein, and my purpose here is to stick as close to his text as possible. The intent here is to produce a reading of the *Investigations*, not a detailed commentary on Wittgensteinian scholarship.

I certainly would not claim the last word on the *Investigations*. Thanks to many years of hard work and the hard work of the many scholars who have tackled the *Investigations*, I can admit to experiencing less puzzlement now than when I started reading the book, and this is something I would like to impart to others, particularly students. I think the *Investigations* deserves its reputation as a great, original work of philosophy, and it deserves to be read. Sometimes I get the impression that we are getting to a point in the appreciation of Wittgenstein that is straying from the original texts. Once again, Wittgenstein is mostly to blame for this state of affairs. The *Investigations*, as we will see, aims at a high degree of precision (even that the book has this aim is far from obvious) and so is devoid of ornament of any kind. There is no fluff to cushion the shock of reading the book. Hence we naturally turn to anything else—lecture notes from students, Wittgenstein's own notes, anything to make the work more accessible. This is fine as long as we then read the book. A similar situation occurs in modern art—we find it inaccessible, so we turn to notes made by the artist—preliminary sketches and so on, so that we can understand the work. But this should not be mistaken for viewing the work itself. I'm sure many would agree that an appreciation of the text is of primary importance.

There are, of course, a number of good books commenting on the *Investigations*. There are a few points that I hope will distinguish my approach. First and foremost I aim to make the book accessible to students or beginners—and to do so without distortion. In general, I'd like the *Investigations* to show itself. Wittgenstein has a lot to offer to even the casual student of philosophy, but beginners can be put off by the lack of traditional style, among other things. While I don't intend to rewrite the book by any means—I think the style and order to the book is intentional, even artistic—I do think many readers will benefit from some general background. However, to do proper justice to the "background" of the *Investigations* would require a few separate volumes (at least). My aim is to supply what's needed so that students can get the general drift of what's going on and then can head back to the text at their own pace. If a reader is patient, open-minded, and does not try to force the work into any particular mold, Wittgenstein will answer most of our initial questions ("What is going on?" "What has grammar got to do with anything?" "Is this some bold new psychological theory?" "Why can't you just say what you think?"). Always remember Wittgenstein is a great talker but a terrible listener. My text is meant to help you listen.

I am also aiming at a certain degree of completeness. Because this work is introductory there will be depths and controversies to the *Investigations* that we will not touch. It is not my intention to slide over any important section, but certain parts will get shorter shrift than others. In lieu of dissecting every bit of the text, I have tried to comment on what I think are representative texts from each major section or idea of the *Investigations*. My hope is that this will give the reader enough direction to fly solo. I also want to say a good bit on part II. Part II, I think, is somewhat overlooked and sometimes little understood.

There is a tremendous temptation to try to understand Wittgenstein through biographical information, his conversations with students, and various other of Wittgenstein's published notes and writings. All of this is extremely valuable, and the student may find many or all of these sources helpful. But all of this would take a great deal of sorting and weeding out. Reading *Remarks on the Foundations of Mathematics* or *Philosophical Grammar* would take as much work (or more) than reading the *Investigations*. This approach would throw some light on the *Investigations*, but it would be slow going and would probably decrease the value of the present introduction. In what follows, I have tried to explain the text by sticking to the text.

The only point at which I have deviated from this plan of not relying on outside texts is by including some biographical and cultural information and some remarks on the *Tractatus Logico-Philosophicus*. While I don't want to include a reading of Wittgenstein's earlier classic here, it is clear that, as Wittgenstein instructs in his preface, the *Investigations* should be seen against the backdrop of the *Tractatus*. The *Tractatus* is a wonderful but difficult book that is still the center of controversy. Much of this difficulty has come from a failure to appreciate the intellectual arena in which Wittgenstein was working. Wittgenstein's philosophical work was done mostly in Cambridge, so he is most often associated with analytic philosophy. However, Wittgenstein's intellectual formation took place in Vienna, and I agree with those who think his work must be seen in this light.

Finally, I wish to shed some light on the relationship of the *Investigations* to ethics and aesthetics. Although these areas are somewhat neglected in commentaries on the *Investigations*, I believe they are integral to understanding the work. Just as we have come to realize that the *Tractatus* embodies an ethical and aesthetic stance that has deep connections to Wittgenstein's cultural background, I think we will also see a similar relationship in the *Investigations*. Although Wittgenstein expanded his philosophical horizons as time wore on, he never intellectually wandered too far from his Viennese roots.

BIOGRAPHICAL BACKGROUND

The subject of many biographies, novels, and even films, Ludwig Wittgenstein remains one of the twentieth century's most intriguing figures. While at Cambridge University, first as a student (1911–1914) and later as a professor (1929–1947), Wittgenstein was noted for his austerity. His rooms were sparsely furnished and his attire very plain. As a teacher, Wittgenstein rarely, if ever, took part in the displays of status and privilege that would normally be accorded to faculty members, let alone the Cambridge Professor of Philosophy. However, this outward simplicity belied a very complex personality. And though the lifestyle of Wittgenstein's later years was extremely humble, the ambiance of his youth was anything but.

Born in 1889, Ludwig Wittgenstein was the youngest member of one of Europe's wealthiest families. Ludwig's father, Karl, was a major force in the Austrian steel industry, a self-made multimillionaire. Karl's family was Jewish in his grandfather's time but had converted to Protestantism, probably motivated by anti-Semitism. Anti-Semitism, which was soon to play a dominant role in the emergence of National Socialism, has had a long history in Austria. Because of Ludwig's mother, the children were all baptized Roman Catholics. In contrast to other German-speaking countries, the Catholic Church played a very significant role in Austrian society, particularly among the aristocracy. However, it is unlikely that the Wittgenstein children were baptized to ensure social status. The Wittgenstein's had little involvement with Austrian politics or the titled nobility. When it was offered, Karl refused to have the aristocratic "von" attached to his name. Apparently the family was not overly religious, and Ludwig's own interest in practicing Catholicism lapsed in grade school.

Where the arts were concerned the story was completely different. The Wittgenstein's were passionate about the arts, particularly music. The Wittgenstein children, who were held to very exacting standards by their father, were not expected simply to appreciate music but to be accomplished musicians. Paul Wittgenstein became a well-known concert pianist, and when he lost his right arm during the First World War, he commissioned Ravel to compose a concerto for the left hand. Ludwig's brothers, Hans and Rudolf, also wanted to pursue careers in music. But Karl refused to allow it, insisting instead that they study engineering and join the family business. Both Hans and Rudolf committed suicide.

The grand "Palais Wittgenstein," as the Wittgenstein mansion was known outside the family, was a magnet for the cultural elite of Vienna. Many of the great musicians and artists of the day, such as the composer Brahms and the artist Gustav Klimt, were family friends, and many more greatly benefited from the family's extensive patronage of the arts.

In Wittgenstein's day, Vienna drew those figures that were near the pinnacle of the arts and sciences in modern Europe. Mozart, Beethoven, and Brahms all found their way to Vienna in their time. Vienna was home to Schubert, Gustav Mahler, the Strauss family, and Arnold Schoenberg. Viennese scientists included Ernst Mach, who had an influence on Einstein; Ludwig Boltzmann, the father of statistical mechanics and early champion of the atomic theory; and of course Freud and the founders of psychoanalysis. Literature in Vienna was no less distinguished, with the likes of Robert Musil, Arthur Schnitzler, and Georg Trakl. Otto Wagner and Adolf Loos are lauded as founding figures in modern architecture. In addition to Klimt, the notable artists working in Vienna during Wittgenstein's life included many leaders of the German expressionist movement, such as Oskar Kokoschka, Egon Schiele, and Richard Gerstl. Philosophy in Vienna gave us not only Wittgenstein but also the likes of Moritz Schlick, Rudolf Carnap, and Karl Popper. The majority of the above luminaries worked in Vienna during Wittgenstein's life, and he knew or worked with many of them. We have already noted that Brahms and Klimt were family friends. Wittgenstein met with the architect Adolf Loos on several occasions and worked with Loos's student, Paul Engelmann, on the design and construction of Margaret Wittgenstein's house in Vienna. He likely attended lectures by Boltzmann and was intent on studying with him. Both Carnap and Schlick expressed the depth of Wittgenstein's impact on their work. He left, anonymously, a large portion of his substantial inheritance to Georg Trakl (Rainer Maria Rilke also benefited from Wittgenstein's largesse). If we add the names of Gottlob Frege, Bertrand Russell, and Alfred North Whitehead, founders of modern logic, Wittgenstein's intellectual circle included many of the prime movers in the birth of contemporary arts, sciences, and philosophy.

The list of geniuses associated with Vienna during Wittgenstein's lifetime is indeed long and impressive, but there was also a darker side to Viennese life. Many Viennese youth, particularly from the upper classes and many prominent intellectuals, including the aforementioned Boltzmann, abruptly and often inexplicably ended their lives. Despite the conspicuous wealth and cultural splendor of Vienna, poverty and homelessness were equally obvious, yet often callously ignored by the wealthy. Anti-Semitism was openly practiced. Adolph Hitler was educated and eventually indoctrinated into the tenets of National Socialism in Vienna under the tutelage of the future mayor of Vienna, Karl Lueger, who made anti-Semitism a major plank in his political party (though he was not the first to do so).[2]

To the casual observer, Vienna was a city of magnificent archi-tecture and grand boulevards dotted with cafes and shops offering the finest in luxuries. A growing, wealthy middle class, enjoying the benefits of a booming economy, built lavish homes, spent excessively, and patronized the arts to signify their wealth and taste. But beneath the surface, Viennese society was fractured by the many tensions that were symptomatic of the broader decline and approaching demise of the Austro-Hungarian Empire. The Empire, which would dissolve altogether in 1918 after a crushing defeat in World War I, had been a dominant power in Europe since the Middle Ages. But by the late nineteenth century it had become a loose federation of various na-tionalities—Austrians, Hungarians, Serbs, Croats, Czechs, Slavs, to name a few. Very little united these people other than the recognition of Franz Joseph (1830–1916) as emperor, and they were at odds more often than not. Each group at various times sought independence or at least recognition of its unique culture and language. Language was a particularly contentious issue in the region. Most other nationali-ties resented havin₃ German as an official language and often refused to speak it. Outside of Austria, the conflict over language sometimes grew violent. Within Austria, this situation was partly responsible for generating a strong pro-German movement and a desire among many in the middle-and lower-middle classes for unification with Germany. Sadly, the Austrians would get their wish with the Anschluss at the start of World War II.

While the majority of the bourgeois and the aristocracy in early twentieth-century Vienna partied incessantly, apparently blithely unaware of the disaster on the horizon, a group of young intellectuals started to criticize the pretense and façade that dominated Viennese culture. Clearly the middle class in Vienna was obsessed with art. But for these young intellectuals art had become mere decoration and ornament. The Viennese collected art almost as indifferently as one might collect stamps, coins, or baseball cards. Owning expensive art was little more than a sign of status. The meaning of the art—its depth—particularly any moral significance—escaped them entirely. Another feature of art for the middle class that infuriated these young intellectuals was its use as a means of recalling the past glory of the Austrian Empire. Most bourgeois Viennese were only interested in art that imitated past masters or dwelt on historical themes. This not only stifled artistic innovation but also caused social stagnation by blinding the middle class to the problems of the present.

These young Viennese thinkers brought the darker side of life in Vienna into focus, revealing their society as morally bankrupt. The real passion of the Viennese middle class was business, practiced with a ruthlessness that might make Machiavelli blush. The successful Viennese businessman enjoyed a decadent, hedonistic lifestyle, cloaked with the words and ritual of pious Christianity and a meticulous adherence to the manners of Old World European civilization. Autocratic fathers ruled their families absolutely and favored a repressive educational system where the students were expected, master a demanding curriculum and absorb the Christian morality that the adult population preached but did not practice. Children were allowed to succeed only on their fathers' terms, and failure was not tolerated. Family life could be as difficult for the wives as it was for the children. A man married to advance his business interests and social standing; love was not of primary importance, if regarded at all. The concerns of women were not counted, and women were not expected to have lives outside the home. As for the rest of society, the wealthy, noble, and famous were to be courted and fawned over, while the poor, unfortunate, or unsuccessful were best forgotten. As far as social attitudes were concerned, the Viennese elite openly practiced racism and anti-Semitism. It is a small wonder that Freud's practice, even though it was more or less officially disdained, was so successful in such an environment

Among the Viennese intellectuals who critiqued and tried to alter this state of affairs were Arnold Schoenberg in music, Adolf Loos in architecture, and perhaps most importantly the journalist and social critic Karl Kraus. Kraus's journal *Die Fackel* (The Torch) was a lightning rod for the criticism of the superficiality and what he and many others saw as the moral degeneracy of Viennese society.

A thorough examination of these thinkers would be beyond the scope of this introduction, but we will return to some of their ideas in the conclusion. For now, we can say that they believed that many of their fellow artists had been alienated from the true meaning and purpose of art. They thought that many of their contemporaries had sold out to the middle class's desire for art as mere decoration. Art, they believed, had become all about form and lacked content. Even in architecture, function, logical simplicity, and clarity of design had become lost in layers of clutter that was supposed to be beautiful but was actually useless, signifying nothing. The architect Adolf Loos's seminal article "Ornament and Crime" lamented the fraudulent substitution of decoration for quality in materials and craftsmanship. Loos's own architecture integrated the natural beauty of the materials with a functional simplicity in design and construction. Wittgenstein counted Loos's ideas as one of his principle influences.

In general, these thinkers held that art should reject ornamentation and style, and the artist of every discipline should strive for purity. Above all, the purpose of art should be moral and reveal the character of the artist, meaning that only a person of integrity can create true art. For Kraus this was most evident in language. For Kraus, many of the horrors of the modern age were caused by the corruption of language. It was Kraus's belief that in its pure state certain evils cannot be spoken in German. An extraordinary statement to be sure, but one about which Kraus was passionate. He spent his life searching to purify the German language. Kraus was fond of saying, "I cannot get myself to accept that a whole sentence can ever come from half a man." For Kraus, language revealed the person, and he saw no distinction between ethics and aesthetics. The artist who simply manipulated a medium merely for money, style, or conformity to a particular school was amoral at least, and therefore usually the subject of a scathing, often satirical, polemic in *Die Fackel*. Kraus believed an artist lacking a moral dimension was worthy only of contempt. Kraus revered authors such as Kierkegaard and Tolstoy whose intensely personal moral dilemmas became the subject of their works and whose lives reflected simplicity and lack of pretense. As is the case with his friend Loos, Kraus had huge impact on Wittgenstein. Wittgenstein was rarely without the latest edition of *Die Fackel*. He even had it delivered to him while in seclusion in Norway in 1913. Probably because of Kraus's influence, Wittgenstein became an avid reader of both Kierkegaard and Tolstoy. He claimed that reading Tolstoy's *The Gospel in Brief* saved his life. Again we will return to these ideas in depth in the conclusion.

Wittgenstein's plans to study physics with Ludwig Boltzmann were thwarted by Boltzmann's suicide in 1906. Possibly trying to accede to his father's wishes, but also through his own early inclination, Wittgenstein registered as a research student in engineering, specializing in aeronautics at the University of Manchester in 1908. At some point, apparently coinciding with reading Russell's *Principles of Mathematics*, published in 1903, Wittgenstein became interested in logic and the foundations of mathematics. After reading Russell's work, Wittgenstein sought out and had some discussions on logic with the brilliant and original German logician Gottlob Frege. Frege was one of the founders of modern logic, and he spent most of his career in an attempt at proving that mathematics was a branch of logic, a view Wittgenstein shared. Frege's command of the science of logic greatly impressed Wittgenstein during these meetings, but apparently Frege was more puzzled by Wittgenstein than anything else. Wittgenstein followed Frege's advice and went to Cambridge to study with Bertrand Russell.

At the turn of the twentieth century, Russell and his colleague G. E. Moore started a philosophical revolution at Cambridge that came to be known as analytic philosophy. The philosophy of the period had been dominated by German idealism, which Russell and Moore believed had needlessly confused philosophers by blurring issues with layers of convoluted idealist metaphysics. Russell and Moore relied on logic and a realist theory of knowledge to banish confusion from philosophical concepts, and therefore, they believed, to actually solve the philosophical problems that had plagued mankind for over two thousand years. In much the same way, the logical positivists, such as Moritz Schlick and Rudolf Carnap of the so-called Vienna Circle, turned to logical analysis and empiricism in order to purge scientific discourse of metaphysical speculation.

Wittgenstein began attending Russell's lectures in 1911, and then registered formally as a student in 1912. Though he was soon impressed with Wittgenstein's genius, Russell at first did not know what to make of this intense young man who would discuss logic and mathematics incessantly, sometimes long into the night. It was not long before Russell began to think of Wittgenstein first as a protégé, then as a colleague, friend, and collaborator. However, Russell and Wittgenstein eventually came to a parting of the ways. Russell was a committed philosopher, but unlike Wittgenstein it was not his ruling passion. Russell told of one late-night philosophy discussion during which Wittgenstein nervously and silently paced the floor. "Are you thinking about logic or your sins?" asked Russell. "Both," replied Wittgenstein. I don't think Russell appreciated the depth of that remark, but I believe Wittgenstein was absolutely serious. Indeed, for Wittgenstein, as a true Krausian, philosophy required an intensely personal, moral commitment.

Although he was the son of a wealthy aristocrat and could have avoided active military service, Wittgenstein enlisted in the Austrian army at the outbreak of World War I in the summer of 1914. He had already begun his first great work, the *Tractatus Logico-Philosophicus*, and he continued to work on the book throughout the war, even carrying the manuscript with him in his knapsack when he was finally transferred to the front, after repeated requests. At the end of the war, despite his wealth, connections, and status, Wittgenstein had no success in getting the book published. Thanks to the intervention of Russell, the book was finally published, first in German and then in an English translation with a German parallel text in 1922. Wittgenstein believed he had solved the problems of philosophy once and for all, so he promptly gave it up. He also gave away the immense fortune he had inherited at the death of his father and settled into a career as a grade school teacher in a remote Austrian village.

However, Wittgenstein eventually realized that his temperament and background left him ill-suited to the simple country life. The *Tractatus* came to be considered a philosophical classic, and intellectuals from Cambridge and Austria started to seek him out. Apparently he came to believe that he had not quite settled all the problems of philosophy. He was lured back to Cambridge in 1929. As it turned out he had completed the requirements for a PhD, except for a doctoral dissertation. He submitted the *Tractatus*. Moore and Russell conducted a brief oral examination. Wittgenstein brought the proceedings to a close by clapping each on the shoulder, saying "Don't worry, I know you'll never understand it." Moore's examiners report stated: "It is my personal opinion that Mr. Wittgenstein's thesis is a work of Genius; but, be that as it may it is certainly well up to the standard required for the Cambridge degree of Doctor of Philosophy." Soon Wittgenstein would begin his career as a teacher and eventually become the Cambridge Professor of Philosophy, which he would hold until his retirement in 1947. It was during this second tour at Cambridge that Wittgenstein developed the ideas that would become *Philosophical Investigations*.[3]

NOTES

1. All quotes from the *Tractatus* are from:
Ludwig Wittgenstein, *Tractatus Logico-Philosophicus*, trans. D. F. Pears and B. F. McGuinness (New York: Routledge and Kegan Paul, 1974). Each individual section of the *Tractatus*, hereafter TLP, has its unique identifying number. All quotes are referenced by this number.
All quotes from *Philosophical Investigations* are from:
Ludwig Wittgenstein, *Philosophical Investigations*, eds. Rush Rhees and G. E. M. Anscombe, trans. G. E. M. Anscombe (Oxford: Blackwell Publishers, 2001). This edition of *Philosophical Investigations*, hereafter PI, was issued as a fiftieth anniversary commemoration and includes the final revision of Ms. Anscombe's translation. For references to part I of the *Investigations* this presents no problem, since each section has its own unique number. References to part II present a slight problem because we have to go by page number and the pagination in this edition differs from the previous editions. To solve this difficulty I have cross-referenced the earlier edition:
Ludwig Wittgenstein, *Philosophical Investigations*, eds. Rush Rhees and G. E. M. Anscombe, trans. G. E. M. Anscombe (Englewood Cliffs, NJ: Prentice Hall, 1973).

References to page numbers have a "p." (the "e" following the page number refers to the English translation, otherwise the number in a reference refers to an individual remark in part I.

2. The original name of the party was the Christian Social Association. When he took control of the party, Hitler styled it National Socialism. An excellent study of the topic is by Brigitte Hamann, *Hitler's Vienna: A Dictator's Apprenticeship* (Oxford University Press, 1999).

3. Several good biographies of Wittgenstein exist. Recommended are:

Ray Monk, *Ludwig Wittgenstein: The Duty of Genius* (New York: The Free Press, 1990).

Brian McGuinness, *Young Ludwig: Wittgenstein's Life 1889–1921* (Oxford University Press, 2005).

Norman Malcolm and G. H. von Wright, *Ludwig Wittgenstein: A Memoir with a Biographical Sketch* (Oxford: Clarendon Press, 2001).

Paul Engelmann, *Letters from Ludwig Wittgenstein with a Memoir*, ed. B. F. Mcguinness, trans. L. Furtmuller (New York: Horizon Press, 1968).

O. K. Bouwsma, *Wittgenstein: Conversations 1949-1951*, eds. J. L. Craft and Ronald E. Hustwit (Indianapolis: Hackett Publishing Co., 1986). Not a biography but a good insight into Wittgenstein's personality and certain ideas that occupied him during the last years of his life.

Also not strictly a biography but an excellent guide to the world in which Wittgenstein grew up:

Allan Janik and Stephen Toulmin, *Wittgenstein's Vienna* (New York: Touchstone, 1973).

❶

Building Blocks

What is it that makes the *Investigations* an especially tricky book? One glaring and immediate difficulty is the book looks like a collection of disconnected paragraphs, perhaps a mere collection of aphorisms or sayings. Further, the paragraphs seem to be pulled out of thin air. They begin with a quote (in Latin no less) from Augustine's *Confessions* and then seem to ramble over various topics, sometimes with abrupt breaks into some new idea, often retracing previous thoughts. Then it all seems to stop in the middle of nowhere. All along one waits patiently (sometimes desperately) for Wittgenstein to make a point, but by the end very often we feel it hasn't happened.

Many explanations have been offered for this state of affairs. Critics have attributed the book's form to the author's mental impairment, to his dyslexia, sexual orientation, or his use of a secret code. Wittgenstein's own explanation from the preface may strike the reader as at least overmodest.

> After several unsuccessful attempts to weld my results together into . . . a whole, I realized that I should never succeed. The best that I could ever write would never be more than philosophical remarks; my thoughts were soon crippled if I tried to force them on in any single direction against their natural inclination. And this was, of course, connected with the very nature of the investigation. For this compels us to travel over a wide field of thought criss-cross in every direction. The philosophical remarks in this book are, as it were, a number of sketches of landscapes which were made in the course of these long and involved journeyings.
>
> The same or almost the same points were always being approached afresh from different directions, and new sketches made. Very many

of these were badly drawn or uncharacteristic, marked by all the defects of a weak draughtsman. And when they were rejected a number
of tolerable ones were left, which now had to be arranged and sometimes cut down, so that if you looked at them you could get a picture
of the landscape. Thus this book is really only an album.[1]

On the surface Wittgenstein seems to simply be issuing a dis-
claimer: "I tried to turn out a book that isn't a mess, but this is the
best that I could do." However, I think there is a little more to it. In
order to understand Wittgenstein's method of composition, the comparisons he makes here with sketching, drafting, and so on should not
be overlooked. Art, especially music, was central to Wittgenstein's
life. Wittgenstein grew up in a very artistic household and was himself
a talented musician as well as—at various times—a sculptor and an
architect. Given this background, I think it would be rash to assume
Wittgenstein had no literary aspirations for his work and so was happy
to publish a haphazard collection of thoughts. On one level I do think
Wittgenstein is serious here—in the sense that he is being honest and
to the point. The *Investigations* is in many ways more like a collection
of research than a traditional work of philosophy. His first period at
Cambridge produced the *Tractatus*. During his second stint at Cambridge, Wittgenstein developed a new method of inquiry that he used
to investigate many of the same philosophical topics that captured his
imagination during the *Tractatus* period. He worked diligently, making voluminous notes.
  Looking at the above passage from the preface to the *Investigations*, I think he is saying that tried to take these notes and work them
into a systematic presentation but found that a systematic philosophical work was contrary to his results. As we probe the *Investigations*, I
think we will see why this is the case.
  Instead of trying to create a systematic philosophical treatment,
Wittgenstein tried a novel approach, but this approach is guided by
a particular aesthetic. The *Tractatus* has a very precise, rigid, logical
structure. There is no ornamentation or flourish to the work, and
we can certainly see that this is in keeping with the main theme
of the work—whatever can be said can be said clearly, or not at all.
This approach has much in common with the modern aesthetic of
Wittgenstein's architectural mentor, Adolf Loos, and is evident in
Wittgenstein's own work as an architect.[2]
  However—and this is a point we will have to amplify in what follows—Wittgenstein's ideas have undergone some modification by the
time of his second sojourn at Cambridge. The need for logical purity

still guides his work, but logic no longer appears as a rigid structural background for language and thought. Rather, he sees logic, language, and meaning as more "fluid"—part and parcel of the tangled weave of human life.

The apparent "formlessness" of the *Investigations* might dissipate if we look at it in terms of modern art or music. Imagine a composer having a grand idea, and he works out several themes to express the various parts of this idea. These individual musical passages are distinct, yet related to the work as whole. These relationships do not form a smooth progression because it is not the composer's idea to build one theme on another. Rather, the musical passages are related in a variety of ways. Sometimes the composer will announce a theme and then abruptly move off into something similar, yet because of the uniqueness of the new theme, he gives it its own key. He may return to the original theme, but he wants to express it in a new light, perhaps because of something "discovered" in a related theme, so he inverts the passage or modulates the key. The result is more like a Bach fugue or perhaps Mussorgsky's *Pictures at an Exhibition* than a Mozart symphony. We might also think of a work of art such as Picasso's *Guernica*, which apparently was supposed to be viewed from right to left as people entered the exhibition hall.

A comparison with architecture may also be instructive. An architect may try to make a house livable and intimate. He may also try to accomplish many other effects, such as making the space interesting or making the occupants feel secure. The architect has many "themes" as well, but he has only the arrangement of space and materials to work with. One room may have many uses, and when approached from different angles can seem to be very different, yet all the uses intersect to make a whole. For example, the library is usually used for reading, so the light must be good; hence large windows, which could also accommodate a view for meditating, might be in order. The walls should be for bookcases, of course, and a good height for lots of books, but not so high as to detract from the coziness of the room—should the scholar need a nap after reading several pages of Wittgenstein. To create a contemplative mood, rugs and some sort of acoustic tile, perhaps, would be preferred for absorbing sound, rather than, say, marble and terracotta. Thus, the same room can be seen from many points of view and incorporate an array of different materials, giving rise to many complexities that are resolved by the skillful architect into a whole.

The comparisons with art and architecture are only meant to be illuminating and suggestive. Wittgenstein never announces that his work ought to be seen as literary art. But again, it doesn't follow that we should assume he had no literary aspirations for his work. On the contrary, the place that art had in his life, his various artistic endeavors in other fields, the care he took with his work, and its thoroughly modern character, suggest otherwise. We will examine this topic to a greater degree in what follows. For now, although the temptation to do so is understandable, I only want to caution the reader against looking at the *Investigations* as a badly drawn pastiche. The structure of the book is far from "standard."

In many ways the structure of the *Investigations* mirrors its theme: language. Wittgenstein tells us that "Philosophy is a battle against the bewitchment of our intelligence by the means of language."[3] Although his ideas underwent considerable development over the course of his life, Wittgenstein claimed, from the period of the *Tractatus* onward, that the source of the problems of philosophy and their solution lay in language. What Wittgenstein means by "language" is a large part of the *Investigations*, and elucidating this idea will occupy an equally large part of our study. But for right now I think it is helpful to realize that for Wittgenstein "language" means our words, what words we choose, how and when and why we choose them—our sentences, our paragraphs, our descriptions, etc. Although care must be taken here, and a great deal of elucidation is necessary on this point: according to Wittgenstein, we should not confuse "language" with ideas, or the essence of language, the accompaniments of language, or even the structure of language. Again, this is a major them of the *Investigations*. "Language" is just what we speak and write.

It only takes a little reflection to see that language, what we ordinarily speak and write, is extremely messy. It is jumbled, tangled, flexible, twisted, and twistable, and as such it is a source of amazement, humor, and of course artistic expression. Clearly poetry very often trades on the inherent ambiguities of language. A good deal of modern poetry seems to focus on how far we can stretch language in the service of art. Reading Joyce or Faulkner shows that this idea is important to modern prose as well. In literature this feature of language is expressive. In music and painting, stretching and bending harmony or color and line beyond traditional parameters allows the artist to reach new heights. But for Wittgenstein, in philosophy, the inherent flexibility of language is a source of error.

Hence Wittgenstein addresses philosophical problems by dealing with them at what he sees as their source: the misuse of language. This is not to say that Wittgenstein's *Investigations* consist of reading philosophical works and declaring, e.g., "Ah ha, Descartes has used the word *soul* incorrectly!" Wittgenstein goes deeper than that in showing us that we misunderstand how language functions. Because we fail to understand the workings of language, we fail to understand its limits, or as we shall see its logic—what it can and can't do—and so we fall into error.

Anyone who struggles long enough with Wittgenstein's text will see him returning to the above point over and over again. But right away we usually hit a major stumbling block in interpreting the text. As I mentioned earlier, we often think that Wittgenstein is defending a theory of language that will deal effectively with its misuse. But, really, this is not the case. The job of a scientific theory is generally to explain some fact of nature, and this is why the term *logical theory* is something of a misnomer. Unlike a theory of gravity that tells us why objects are attracted to one another, logic doesn't really "explain" anything in the sense of providing causes or reasons for an effect. Logic, as Wittgenstein sees it, when it is useful, is a tool for analysis and description. If there is a logic to language, as we will see, we may only analyze and describe that logic. In this sense Wittgenstein's work in the *Investigations* is logical—merely descriptive, not explanatory. Logic does not tell us why something is so—as Freud's theory of the unconscious attempts to "explain" nervous disorders—it only tells us that it is so. Thus in the *Investigations*, Wittgenstein tries to display, not explain, the workings of language. Wittgenstein's response to a theory of the operation of language is most often—"Well, let us see what language would actually look like if we accept this as the way language actually operates." As students of philosophy, we are constantly looking for explanation and theory, and Wittgenstein responds with "Well, look at it this way. Look at the theory in operation. If it is wrong it will fail." This approach on the surface seems counterproductive, but we will see that this is the only way to show or display the problem of language and its solution.

Historically, when one philosopher thinks another is wrong about something, the response is usually to critique the idea and provide a better one. Thus, Aristotle thinks Plato's theory of ideas is wrong. He points this out and offers an alternate theory of ideas. But what if the whole enterprise is misguided? Let us for the sake of argument say that it is impossible (for whatever reason) for *any* theory of ideas to be correct. If this were true then the proliferation of theories on this topic would be pointless. The only way to help the situation would be to show those seeking the best theory of ideas that their search is in vain.

Point of view and perspective often dictate an approach to a problem. Consider the difficulty that we would encounter trying to convince anyone that the earth is round, using ordinary observation. Because of our particular position in relation to the earth, it would be extremely difficult to prove to anyone that the earth is not flat. However, you could put the doubting Thomas in a boat and tell him to keep sailing east. For the entire journey he could keep affirming that the world is flat—until he got back to where he started, at which point he would have to cede the argument.

Trying to understand the workings of language leaves us in a similar predicament. You cannot use language to dissect and analyze language in order to search for its ultimate foundations. Any theory of language is expressed in a language, and so you go around in circles. This point might seem difficult at first, but it is important for understanding the *Investigations*. In our hypothetical situation above, since any observation will produce the same conclusion—"the world is flat"—we cannot solve our problem with more of the same type of observation. We have to try something else. If you were reading a book and thought the author made some sort of mistake, you couldn't check this out by buying another copy of the same book. If you wanted to find out how your television worked you wouldn't be able to do so by just simply watching more television. You would have to buy a book on the subject, look at the schematics, take it apart, or something of that nature. It seems as if we should be able to do the same thing with language. After all, we simply want to discover the components of language, the nuts and bolts, just as we would with anything else. However, Wittgenstein wants us to realize that language presents us with a unique challenge. Think for a moment about trying to give the final or ultimate definition of a word. We might define a circle as a geometric figure in which every point on the circumference is equidistant from the midpoint. But each of those words can be defined, and so we would have an additional twelve definitions. And each of those definitions could spawn more definitions, and so on. So instead of an analysis that finds some sort of bedrock or ultimate description, we have gone in the opposite direction and greatly multiplied the object of our inquiry, failing to produce the desired result of exactly defining the word. The reason is simple: talking about language begets more language. Any sentence that purports to analyze or describe language can itself be analyzed or described. Now of course we might want to argue that the point is not the language—the point is the ideas on which the language is founded. Unfortunately, this approach will also fail to solve our problem. Although this case will have to be made more completely in what follows, Wittgenstein wants to show us that it is essentially impossible to separate thought and language. Any idea or thought, certainly one that supposedly is foundational for language, that has no expression in language, is certainly useless and might as well be nonexistent. For all practical purposes language and thought are the same—we think in language. So it would be incorrect to say that we can use language to somehow get to those ideas that are at the base of language. Thus, if language has failed you because of its flexible nature and it has led you into error, the best someone can do is show you how to follow out the thread and show you where the cloth unravels. This is what Wittgenstein does in the *Investigations*.

Wittgenstein thinks most philosophical problems are generated in the following way. In essence, the philosopher often "borrows" words that have a clear meaning in their original context and then transports them to a context where they work less well—or perhaps not at all. For example, we often say: "I see what you are talking about." Taken literally—restricting the meaning of *see* to something done with the eyes—this statement is nonsense. But *see* is a very elastic word, and we understand its meaning in this context. The problem arises when we think that *see* has some sort of special, independent meaning of its own that it brings with it wherever it is moved. If we took the above idea as literally true—that all uses of the word *see* must have a visual reference—then perhaps a philosopher might explain the statement "I see your point" as meaning "seeing with the mind's eye." Now, again, this is all right as long as we don't think of "the minds eye" as a theoretical entity. But, Wittgenstein tells us, this is just what happens in philosophy with this very word. Philosophers often seem to think that the word *seeing* must always have the same basic meaning—that of some sort of visual experience—and then they construe "mental" seeing on the model of physical seeing. We say something like: "The mind 'sees' the truth." If we take this statement literally, then of course this "mental seeing" is something odd, both like and unlike seeing with the eyes, and so "mental seeing" requires a theory to explain it. And so beginning with an assumption about the word *see* we set off on a theoretical quest, but with no hope of getting back to where we started. No amount of theorizing can explain "mental seeing" because there is no such thing. The theoretical entity "mental seeing" is a chimera conjured out of the labyrinth of language. Chasing it is like being the doubting Thomas in the boat mentioned above, blissfully sailing along insisting the world is flat. The only hope is to get back to where we started—to bring the word *see* back to its original home.

So the solution to the problem lies in showing that there is no actual "mental" seeing. Proving this is not done for Wittgenstein empirically, and rightly so. The idea of "mental seeing" or the "mind's eye" in the above paragraph did not arise as the result of scientific investigation, and so it is not to be dispelled scientifically, through experiment, etc. This idea of seeing, Wittgenstein tells us, was just a "dream of language." We may of course talk about "understanding" in terms of seeing—"I see your idea." The problem is that the word *see* in this context doesn't carry the implications of physical seeing. It was the philosopher that brought along this excess baggage and dropped it where it didn't belong. A correct analysis of "understanding," or comparing understanding to actual seeing, should convince us that a concept of understanding constructed in visual terms is okay as long as we don't take it as indicating a theoretical object—as something that requires scientific or empirical investigation. So, just what is the correct "theory" of understanding? What is Wittgenstein's epistemology? Wittgenstein is not going to answer that question, and trying to pull an answer to that question out of the text is only going to lead to further misunderstanding. However, if you have a picture of understanding that rests on a misunderstanding of language, then Wittgenstein just wants you to let that picture go.

Demonstrated here is one of Wittgenstein's key points that bears remembering when reading the *Investigations*. To try to analyze, understand, augment, or otherwise tinker with an idea or concept apart from its application or actual employment will probably result in a useless idea or concept.

Of course, this is just an overview. The book considers many other concepts besides understanding. But I think if you keep the above ideas in mind, then understanding the work is hopefully a little easier.

NOTES

1. PI ix.
2. Cf. Bernard Leitner, *The Wittgenstein House* (New York: Princeton Architectural Press, 2000); see also Engelmann, 1968.
3. PI 109.

The Old Way of Thinking

The Problems of the *Tractatus* and the Search for Solutions

In his preface Wittgenstein tells us that the *Investigations* is perhaps better understood when compared to his "old way of thinking." That old way of thinking refers to the *Tractatus Logico-Philosophicus*. By this time Wittgenstein is convinced that the *Tractatus* contains "grave errors." As is usual with Wittgenstein, the reader's hope for something more specific is in vain. What are the errors? What about the *Tractatus*, if anything, is correct? An exhaustive answer to these questions is well beyond the scope of this book. We will, however, examine a number of points common to both books with the aim of throwing some light on the *Investigations*.

Throughout his career, Wittgenstein's constant focus was language. The *Tractatus* view of language had, for Wittgenstein, developed out of very deep cultural and philosophical roots. We have already spoken about this background, and from that discussion hopefully we can see some of the ethical, aesthetic, and philosophical requirements that stimulated Wittgenstein's search for logical purity. Purity in logic and thought and purity of expression went hand in hand for Wittgenstein. To achieve this purity of language and so of thought, the *Tractatus* attempts to uncover the uncluttered, logical essence of language.

Meaning, according to the *Tractatus*, is possible because language's logical structure corresponds to or mirrors the structure of the world. Roughly put, when language—or the language user—sidesteps or circumvents this correspondence relationship the result is something other than sense. What exactly Wittgenstein means by "the world" is not clear or, rather, it may have been clear to Wittgenstein, but scholars disagree. Since he says in the *Tractatus*[1] that the world is a collection of facts, not things, it is very possible that when he is speaking of the world he is speaking of what we commonly call our experience. This idea, of course, raises many knotty philosophical questions about the relationship between experience and objective or independent reality. Although this issue is extremely important and ultimately has bearing on the *Investigations*, because of its complexity, I would like to leave it aside for now.

Let us, for the sake of the discussion, stay as close as possible to the text of the *Tractatus* and think of the world as a collection of facts or what we may call the facts of experience. These "facts" are complex and so are analyzable—they can be broken down into their basic components, which Wittgenstein calls "objects." Since these "objects" are the basic components of all description, they are indescribable. Although the analogy lacks precision, for the sake of a rough understanding we might compare Wittgenstein's "objects" to Locke's "simple ideas," Hume's "simple impressions," Leibniz's "monads," Whitehead's "actual entities," Moore's "sense data," etc. In the *Investigations*, Wittgenstein compares his "objects" of the *Tractatus* to Russell's "simples." This comparison, as we might expect, is the most precise, but for our purposes the other ideas are not too far off.

Objects, then, are the utterly simple components of our experience or "the world." Since description is complex, objects cannot be described; they can only be named or labeled. Here we encounter the Tractarian "theory" of meaning. In Wittgenstein's early thought, objects can form a variety of (perhaps infinite) possible combinations with each other. He calls the combinations they do form at a given moment "states of affairs." It is these "states of affairs" that we wish to describe, talk about, know about, etc. We do this through propositions, e.g., "The book is on the table." Hence, a meaningful proposition is an arrangement of names of objects that mirrors or pictures an actual or at least possible arrangement of objects or state of affairs you want to describe. This idea is sometimes called the "picture theory" of meaning. The proposition, through an arrangement of names, pictures reality in the way that a model or drawing could describe an event that had happened previously, or the way an engineer's drawing "describes" a machine.[2]

We will have to return to other relevant ideas in the *Tractatus*. But this basic discussion will suffice for an examination of the opening of the *Investigations*—roughly the first sixty-five paragraphs.

We have seen that a major focus of the *Investigations* is the distinction between how we believe language functions and how it actually functions. The initial linguistic misconception that Wittgenstein examines is his idea which was at the heart of his *Tractatus*: words have meaning through reference to an object—or words have meaning by naming something, and the meaning of a word is the object for which it stands. Apparently Wittgenstein thinks this is a philosophical theory with a long pedigree. He wants to demonstrate this fact by opening the *Investigations* with a quote from Augustine's *Confessions*—in Latin. In the quoted section Augustine describes learning language through finding out the names of things, which seems to support Wittgenstein's claim that "meaning as naming objects" has been a dominant theory of meaning in philosophy. If this is actually Wittgenstein's view, then I think he is somewhat mistaken here. The very strict nominalism to which he is apparently referring—all words act primarily as labels for objects—is actually quite rare. Roscelin (c. AD 1000) perhaps held it, and perhaps so did the philosopher Cratylus of the Platonic dialogue of the same name. This idea has never survived too much criticism. Nouns might be seen as referring to objects, but conjunctions, verbs, and articles are difficult to press into such service. Although Wittgenstein made use of the idea that meaningful words are names in the *Tractatus*, as we saw above, his theory is much more sophisticated. Conjunctions and so on are handled as part of logic, which acquires meaning by being rule-governed. Clearly, the more common reference theories in philosophy acknowledge that there is more to meaning than naming and hold that words function as signs or refer to things by way of ideas or would make a distinction between the meaning of a word and what the word refers to. (In fairness to Augustine, he also probably held one of these more sophisticated theories of language.) It is also more precise to say Wittgenstein's critique here at the beginning of the *Investigations* is not intended to focus on any particular reference theory. More to the point, he wants to analyze the general notion that words acquire meaning by naming objects, an idea that usually plays at least some role in most reference theories of language. Certainly the section of Augustine's *Confessions* that Wittgenstein quotes gives a fairly common account of the theory that Wittgenstein wants to critique, whether it is the whole of the theory or a part, i.e., people learn language by learning to name objects, and the meaning of words consists in this relationship.

For Wittgenstein in the *Investigations*, words sometimes function as names, but this is an inadequate or primitive description of meaning. One of the aims of the beginning of the *Investigations* is to show that meaning as reference is a simplistic version of the way language operates.

In the opening section of the *Investigations*, Wittgenstein makes a sustained effort at "deconstructing" the reference theory of language, and we are introduced to many of Wittgenstein's analytical tools, such as an analysis of grammar, meaning as use, language games, and forms of life—all of which we will be addressing shortly. But before we begin I would like to caution the reader on a particular point. When one begins reading the *Investigations* it often seems as if Wittgenstein is engaged in anthropology, psychology, or presenting a social theory of language. Although what Wittgenstein has to say would be of enormous use in many of these fields, his investigation is primarily a logical one.

That Wittgenstein's investigation is logical may not be readily apparent, and because of its complexity we will have to develop this idea over time. For right now we should note that Wittgenstein in the *Tractatus* thought of logic as formal, symbolic logic and that this formal structure is the way to describe the logic of language. Or perhaps more precisely we should say that symbolic logic was *the* logic and all logical disciplines—math, language, etc., must be described by it. In the *Tractatus* Wittgenstein held that symbolic logic, once properly understood, was the only instrument that had the necessary clarity and rigor to uncover the essence of language and so purge language and therefore thought of the damage done by bad philosophizing. In the *Investigations*, however, the logic of language is not revealed by an external formal structure. Rather, sentences on their own are meaningful or not, and so language must have its own internal logic—what Wittgenstein terms its *grammar*. Through analysis, the logic of language can be made to reveal itself. So, when Wittgenstein talks about things like language games, meaning as use, forms of life, and so on, he is addressing the logic of language. Again, it may appear as if Wittgenstein is expounding an anthropological theory, but actually he is describing the operation of language and the means to analyze it.

Wittgenstein's general procedure in the opening of the *Investigations* is something like the following: "let us imagine a group of people doing x" and then he describes a "primitive" society. Again, though it might appear that he is talking about the evolution of language, he is in fact applying a particular picture of how language functions and trying to see where it leads. Very often we see it leads nowhere. So, for example, he first uses the technique above to examine the idea that words function as names. Rather than leaving the idea in the abstract, Wittgenstein puts it into practice. For example, let us imagine a group of people whose language consists of names. Let us look at their activities—their daily lives—and see if we recognize these people and what they are doing. Wittgenstein wants us to imagine these language users doing very ordinary things—building, shopping and so forth—and then to compare these activities to our lives and our language. We will see that our actual employment of language and our lives are vastly more complex. This point is significant. In a very real sense misunderstanding our language and how it operates can ultimately give us a false picture of ourselves and our society. Wittgenstein in the *Investigations*, as he did in the *Tractatus*, sees the mission of the philosopher as clearing away these misconceptions, allowing the truth to emerge.

In Wittgenstein's view, it is also crucial to realize that apart from their actual employment, words have no meaning, or at least not the meaning that we think they do. Much of the *Investigations* is dedicated to understanding this fact in its various guises. Again it is important to note that Wittgenstein in the *Investigations* is making a logical point that is similar to one made in the *Tractatus*. Both texts agree that our ability to make sense is dictated by the logic of language. However, in the *Tractatus*, that logic ultimately is a formal structure independent of language. In the *Investigations* the logic of language, the source of meaning, is found only in the use we make of words. Time and again philosophers have tried to explain meaning by something other than use—metaphysics, psychology, reference—even logic. But although Wittgenstein was an ardent practitioner of this last idea in the *Tractatus*, he came to see that one can't use language to get around itself—that is, to show what is behind language or what supports it. He came to believe that this enterprise would be redundant, and so theories of the "true" way language functions apart from how it is actually used are doomed to failure. The philosopher can only describe the workings of language, not explain or dictate. He or she describes language by describing its actual employment. Hence, for Wittgenstein, the philosopher is generally circumvented in his or her attempts to give meaning to grand philosophical abstractions. Since, as Wittgenstein will show, language, in order to be meaningful, must be a shared activity, no one individual can "impose" a particular meaning on a word. So I think we will see, for example, that philosophical theories employing words like *good, true, being*, etc., are spun in abstraction from real life and the actual employment of these words necessarily turn up empty. For Wittgenstein the arena of the philosopher is the logic of language. But here again we must use caution and avoid the temptation to think we are thereby entering into a metaphysical, psychological, or scientific arena. For Wittgenstein, logic itself says nothing—on its own logic makes no claims. The same can be said for the logic of language. When language is used it is meaningful. To talk about the workings of language is to talk about the grammar of language—nothing more.

It may be objected that Wittgenstein has a theory that there is no theory of language. But I don't think this is quite correct. Rather, Wittgenstein engages in no scientific or theoretical activity whatsoever. He offers no explanations, causes, or predictions—only a method by which to examine language and weed out false accounts of the way language works. Again his approach focuses on the logic of language, and logic is neither true nor false. This point is very important, and it may seem paradoxical because logic books are full of things like "truth tables" and statements like "if the premises are true the conclusion must be true." However, propositions of logic, e.g., "If P then Q," make no claim that can be tested empirically. This proposition says only that *if* P happens to be the case *then* Q is also the case. It does not say that P exists. In fact P may be anything at all—real or not. So we can see that logic, which is devoid of content, is neither true nor false. Although we might encounter the phrase "logical theory," this should be seen as quite different from, say, the theory of relativity, which offers predictions that can be tested by observation. Indeed, Wittgenstein, even in his earliest writings, held that theorizing had no place in logic.[3]

Let us turn to an examination of some of Wittgenstein's analytical tools. When we speak of the logic of language as Wittgenstein sees it in the *Investigations*, a crucial idea found in the opening of the *Investigations* is that of "language games." This idea is difficult and much debated. I think the most significant misconception is that with this notion Wittgenstein is presenting a theory of language. Again, this would run counter to several clear statements to the contrary in the *Investigations*.[4] Rather than a theoretical entity central to, say, a social or evolutionary theory of language, I think the idea of "language games" can more fruitfully be seen as an analytical tool that helps describe the workings or logic of language.

As we noted above (p. 10), at the outset of the *Investigations* Wittgenstein notes that it is an oversimplification of language to assume that words only function as names. Beginning at paragraph 2, Wittgenstein asks us to imagine a community of builders whose language works according to the above model. In this imagined language there are only names. So we never hear something like "Hey Joe, would you bring me a two by four, and some time today, okay?" We hear only, "Beam!" and then Joe who, we assume, has been taught to respond in this manner, brings a plank of wood. Notice how much of the original sentence would be simply impossible for this community. Complex expressions of time (related to tense) and volition (the subjunctive) can't occur. The members of this community more closely resemble automatons than humans. In fact, it is difficult to imagine anything being built with such a simple form of communication. Here, Wittgenstein is presenting us with what might be called a subset of our language and an inadequate description of how our language actually functions. In other words, if we thought of a situation in which we actually employed the naming-as-meaning model—imagined it in actual use—it would be nothing like what we call language, and it would be difficult to imagine the language's users carrying on our ordinary daily activities. In actual employment the model fails to capture what we call language. Thus this comparison is very instructive: it helps "deconstruct" a theory, and it tells us something about the complexity of our own language.

Wittgenstein uses this technique of a "language game"—imagining a linguistic theory put into actual practice—many times in the *Investigations*. However, because Wittgenstein uses this term in a number of ways, it would be useful to examine the text in which he describes these uses.

> In the practice of the use of language (2) one party calls out the words, the other acts on them. In instruction in the language the following processes will occur: the learner names the objects; he utters the word when the teacher points to the stone.—And there will be this simpler exercise: the pupil repeats the words after the teacher—both of these being processes resembling language.
>
> We can also think of the whole process of using words in (2) as one of those games by means of which children learn their native language. I will call these games "language–games" and will sometimes speak of a primitive language as a language-game.
>   And the processes of naming the stones and of repeating words after someone might also be called language games. Think of much of the use of words in games like ring-a-ring-a-roses.
>
> I shall also call the whole, consisting of language and the actions into which it is woven, the "language-game."[5]

There are a few distinct ideas here that require sorting out. First, as an example, let us consider the simple language of the builders: A says, "slab!" and then B brings a slab. Now learning this language will include rote training in these words. This training will mirror the language—naming and using names. The crucial difference between learning the language and using the language is that, for example, repeating the words "slab," "beam," "brick" after the teacher does not accomplish the same thing. Repeating the word "slab!" in the classroom in order to learn, e.g., how to pronounce the word, doesn't result in a slab being brought to the person who said the word. Hence the process of learning the language of the builders is a subset of the language—the words are the same but the use is different. In order

to distinguish processes of learning language from its actual employment, Wittgenstein terms the means by which the language is learned
a language game. In the same way the words in a nursery rhyme like
"ring around the roses" are part of a child's game and are not to be
taken literally. When children sing "ring around the roses—pocket full
of posies" and hold hands and dance in a circle, the words simply accompany the actions. They are not, for example, meant to convey any
information about roses or posies. Hence a "primitive" language, such
as the language of the builders, since a subset of our language would be
considered a language game, not unlike a child's nursery rhyme.

However, there may be something of an ambiguity in the last sentence of the text cited above. The original German reads: "Ich werde
auch das Ganze: der Sprache und der Tatigkeiten, mit denen sie ver-
woben ist, das 'Springspiel' nennen."

While I do not want to take general exception to Anscombe's very
successful translation, here we have an important statement for understanding the work as a whole, so I want to look at it closely.

The first ambiguity is in the words *das Ganze*. It certainly can be
translated as "whole" as long as we do not confuse this with an ad-
jectival use as in "I've wasted the whole day." In German this would
"ganz" (lowercase *gl* no *e*). Here, as indicated by the capitalization,
"whole" is a noun as in the "the whole thing" or as in "the project"
or "the book"—"The whole thing is a waste of time."

But what "whole" are we talking about? The translation says "the
whole" consists of language and the actions into which it is woven.
If we take this whole as referring to all of language and its associated
activities, we would be talking about something quite large—actually
pretty much everything we humans do and say—art, math, engineering, science, architecture, cooking, shopping, sports—everything. All
of it would be reduced to a language game.

Although the concept of the human universe as a language game
might have great metaphysical appeal, it is for this very reason that
I doubt that this is what Wittgenstein means. Such an idea would
represent one of those grand, unifying, philosophical "theories of
everything," something to which Wittgenstein in the *Investigations*
is very much opposed. Wittgenstein is always focusing on the multi-
plicity and differences in language and trying to counter our tendency
to make incorrect associations and connections. Also, reducing the
human condition to a "game" tends to trivialize it, which again runs
counter to the spirit of Wittgenstein's works.[6]

It has most often been suggested that Wittgenstein is saying something like *language is playing a game with words*. This interpretation

THE OLD WAY OF THINKING 17

is certainly more correct. However, the text does not say language is a game in the sense of making a statement of a theory about language. Wittgenstein often compares our language to simpler forms he calls language games, but this generally points out that our language does not operate on this simplified level. Our language is not like the games used in learning language—it is not a nursery rhyme. It is far more complicated—a fact Wittgenstein is trying to get us to appreciate. While he does speak frequently about paying attention to the games we play with words, I think he means this on the grammatical, logical, or descriptive level. Language in its daily use can be compared to a game. As with a game of soccer (indeed, one biographical note claims this idea occurred to Wittgenstein while he was watching a soccer match[7]), language has rules, boundaries, guidelines, good players and bad, characteristic activities, and so on. The idea is that looking at language as a game, concentrating on the rules and the boundaries, etc., prevents us from trying to understand language from a metaphysical or psychological viewpoint. Looking at language as a game played between speakers makes us appreciate language in its daily use, and it is in this arena that language is meaningful.

Given this I would prefer a different or more literal translation and interpretation of the above passage:

> I will also designate the whole thing the "language game": the language and the activities with which it is interwoven.
> Or I will also call the whole thing, the language and the activities with which it is interwoven, the language game.

The chief difference here is that "the whole" is not meant to incorporate all of language and its activities. Rather, when you are analyzing language or a subset of language, it is important to also see the activities that are characteristic of that language. When we look, for example, at the language of the builders, Wittgenstein wants to call the words plus the actions a language game. Building is not the same thing as the language of the builders. But to see how language functions and the meaning of the words, you have to put language into its context—that is, where it properly operates. You have to see language in action—language and its characteristic activities, a language game.

The need to see language in action becomes most apparent when you look at a subset of language. In the language of the builders we would not know what *slab* meant unless we described the activities that took place around the term. It is just as clear that in teaching such a language the activities must be included. The student must know what to do when *slab* is called out. That these characteristic activities play an integral part in language often escapes our notice when we look at or use language as fluent speakers. These features are such an integral part of language and meaning that we take them for granted and they escape our notice. So we forget about the importance of context and characteristic activities in meaning when reading a newspaper or a novel or when philosophizing about language. The result can be the substitution of psychology and metaphysics as an explanation of meaning, when an analysis of use is called for. Seen in this light language games are another analytical or logical tool, not explanatory or theoretical entities.

Another important and related idea found in the beginning of the *Investigations* is "form of life."

"And to imagine a language means to imagine a form of life."[8]

The German word *Lebensform*, which is translated as "form of life," could also be translated as "life-form," which is used in the most recent edition of the *Investigations*,[9] or "way of life." "Way of life" would perhaps convey the continuity of the culture and traditions of a society— as in "the way of life of native Americans." "Form of life" of "life-form" would have a more biological use. I'm not sure why the translator chose "form of life" over "way of life." It may be that Wittgenstein intended this more technical or biological sense for Lebensform. Wittgenstein cited Oswald Spengler and his work *The Decline of the West* as a major influence. Through this work, Wittgenstein became interested in the relationship between morphology and history.[10] The idea here is that like an organism, a culture has a form that is unique to it and form evolves over time, going through a process of growth and decay. It is possible Wittgenstein thought that there is a "morphology" to our lives and the use of language. That is, our language and lives exist within certain rough boundaries or forms that change and mutate over time. The idea of cultural and social evolution, as well as the uniqueness of certain cultures and divisions between cultures, was prevalent in German thought at the time—particularly in fin-de-siècle Vienna. This idea became one of the cornerstones of National Socialism. Its progenitor is probably Hegel, but it is certainly found in Nietzsche, who influenced Spengler. However, once again I would caution the reader to be wary of putting "form of life" in the category of the natural sciences and/or a theory regarding language formation. Wittgenstein is clear that this is not what he is doing. (". . . we are not doing natural science; nor yet natural history."[11])

Therefore, we should resist the temptation to treat "form of life" in a technical sense—as part of a technical vocabulary. As von Wright has pointed out, the *Investigations* is remarkably free from technical terms and jargon of any sort, a fact that is often unappreciated.[12] If we compare Wittgenstein to other German thinkers of the same period, say Husserl or Heidegger, Wittgenstein's prose is incredibly straight-forward. Again, paradoxically, this directness makes the text more dif-ficult sometimes because we have come to expect jargon and theory. When it is absent we feel obliged to provide it. We make the very mistake that Wittgenstein is trying to guard against: layering "theo-retical" meaning over the actual meaning.

Instead of treating "form of life" as a technical or theoretical term it should be treated as an extension of the ideas already introduced with "language games" and meaning as use. In other words, to under-stand the meaning of a term or phrase—to understand language—Witt-genstein believes you must see it against the background of its charac-teristic circumstances and activities. It is against this background that the word is used, and it is only within these circumstances that we can see the actual employment of a word. Without analyzing the actual employment of the word, meaning gets "theoretical" or confused. As we will see, when we disregard the use of a word, we are tempted to substitute theory for use as an explanation of meaning.

Clearly, when we imagine a language, such as the case of *slab* in the language of the builders, it is difficult, if not impossible, to understand the meaning of the word *slab* without imagining or knowing what's to be done when the word is uttered. If we think, for example, the meaning of a word is merely the object the word refers to, then I think the mean-ing is settled when I ask, "what does *slab* mean?" and someone points to a slab. But if we ignore the context and the characteristic activities surrounding the use of the word, then this "name-object" relationship seems very mysterious and demands an explanation. How is the object "attached to the name"? Perhaps upon reflection we think the name somehow "reaches" to the object. Wittgenstein would alert us that the here addition of "somehow" is a tip-off to potential problems. The dif-ficulty is that how the name "reaches" the object is left unexplained, and perhaps we assume there is some psychological process involved. We know nothing of this process, but we again assume that psycholo-gists or philosophers will figure it out eventually. This, according to Wittgenstein, is where we go astray. We have forgotten about the es-sential activities that accompany the explanation of the meaning and the many other assumptions that are necessary here (e.g., that I look in the direction that someone points). When I ask the meaning of the word *slab* it is essential that someone points to a slab, or does what is supposed to be done with slabs, or shows me an example of a slab. In general, this type of thing is all we ever do in explaining the meaning of a word—or at least all that is required. Whatever psychological process that might accompany the use of the word, e.g., feelings, emotions, images, and the like, they are not required for the explanation of the meaning of the word *slab*. The psychological process doesn't enter into the actual employment of the word in this language game. It is important to note that meaning is not understood or conveyed through the rule taken abstractly, but through the practice of using the rule. Only in the whole context of building does *slab* as it is used in the language of the builders make any sense. And this is only a subset of language. Imagine how much more this is the case in our own language. Thus we see that in understanding a language we must consider the entire context of the language, and we see that a language operates within a boundary or "form of life." Hence "form of life" should not be seen as a theoretical or technical term but should be looked at as simply descriptive of the way language operates: it is interwoven with our lives.

Thus we have three concepts that Wittgenstein uses in the beginning of, and throughout, the *Investigations*—meaning as use, language games, and forms of life. These concepts are perhaps best seen as different tools in a toolbox that is constructed or gathered for the same general purpose: differentiating actual descriptions of language from false ones. However, we should strongly avoid the temptation to think of these ideas as a part of technical vocabulary or as part of a theoretical apparatus. Wittgenstein is not trying to explain anything. I think we might see these ideas as concepts crafted to allow a better view of how language operates. The microscope doesn't explain cellular biology—it was invented so that we can see the cell more clearly. I think it is the same for these ideas and others found in the *Investigations*.

Again, we must keep in mind that Wittgenstein's investigation is logical rather than empirical, and in fact the blurring of this distinction is itself, for Wittgenstein, a source of confusion in philosophy, as we shall see. Wittgenstein's focus will always be language and meaning. Wittgenstein wants to say that questions of meaning have to be settled by an examination of language and how it operates, not in an empirical investigation of causes and effects. It would be a (possibly tragic) mistake to explain the meaning of a stop sign to a new driver by using a psychological explanation, as if the process were automatic. "Well, the red color and this shape are a signal to my brain that enervates my leg muscles to apply x amount of pressure to the brake." However true this might be, this hardly explains the meaning of the sign. Hopefully the student will dismiss the driving instructor who tells her this as an overzealous academic and conclude: "So when I see this sign I'm supposed to stop."

As I said, the first sixty-four paragraphs of the *Investigations* is mostly devoted to a sustained critique of the *Tractatus* theory of meaning. This theory is often referred to as "logical atomism," and these passages are often described in philosophical terms, such as the "dismantling of logical atomism."[13] While this description may be apt if we approach the *Investigations* as academic philosophers (and it's hard for us to do anything else), we have to avoid letting this idea cloud the issue. We have to resist the temptation to think of Wittgenstein as engaging in a traditional epistemological or metaphysical debate. He is not trying to show that the logical atomism of the *Tractatus* is an incorrect metaphysical theory, in the way, for example, that Aristotle critiques Plato's Theory of Ideas. Aristotle argues against Plato's theory and provides one of his own that he thinks is a better explanation of how the mind works. Aristotle is taking a more scientific approach to epistemology, making claims about the nature of the mind, and this is something that Wittgenstein does not do.

Wittgenstein here does not generally engage in a theoretical debate in the sense of attacking a particular philosopher or a particular theory. His focus is language, and as we noted he certainly believes that the philosopher's task revolves around the examination of language. I don't believe he ever in the *Investigations* examines any particular idea in abstraction from its language. Rather than critiquing logical atomism as a theory, Wittgenstein might be more fruitfully understood as trying to circumvent the need for this kind of understanding of language. I think Wittgenstein is trying to show us that if we look at the way language actually works and is employed, then an idea such as logical atomism is not so much wrong as inexpressible.

For starters, the expression of the idea of logical atomism requires a certain precision or perspicuity in language that just doesn't exist. Logical atomism attempts to say that language is composed of discreet elements (names) that are joined together. But what would be the meaning of the sentence: "Language consists of a series of names strung together"? Presumably, if the sentence were meaningful it would have a use—it could be put into practice. But that would mean it would be a good description of language and its operation. However, when we tried to construct a language game based on this model—the language of the builders—the result was nothing that looked like language as we know it. To put this language into practice, we only succeed in banging our heads against the boundaries of language.[14] We could not force our language into this form. The logic of language is not as was supposed in the *Tractatus*—sentences cannot be broken down into discreet bits or names which refer to objects. Language is by nature fuzzy, elastic, and disjointed, but it generally works quite well just as it is, unless you layer unnecessary baggage over it—as we are in this case by trying to make language correspond to a particular theory. Of course, because of this inherent flexibility and the additions we make to language, it does require some untangling now and then, and Wittgenstein is more than happy to try to help in this regard.

The above paragraph illustrates another idea from Wittgenstein's "old way of thinking" that played an important part in the *Tractatus*: showing and saying. In the *Tractatus*, as we noted above, Wittgenstein wants to sharply delineate what can be said from "nonsense." What can be said, meaningful propositions, are constructed out of names of objects. These are the propositions of natural science. Propositions, then, speak about what Wittgenstein calls states of affairs. A proposition is able to accomplish this because the form of the proposition logically pictures a state of affairs. It is this form, then, which is responsible for the "sense" of the proposition. Since this logical form is not itself a natural object then we cannot form meaningful propositions about it. To attempt to do so would involve us in hopeless circularity. We cannot use language to discuss the logical building blocks of language. Hence the logical form of a proposition cannot be "said" (or talked about) but it is displayed or "shown" in the proposition. As in the case of a model drawn to scale, the proposition pictures reality. The propositional elements stand in the same relation to each other, as do the elements of reality. The proposition shows its sense.

I think this distinction between what can be said and what can be shown was an important idea for Wittgenstein that he never let go of completely, and indeed I think he makes great use of the idea in the *Investigations*. Here, I think his use of primitive language games, like the language game of the builders, is intended to show what cannot, strictly speaking, be said. So for Wittgenstein, we cannot say, for example, that the *Tractatus* picture of language is false in the empirical sense. Since the construction is logical, we were not speaking of anything empirical to begin with. The *Tractatus* conception is an attempt at a presentation of the logic of language—as Wittgenstein understood the topic at that time. Logic cannot be right or wrong or true or false in the scientific sense as Wittgenstein points out in the *Tractatus*. It makes no predictions and so it cannot be disproved scientifically—that is, by observation. I think it can be said that given certain premises, the *Tractatus* idea is not logically inconsistent. What makes it "wrong" is that you can show that it fails in its intended application—or, as I would prefer, the language to make it work is lacking. (Interestingly enough the language to make it incorrect or false is equally lacking.)

In this regard, a number of writers have spoken of the "pragmatic" or "therapeutic" nature of Wittgenstein's thought. Sometimes Wittgenstein's remarks are compared to Zen koans or riddles—e.g., "What is the sound of one hand clapping?" The idea in a Zen koan is to illustrate the pitfalls and traps into which language can lead us. The above mentioned "question" is very baffling if you try to treat it as an actual question that can be answered. It is less baffling (or not at all) when the sentence is seen as a pseudosentence—a group of words that is masquerading as a question. As such the question can only be "unasked" or discarded. Trying to answer the question in the usual way merely leads nowhere. Notice that this really cannot be "said." "Saying" some questions are meaningless is obvious—it merely begs the questions "Which ones?" or "How will I know the difference?" Though we will fully explore this idea later on, trying to strictly delineate all the rules for what counts as a question will only compound the problem—not solve it. When we try to draw exact boundaries or limits for the use of a word we run the risk of cutting it off from its actual use and thereby its meaning. For example, consider the definition: "All questions seek factual information." But what about the rhetorical question or the complex question ("Have you stopped beating your wife?")? What about something like: "Is that the best you can do?" Again, there will be more on this later. For now we can say that Wittgenstein solves a philosophical problem by showing us that it evaporates once we see the mistaken conception of language that generated the problem in the first place.

Wittgenstein's oft-quoted remark "What is the aim of your philosophy?—To show the fly the way out of the fly bottle,"[15]—is very indicative of the above-mentioned trends in Wittgenstein's work. What has to be avoided is turning the investigation into an empirical investigation into the actual employment of words—or the search for a pragmatic or social theory of language. Wittgenstein is not writing a dictionary. His results are far more general and his early provisional title for the *Investigations—Philosophical Grammar*—is perhaps more apt description of what Wittgenstein is up to. Wittgenstein says on this:

> Such a reform for particular practical purposes, an improvement in our terminology designed to prevent misunderstandings in practice is perfectly possible. But these are not the cases we have to do with. The confusions that occupy us arise when language is like an engine idling, not when it is doing work.[16]

The language game of the builders and the imagined natural history that surrounds it is not intended to be seen as the description of a possible language in the sense of a hypothesis to be studied. Its "failure" when compared to our language is not intended to be seen as proof that such a thing doesn't occur or could never work. The "failure" of the language game of the builders should not be seen strictly as a practical failure. The failure is logical. We might say that the language of the builders misses certain key elements that would make it a language comparable to our own, as we noted above. But the problem goes much deeper. The linguistic tools that we need in order to see the language game of the builders as a language comparable to our own are simply lacking. Strictly speaking, this is not a defect in the language game of the builders. It is a condition of our own language. Imagine saying "the language of the builders is complete." Only the addition of some theoretical entities could make this so, and this is precisely the point where we go wrong. For example, how could we account for the lack of verbs or some indication of time and tense? We would have to import something extralinguistic; that is, something not in the language game of the builders but is present nonetheless. Psychology is certainly a popu'ar idea that is resorted to in these circumstances: "When the master builder says *slab*, he *intends* that the slab should be placed here now, instead of later." But what in this language game shows this intention? What is it about what the master builder says or does that indicates this intention? From what we have been given in the language game clearly nothing stands for intention. There is nothing in the language game that can be *said* about *intention*—no word in the language of the builders exists for it. We are supplying this concept taken from our language so that their language can be on par with ours. *Intention* or *intending* exists in our language as a complex language game with characteristic activities and circumstances. We might say of an animal that is stalking its prey that he "intends" to eat it. But notice that even though the animal doesn't have a language, this situation contains all the characteristic activities and circumstances that are associated with intending. But it would be incorrect to import this concept into the language game of the builders where these circumstances and activities are entirely lacking. Thus it is a condition of our language that we cannot *say* in this case "The master builder *intends* . . . etc." In other words, *intention* makes sense within our language and what exists in our language that makes *intention* meaningful does not exist in the builder's language, and trying to use *intention* in connection with the language game of the builders is a fundamental error.

I think at this point it is important to note here that Wittgenstein in the *Investigations* takes the existence of our language and its workings for granted; it is a given. He never tries to explain how language evolved, nor does he discuss or try to explain its fundamentals in any great detail. Rather, there is in the *Investigations* a description of language, and we are reminded that this is the function of grammar. What we do get is a survey of the boundaries of our language. Generally, the logic of our language, from which language gets its sense, is found in the use of words in particular circumstance, along with certain characteristic activities. Outside of this is generally nonsense—or the words are not doing what was supposed. I will try to make this clear in some detail in what follows.

Wittgenstein compares words to tools. This analogy is important, and I would like to spend some time on it. He first notes that descriptively the functions of the tools in a toolbox are various. Hammer, nails, ruler, etc., each functions in different ways. However, that the functions of words are equally various often escape our notice, or there has been a steadfast attempt on the part of philosophers to lump words into one category. But if we think grammatically, the variety of functions for words is obvious. Words modify, name, express action, are subjects and objects, are transitive and intransitive. They also warn, instruct, edify, soothe, and seduce. The similar appearance of words lulls us into thinking they all do the same thing, but examination teaches us otherwise. The problem is that our initial impression—"all words are alike"—won't fit into our grammar—our description of words. Very often in philosophy when observation is at odds with our beliefs or inclinations then theory comes to the "rescue." Wittgenstein notes one such attempt to reduce the various functions of words to a common denominator: "Every word in language serves to signify something." We have so far said *nothing whatever*.[17]

This might seem like a very puzzling remark. Why should it be the case that the speaker here has so far said nothing whatever? It seems like a very good sentence—maybe even profoundly true. But if it is true we should like to know what the sentence is about. It is certainly not a specific statement about every individual word in the language. The sentence does not convey any information about every word in the language in the way that I might say everyone in a particular room is over forty. It seems closer to a very general statement, such as "every human being has a gender"—that everyone is either male or female. We might say that we are here talking about the natural properties of human beings and that there is an empirical correlate to the statement. However, "every word serves to signify something" makes a very general statement about the *function* of words or how we use words. It does not say anything about the empirical world. The statement, therefore, addresses meaning or grammar. Wittgenstein will later call this kind of statement a grammatical remark.

The question is: does this statement really say anything meaningful? Here we must treat the statement logically; that is, for Wittgenstein, look at what use it might have. Wittgenstein wants us to see that it is in the use of the statement that we see its meaning. We must ask where the statement can fit into our language and ultimately our lives. What are the circumstances of its employment? Certainly we can see that no matter how true or profound this statement appears, if we can't do anything with it in this context—if it gives us no information that we can put to use about the function of words—then maybe what seemed so profound is really nonsense.

Wittgenstein asks us to look at an analogous statement: "All the tools in the toolbox serve to modify something." If we layer on the appropriate "theory," we can certainly make sense of this statement. The hammer modifies the nails, the saw modifies the length of the wood, the ruler modifies our knowledge of length, etc. Now, things that at first appeared to have different functions have one function thanks to the "theory"—but what have we gained? Explanation? Clarity? Do we have a better understanding of the tools? Are we better builders? Actually we are worse off. This categorizing offers nothing at all. We have said nothing. The same may be said for the idea that all words serve to signify something. If we look at the functions of words it is clear that these functions are various. Lumping these functions together under one heading is superfluous or at least not an explanation of the meaning of words. Grammar points out these distinctions, and so understanding the functions of words requires us to pay attention to their grammar.

If we look at the function of the tools in a toolbox and we try to characterize their function, then to categorize this function under one heading actually inhibits our knowledge of that function. We literally couldn't do anything with this information. Imagine someone instructing you on the use of a ruler by telling you that it modifies our knowledge of length. This statement might be true, but it would not help you learn to use the tool in the way that the instruction "lay the ruler along the wood from beginning to end and read off the number at the end" would. It is important to notice the characteristic activity and context involved in understanding the function of the tool.

The same could be said of the idea that the function of words is limited to signification. There is very little that could be done with the information contained in the idea that every word serves to signify something. Could you teach someone even a rudimentary word such as *please* using this rule as a guide? Think of how this is normally done. The child asks for a cookie. You hold up a cookie and tell him "say *please*." When he says it you give him the cookie. No question of reference ever arises in this description.

At remark 27 Wittgenstein asks us to think of exclamations and their various functions:

Water
Away
Ow
Help
Fine
No

All of these words can have a variety of functions that can only be seen when looking at the use of the word. The simple word *away* can be an adjective and an adverb, a command or a cry depending on the context. If we consider *away* as a bare word on a page, then to describe its meaning requires that we invent a context. We could of course describe all possible uses of *away* as you might find in a dictionary, but this amounts to little more than supplying all possible contexts.

Again, if we do not pay attention to the use of words, Wittgenstein wants to show that this will leave gaps in our understanding that we tend to fill in by resorting to a theory of some kind. In philosophy there is a strong tendency to invent an ontology of meaning—a tendency to which Wittgenstein readily admits he succumbed in writing the *Tractatus*. The reasons for the popularity of explaining meaning through an ontology or metaphysics among philosophers are various, and Wittgenstein explores most of them. In general, meaning has always seemed to be bound up with something more than the word. Words have often been viewed as mere conventions, while meaning is something important that touches the realms of psychology, epistemology, and metaphysics. Meaning, of course, involves understanding, and what is understood here seems to be clearly transcendent, sometimes absolutely true. "2 + 2 = 4" is in itself only a trivial, transitory collection of marks on a page—what these marks signify seems to be an eternal truth, something altogether unique and permanent.

Wittgenstein, in the *Tractatus*, was captivated by a particular ontology of meaning—which, as we have stated, is often called logical atomism. Although, as we will see in the following text, Wittgenstein traces the idea to Plato, I seriously doubt that Wittgenstein's actual influence was Plato. The actual genesis was probably Frege or Russell.

At about the time he was writing the *Investigations*, Wittgenstein had been reading Plato, and he may be correct that Plato was the first to explore the idea that a word must name a real object in order to be meaningful. For whatever reason, in the opening of the *Investigations* Wittgenstein feels constrained to connect his ideas to classical thinkers such as Augustine and Plato. Apparently he wants to impress on us that the discussion is worthy of our attention because great minds were much exercised on these matters.

> "What lies behind the idea that names really signify simples?"—Socrates says in the *Theatetus*: "If I make no mistake, I have heard some people say this: there is no definition of primary elements—so to speak—out of which we and everything else are composed; for everything that exists in its own right has to be . . . named without any other determination. In consequence it is impossible to give an account of any primary element; for it, nothing is possible but the bare name; its name is all it has. But just as what consists of these primary elements is itself complex, so the names of these elements become descriptive language by being compounded together. For the essence of speech is the composition of names. Both Russell's 'individuals' and my 'objects' . . . were such primary elements."[18]

The above paragraph is a good description, as Wittgenstein admits, of the basis of the tractarian theory of meaning. Clearly the assumption in the above paragraph is that it makes sense to talk about the objects of our experience as composite. However, this idea is not merely saying things are composite in the sense that a car is made up of parts. Instead, this theory makes the claim that everything can be broken down into ultimate constituent elements. We may be familiar with this idea from hearing about the atomic theory, which states that everything is composed of atoms. But Wittgenstein is discussing an idea that takes atomism even further. Even the atoms or any subatomic particles that can be experienced can be broken down until you hit these "primary elements," "objects," or "individuals." But what are these things? That is the problem—we can't say. The tractarian theory argues that these objects cannot be described because all description is complex or composite. These objects can only be named.

Be that as it may, Wittgenstein wants us to consider just how meaningful the above description of the tractarian theory is. If the description is correct, then it should have a use—a place in the language. If we say this description represents a theory about how language functions, then it belongs to grammar and should describe the use of words. This is a very important point. Whatever else this theory might be, it claims to be a theory of meaning—a theory of how language functions. In addition, the above text from the *Investigations* that refers to ideas in the *Tractatus* appears to be a scientific theory about the nature of the world around us in that a claim is being made about the composition of reality. Although the idea presented may seem like a statement of natural science and appears to be very logical, the idea is not presented as the result of scientific discovery, nor is it testable in any way. No evidence is offered for this theory, nor is any attempt made to fit this theory with other successful or highly confirmed theories, such as relativity or genetics. Also, if we look carefully at the above account, we see that the idea that the world is composite is assumed. The paragraph does not try to offer evidence for the composite nature of things. This is considered to be obvious. Again what the theory does is talk about the relation of names to the ultimate component parts of things.

Hence we do not have a scientific theory in the proper sense, but the "theory" does treat meaning, and this is what interests Wittgenstein. Since we have a logical question—a question of meaning—it would be a mistake to treat it empirically, as a question of science. To do so causes a confusion similar to that experienced by children who might wrack their brains over whether the infinitive "to sleep" is in the active or passive voice. If we try to answer the question as to the voice of verbs by examining the activity mentioned, we are treating a grammatical question as if it were a question of empirical science. The question makes sense in one sphere, but we are transposing the question to a sphere in which it doesn't belong.

This distinction between the logical or grammatical and the empirical is very important to Wittgenstein and is a central insight of the *Tractatus*. In that work, Wittgenstein explains that logic is concerned with the rules governing a symbolism. Logical operators serve only to connect propositions. The propositions may say something about the world, but the operators such as *and*, *or*, or *implies* do not. Since logic deals only with the rules for a symbolism, it is neither psychological nor empirical—it is not dependent on our minds or the natural world. For a variety of reasons this idea about logic can be very difficult to grasp. In philosophy logic is sometimes spoken of in metaphysical or psychological terms—as being something either ideally real or as somehow involved in human psychology.[19] For Wittgenstein, neither is the case. The "truth" of the logical statement, e.g., a = b, b = c, therefore a = c, merely depends on the use given to "=" and the variables a, b, and c. In a correct logical system the use of the symbolism is apparent from the context. If we look at the above statement taken as a whole, it is apparent from analyzing the statement itself that "="

means "the same as." No reference to psychology or nature is required for the understanding of the proposition.

Much the same point is made with regard to meaning in the *Investigations*—again with the exception that logic in the *Investigations* is not restricted to formal, symbolic logic. The meaning of a sentence is not a matter of an empirical investigation. Our philosophical questions regarding concepts or meaning are logical. The sense of a sentence must be derived from the sentence itself—not from any psychological, metaphysical, or scientific facts.

Thus to return to our consideration of reference theories of meaning and problems of names and composite objects, if we take an ordinary object, such as a chair, Wittgenstein wants to show in the *Investigations* that it is difficult to give sense to the statement that the word *chair* names or means a composite. Initially, the question "What are the simple components of a chair?" has no answer or a thousand answers—which amounts to the same thing. The impossibility of an answer is not a failure of science or our powers of observation, but a failure to give sense to the question. "The simple components of a chair" describes nothing. This description could mean chair parts, wood, splinters, design elements, atoms, molecules, or energy fields. There is no end to the possibilities. What this tells us is that in order to make sense of the question a specific context must be supplied.

This idea is very important to the *Investigations*, and it can be easily misunderstood because of its subtlety. Many philosophers explain or write about meaning as if meaning occurred in a vacuum. It can seem as if the meaning of a word is somehow attached to it like an aura that follows the word around. Again, the temptation is to think of meaning as something transcendent and that the word only represents or signifies something beyond itself.

So we start with the idea that the phrase "the simple components of a chair" must have a meaning—after all, I can read and write the sentence so I must know what it means. One would assume that therefore *something* must correspond to the phrase, and so presumably one can look for or investigate these simple parts of the chair. Our inquiry must turn up something. But this is the point where we have made a wrong turn. Wittgenstein wants to show us that there is a great difference between a word or phrase meaning something and seeming to mean something. The phrase "a two-angled triangle" is obviously nonsensical—it is a contradiction in terms. We couldn't investigate two-angled triangles, not because of an empirical limitation—"I haven't got any here to look at"—but because the phrase is meaningless. But the "simple parts of a chair" is equally meaningless, yet this is not as obvious because there is no contradiction in terms involved. We note that the contradiction in terms—the two-angled triangle—gives us a useless phrase. The case is the same with the "simple parts of a chair" in the above example. The phrase begs for a context. As we noted above, the phrase itself does not tell us to which parts we are referring: materials, design, atoms, all of the above. But for the purpose of developing the theory of logical atomism we have assumed a particular context—*simple* is assumed to mean the results of analyzing an object until we can go no further. But if we look at the actual employment of the phrase, no such idea can be necessarily derived. "The simple components of a chair" as a sentence is more of a requirement of a theory of meaning than a sentence with an actual use in our everyday lives.

Here we see Wittgenstein's conception of logic in the *Investigations* in operation. It should be noted that there is a "different," or perhaps to put it better, an "expanded" conception of logic at work in the *Investigations*. This difference is crucial and extends to almost every segment of the work. As we have noted, in the *Tractatus*, Wittgenstein sees logic in a very specialized way: what we might call "formal" logic; that is, strictly defined, rule-governed method for connecting propositions and deriving conclusions from premises. Wittgenstein thought that this formal structure was unique and independently consistent. The structure of formal logic lay behind and "supported" language and meaning. In other words, language had a logical structure and this was made clear through symbolic logic. This idea was responsible for what Wittgenstein calls the "subliming" of logic. Logic seemed to be composed of certain independent inviolable principles—such as the excluded middle (any statement must either be true or not true) or the principle of contradiction (something cannot be and not be at the same time)—that functioned almost like scientific laws. These laws were seen as the fundamental basis of thought, meaning, and language. In a way, since logical reality determined the limits of what can be said or thought, then logic mirrored the reality of the natural world.

But Wittgenstein came to see that language has a logic all its own, and this logic is far more complicated than logicians had supposed. As we alluded to above and we will explore in greater depth as we move along, it is use that dictates meaning. When we say a sentence is meaningless, we are saying that it has no use, or it does not have the use that we thought it did. What we need to see, though, is that this restriction must be logical, not psychological or empirical. If I say that the earth is as flat as a pancake, then I may be said to be wrong or crazy. But if I say the earth is as flat as the color red, I am simply making no sense. The facts here don't matter—empirical science cannot solve my problem. Somehow I've got the words jumbled up. Again, it still may be the case that I am simply wrong or crazy, but this doesn't tell us why the sentence makes no sense. Here the problem with the meaning of the sentence must be described as logical. I have tried to connect concepts that can't be connected, resulting in nonsense. But it must be noted that I have broken no rule of formal logic, yet the sentence is illogical. As we shall see, we can clearly say the sentence makes no sense because it has no use. The circumstances in which we might use the expression "flat as the color red" are lacking—or at least need to be supplied. Thus "logic" in the *Investigations* has a much wider context than it did in the *Tractatus*. As we will see it will be important to distinguish the logical employment of a word—a description of its use or grammar—from its empirical use. It is through noting this distinction and then distinguishing how a word is actually used from false accounts of that use that will clear up our philosophical difficulties. This will hopefully become clearer as we progress.

For now we should note that without the context there is no use and hence no meaning to the phrase "the simple components of a chair." And the reason for Wittgenstein's focus on this phrase is to critique the foundations of his theory of meaning found in the *Tractatus*. There is no external, formal, logical structure that we can rely on to automatically supply meaning or sense. The sense of the sentence is found in its use or actual employment.

In other words, we are owed a sense or a context for "simple components." Wittgenstein is saying that a use cannot be assumed, but this is the very mistake the philosopher makes—the assumption that words have a type of "general meaning" that they carry with them into any context. The above example shows that this is not the case. You could stipulate that the "simple components of a chair" are the pieces that the chair is built out of according to the design of the chair. Now the question has a sense and an answer—or the possibility of an answer now exists. However, in so stipulating the boundaries for these words in this manner the question becomes ordinary—uninteresting. We have circumvented the need to interpret "simple components" as some sort of universal constituent objects. Now, the philosophical problem about the connection of names to objects is nowhere in sight. But this is precisely the answer to the problem—the rejection of the question. Or, rather, this is the rejection of the false grammatical construct that generated the question. Again, making sense of the question by supplying a workable context causes the philosophical problem to drop out of consideration. In general, philosophy tries to force a meaning on a word, or assumes the same meaning travels with it wherever it goes. But this is not the case. Words function in a variety of ways and so can have a variety of meanings.

To make this point clearer Wittgenstein uses the method he exemplified with the builders—constructing a language game that works on the rules specified in the passage he quoted from Plato's *Theatetus*: words or symbols function as names of objects, and propositions are concatenations of names that are arranged to mirror an arrangement of objects.

In this game (PI 48), there are nine squares arranged in three columns of three and numbered from left to right to form a matrix. Squares can be red, black, green, and white and these colors have symbols or names: R B G W. So a "sentence" in this game would be "RRBGGGRWW," which corresponds to the arrangement of squares in which the first two are red and the third is black, the second row is all green squares and the third has a red and two white squares. This game follows the rules stated in the passage from the *Theatetus*, but it fails to answer the difficulties posed above. There is a precise connection between the letters or names and the objects they signify, the colored squares; and an arrangement of names is equal to an arrangement of objects. It would be hard to more precisely follow the requirements of a reference theory as delineated in the *Theatetus* or the *Tractatus*. Yet we should notice that questions of meaning still remain unresolved. As with "the simple components of the chair," it is difficult, if we think about it, to precisely fix meaning of "simple components" in this language game. Although the colored squares are supposed to be "simples" or "objects" in this game, their simplicity is not absolute. We can certainly think of other contexts in which this "simplicity" would vanish. In other connections these "simples" could certainly be composite. We might wish to refer to the color and shape or color and position of the square—or refer to the color square as composed of or related to certain parts of the color spectrum—etc. We could even think of the square itself as composite. Hence calling these objects "simples" certainly works in the little model we have created, but we should resist the temptation to think that we have hit on some sort of final analysis—that there are no further questions possible. But Wittgenstein is showing us that precisely this mistake is at the heart of the theory of meaning in the *Tractatus*. By stipulating that the meaning of a word is the object it signifies, we think we have found some sort of bedrock—the ultimate constituents of meaning and reality. But even in our little language game this is not so. If we start to examine our model to see if it is correct, then we see that the actual meaning of the words *simple* and *composite* intrudes and a number of questions and interpretations can arise. What this is intended to show is that the reference theory is supposed to offer a precise theory of meaning that is unambiguous and settles all interpretations: a word has meaning because it functions as a name, referring to one and only one particular object. The game seemed to be a paradigm of simplicity and precision, but if we expand the context a little, this precision is lacking. Again the language necessary to make this idea a description of meaning is lacking. Yes indeed, words sometimes function as names, and because of this language seems to present us with an appealing picture of the way it operates. But once we compare this picture to the "whole thing," we can see that it does not come close to capturing the truth. You would have to swim upstream—fight the natural tendency of language by drawing artificial boundaries to make this work as a theory or description of meaning. As with the language game of the builders we see that the idea behind this language game when compared with our own language lacks the necessary complexity.

It is worth repeating that as in the *Tractatus*, Wittgenstein in the *Investigations* is interested in exposing the limits of language and these limits are logical. However, the philosopher discovers, but does not prescribe, these limits. The philosopher does not tell us what must be the case. Rather, when we properly uncover the limits to language then what is the case is revealed.

NOTES

1. TLP 1–1.2.

2. If further elucidation of the *Tractatus* is required, a very reliable beginning is:

H. O. Mounce, *Wittgenstein's Tractatus: An Introduction* (Chicago: The University of Chicago Press, 1981). Mounce was a student of Rush Rhees who was a former student of Wittgenstein, a longtime friend and ultimately one of Wittgenstein's literary executors.

3. There is no theory of logic in the *Tractatus* in the sense of a scientific or psychological theory that is supposed to be explanatory, i.e., trying to justify logic or explain what it is founded on. The propositions of logic are all tautologies and say nothing, cf. TLP 4.461–4.466, 5.473–5.476, 6.1–6.12.

4. Cf. PI 126–128.

5. PI 7.

6. Cf. Ludwig Wittgenstein, *Culture and Value*, ed. G. H. von Wright, trans. Peter Winch (Chicago: The University of Chicago Press, 1984), 45–46;

G. H. von Wright, *Wittgenstein* (Minneapolis: University of Minnesota Press, 1982), 32; Malcolm, *Memoir*, 58–61.

7. Malcolm, *Memoir*, 55.

8. PI, Prentice Hall ed., 19.

9. PI 19.

10. Wittgenstein, *Culture and Value*, 14e.; cf. von Wright, *Wittgenstein*, 212–215.

11. PI 195e, Prentice Hall ed., 230.

12. Von Wright, *Wittgenstein*, 33-34.

13. E.g., Anthony Kenny, *Wittgenstein* (Cambridge, MA: Harvard University Press, 1973), 103ff.

14. PI 119.

15. PI 309.

16. PI 132.

17. PI 13.

18. PI 46.

19. Throughout the history of logic the topic has been bound up with metaphysical and psychological/epistemological considerations. Wittgenstein was notoriously unschooled in the history of philosophy, but he was acquainted with W. E. Johnson, who taught logic at Cambridge while he was there. Johnson was perhaps an example of the "classical" school and saw logic and inference as connected to mental processes and the nature of reality. Cf. W. E. Johnson, *Logic—Part II: Demonstrative Inference: Deductive and Inductive* (New York: Dover Publications, Inc., 1964). Wittgenstein was well versed in the work of Gottlob Frege, who held a Platonist theory of mathematics—numbers were subsistent entities (the same could be said for the True and the False). Cf. Gottlob Frege, *The Foundations of Arithmetic*, trans. J. L. Austin (Evanston, IL: Northwestern University Press, 1980), 67e ff. And of course "logical atomism" is foundational for the *Tractatus*.

3

The New Way

Up to now, we have introduced some key ideas in the *Investigations*, such as the failure of reference theories of meaning, language games, the importance of context, and meaning as use. After this beginning section Wittgenstein begins to deepen his analysis of these topics and draw out their consequences.

At about remark 65, Wittgenstein begins a long discussion on grammar and rule following—topics he has introduced, but now he wants to develop certain themes regarding these topics. This technique of circling familiar themes and augmenting their analysis is common in the *Investigations*. We have mentioned Wittgenstein's focus on grammar—loosely defined as the rules for the use of a word. When we think of grammar, we might think of classifying words as nouns, verbs, adjectives, adverbs, subjects, and predicates, etc. Wittgenstein means something more complex by the term. Usually in English we distinguish grammar and usage. A word may be grammatically a noun and in a sentence function as a subject or an object. These distinctions for the grammarian are logical or rule-governed, but we should note how much depends on context. "The whole production run had run for days and made each stocking with a run in it." Here the word *run* differs grammatically three times—subject, verb, object, and has a variety of meanings—all regulated by context. In general, usage is driven by context and the habits and preferences of speakers, writers, editors, and English professors. Words get coined or become archaic, slang is derided then accepted, endings are dropped, etc. Words in English are notorious for being equivocal. *Bark* could mean a part of a tree or the sound a dog makes depending on context. When Wittgenstein talks about grammar, he tends to collapse the distinction between grammar and usage—or treats these distinctions under the category of grammar—in general, the description of rules that govern the use of a word.

The idea that grammar must involve the description of the use of a word is important for Wittgenstein. Apparently for Wittgenstein, if grammar is to fully tell us what the function of a word is then its use must be included. We might think that parsing a sentence is a simple affair, a matter of finding a noun representing that which performs an action and a verb representing the action and so on. But Wittgenstein wants to point out that things are not so simple. Words are not nouns or verbs by nature, as if they had been baptized with a particular function. Their function must be determined by use. Referring to the example above, a dictionary or grammar book cannot tell me whether *run* is a subject or object or verb or noun. It may inform me of these possibilities, but the actual case depends on the sentence or context or use. If we look at the phrase "the production run had run for days" and the different meanings of *run*, we see that we can only sort this out with a vast array of circumstances surrounding the idea "a production run." We must know about factories, assembly lines, how they work—to a degree—in order to make sense of the sentence. This context represents essential ingredients to the use of the word. These essential ingredients may be overlooked because these circumstances, etc., do not appear to be "logical" and so can't be important to meaning. But again Wittgenstein wants to point out that the logic of language must include the circumstances under which a word is used. Without this we cannot see a word's actual employment and so the function and therefore the meaning of the word can escape us.

It is important to realize that using a word—speaking or writing—and describing the use of the word—an analysis of grammar—are two different things. The analysis of grammar on its own, since it is descriptive, does not make a sentence meaningful. It would be absurd to say that a sentence was not meaningful until it is diagrammed or parsed. For the everyday, ordinary speaker, language must be meaningful in its actual employment. Grammar describes or gives a snapshot of meaning, and, as such, remains an abstraction. Grammar gives the appearance of rigidity—a solid structure or scaffolding for language, but we must remember the fluidity of language in its ordinary use. A difficulty that Wittgenstein wants to focus on is the incorrect idea that grammar exists as a perfect set of logical rules, rules hidden beneath language that we try to uncover. It has seemed to many philosophers over the years, as it did to Wittgenstein in the *Tractatus*, as if the rules of grammar have a priority over language, as if logic dictated to language and determined meaning, determined what made sense. But Wittgenstein in the *Investigations* wants to say in actuality the reverse is true. Use has priority in determining what makes sense, and grammar describes that use.

Hence to understand the operation of language—or investigate language—we must construct a grammar; that is, describe the use or actual employment of words.

Philosophers might object here and note that meaning must be rule-governed, and this is true. Without consistency of use, meaning is impossible. But it is the nature of these rules and their relationship to meaning that is at the root of a great deal of philosophical controversy. It can seem as if the rules of grammar "confer" meaning on a sentence. When we view language in this way, then the rule seems to be the important thing and the sentence is secondary. The rule stands behind the sentence and supports it, and it seems that this is where we must look for the meaning of the sentence. The sentence becomes irrelevant. Wittgenstein wants to show that this type of thinking can cause us a great deal of confusion. Let us take an example that supposes this idea is literally true. Let us say the rule for the word *circle* is "a closed curve in which each point on the curve is equidistant from the midpoint." Let this be a strict rule for the meaning of *circle*. Now, this rule might work very well as long as we are thinking of circles as defined in geometry. But what would we say about the case of a child learning to draw circles? Few if any of the shapes the child draws will be exact, and so they will not exactly fit the rule. But then, are the shapes the child has drawn circles or not? Most people will recognize the shapes as circles, and most likely the child will tell an onlooker that she is drawing circles. Do we need a new rule or perhaps to augment the original one? And what do we do when we apply this rule for *circle* to a sentence concerning arguing in a circle? Now the rule doesn't fit at all, and it seems difficult to see how we will stretch or amend the rule to apply in this case while maintaining any exactness. What about a person who is confused reading the *Investigations* and says, "He just seems to be going in circles!" Now what can we say about the meaning of *circle* in this case being determined by our rule? There doesn't seem to be any end to the gyrations we must put our rule through in order to make it "responsible" for meaning. However, if we let the use teach us the meaning there doesn't seem to be a problem. The word *circle* in ordinary, everyday English has the flexibility to cover all these cases. Clearly, though, this is an involved topic, and therefore Wittgenstein examines rule-following in depth.

For Wittgenstein, the fundamental idea responsible for many philosophical problems is that speaking a language or understanding the meaning of words is explained as operating a calculus—an axiomatic or rule-governed system like formal logic or mathematics. As we have noted, this idea gripped Wittgenstein very early and is an important part of the *Tractatus*. Many philosophers would agree that there is a connection between meaning, logic, and mathematics. For Wittgenstein, logic entailed the rules governing the use of symbols, and mathematics could be seen in the same way. In the *Tractatus*, meaningful language—the stringing together of names of objects and the logical connection of elementary propositions—followed a similar logical structure.

However, by the time he writes the *Investigations*, Wittgenstein has come to see this conception as flawed. Wittgenstein's idea in the *Tractatus* depended on the reference theory of language—words were meaningful when they named objects. Wittgenstein came to see that if his central insight in the *Tractatus* was correct—language is meaningful as it is—then what makes it meaningful couldn't be exterior to language. Much of the inherent sloppiness of language—its ragged edges, twisted locutions, and frayed syntax—are part of the nature of the beast. Language itself cannot be cleaned up or perfected—but it must be surveyed and investigated because the flexibility at the heart of our living language can be so complex and confusing. Also, as we mentioned, Wittgenstein believes we must expand our notion of logic. "Logic" cannot be restricted to the formal structure Wittgenstein had imagined in the *Tractatus*, and the logic of language is not a formal structure external to language but is found in the operation of language itself.

The first order of business is to see that our grammar is as complicated as the language it describes. Wittgenstein wants us to realize that this state of affairs is not a flaw that needs philosophical correction, but a reflection of the way things are.

At remark 65 Wittgenstein says, "Here we come up against the great question that lies behind all these consideration." Typically, Wittgenstein never spells out the "great question." Apparently he is talking about the underlying concerns of the *Tractatus*—the essence of language and the general form of propositions. The point he is trying to make is that this search for the abstract essence of language is misguided. In the *Tractatus* he looked for a rule or common element that joined all propositions and so formed the basis of language. He tried to answer the question "What is language really?" by finding the common element in language.

Anyone with a background in philosophy will probably recognize Wittgenstein's concern here as "the problem of universals." This has been an extremely knotty problem for philosophy since the time of the ancient Greeks. The problem is generated on a number of levels: epistemology, metaphysics, philosophy of science, etc. Certainly, we can see that language depends to a degree on universality. Language depends in part on nouns, which can seem to signify a natural group, essence, kind, or species—tree, dog, human, and so forth. Philosophers since the time of Plato have debated the idea of essences or species— are they real or are they conventions, or perhaps nonexistent altogether? If they are real, what sort of reality do they have? Are they only ideas—or do they represent perhaps something like the laws governing natural kinds? Many philosophers have weighed in on this issue, and the debate is seemingly never ending. Wittgenstein never speaks of "the problem of universals," and because of his eclectic philosophical background it is an open question whether he is aware of the history of the problem of universals and whether he is specifically addressing this issue here. He is, however, familiar with Plato, and when he discusses the idea of the essence of something as consisting of a common element it does call to mind Plato's theory of ideas. Socrates in the dialogues seeks the definition of a virtue, for example, by looking for a common element that links all actions of that type. If Wittgenstein is critiquing Platonism, it is curious that he does not mention Plato here. He was quite willing previously to invoke Plato's *Theatetus* as a target for his critique of the reference theory of meaning, when he might well have targeted the *Tractatus*. Here when he might have mentioned Plato, he only mentions the *Tractatus*.

Nevertheless, I would certainly argue that Wittgenstein has made a significant contribution on this topic. I do think, however, Wittgenstein is restricting his remarks to language, and more specifically, to grammar. This may have implications for the problem of universals, but I think it would be a mistake to think of Wittgenstein as propounding a theory on essence or on natural kinds or even on ideas. This is not to say that Wittgenstein has nothing to say on these topics; however, he repeatedly states he is not advancing theses.[1] Rather, Wittgenstein wants to caution us that if we look at language, then we will see that there is no one structure that can account for language. Rather, there are many interrelated structures that form a family. Our grammar, if it is to be useful, since it is a description of these interrelated structures, cannot be a pure, rigid calculus, but must be multifaceted and flexible.

To make this point Wittgenstein looks at the concept of *game*. It is tempting to jump to the conclusion that in order to define the word *game* we should look for a common element to all games. But first he tells us we should note that to do so is a stipulation or an assumption about definitions and the way language operates, not the result of looking at the various things we call games—that is, looking at how the word *game* actually functions in our language.

We often think that a word like *game* is a noun—it names a class or group. We might think of a class as a set of objects and that this set is clearly defined. When we are learning this idea we are often told to picture a set as a circle and all the things in the set as "fitting" in the circle like a collection. We may also think that there is a list of rules that determine membership in a set or class. This list of rules functions as a test to determine class membership. If object x passes the test it is a member of the class—otherwise it is not. This model generally sees the world as delineated by natural kinds and language and logic as reflecting this demarcation. Notoriously, this model has difficulty explaining borderline cases and gray areas. For example, if we think of "works of art" as a clearly defined set or class, anything new or novel, no matter how important or well crafted, sometimes it does not get seen as a work of art—perhaps until many years later and sometimes not at all. Consider the length of time it took for impressionism to be seen as great art.

In order to show the limits of a "set" model, Wittgenstein asks us to look at—not think about or just reflect on—how we use the word *game*. There are dozens of different games within each type of game and dozens of types—and perhaps some that defy classification. There are ball games—football, baseball, basketball. There are board games—chess, checkers, Scrabble. There are card games—poker, pinochle, old maid. Plus, there are war games, Olympic games, "head" games—not to mention tag, Simon says, and hide and seek. And what can we say about games of catch or building a house of cards or skipping stones or catching snowflakes on your tongue? When we examine all these games, there are sometimes common features, but sometimes not. Some features—such as rules—are important in some games like chess but unimportant in others like skipping stones. Some games are amusing, such as catch—some are very serious, such as war games. If we *look* closely at the concept *game* in action, then the belief that there is an element common to all games begins to dissipate.

For Wittgenstein, the various things we call *games* can best be described as forming a family, and the relationships and similarities between them he calls "family resemblances." These uses should be described as intertwined like threads of a fiber. In other words, the grammar of *game* is best seen as a related series of uses.

Wittgenstein wants to analyze this concept of "family resemblances" as describing the grammar of a concept such as *game* very carefully. Again, he clearly thinks this issue is important—calling it a "great question." The most obvious objection to the idea that the word *game* represents a series of interrelated uses would probably come from the logician or mathematician who would very likely argue that a word or symbol without a precise definition is meaningless, that a concept without a boundary is not a concept. Initially, such an objection makes sense. Mathematically speaking it would certainly appear that the definition of circle or square is hardly fuzzy. A theorem in geometry such as the Pythagorean theorem—$A^2 + B^2 = C^2$—could not have more precision. Two plus two is exactly four—there doesn't seem to be a family of cases here. We might write the solution to this equation in a variety of ways, but these ways are all interchangeable. It might first appear reasonable that the same might be said for words. Certainly, we think that a definition tries to remove ambiguities. In seeking the definition of *tree* we try to draw a sharp boundary between trees, shrubs, flowers, and other plants. An ambiguity or an anomalous case either represents a failure to understand what counts for a tree or a lack of skill in identifying the individual case. Common sense tells us that the more ambiguity you have in a definition the less meaning you have and the less you understand.

But Wittgenstein wants to challenge the notion that meaning requires sharp boundaries. First we should note that math and logic don't always have the exactness that we might suppose. While "square" and "circle" seem very exact, this precision starts to disappear when we construct these figures on a curved surface. Pythagoras himself, so the story goes, was extremely embarrassed when he found that a right triangle with the sides of length 1 produces a triangle with a hypotenuse measuring the square root of 2 when the equation is solved. Technically, we know, there is no such number—when we try to calculate the square root of 2 we wind up with a repeating decimal—as when we calculate pi. Even "simple" arithmetic produces many a strange beastie—imaginary numbers, irrational numbers, etc. When we look at it, math doesn't represent the bastion of precision we once thought. However, it is important to note that despite the lack of precision, the geometry and arithmetic work quite well.

In general, meaning presents a very similar case. We tend to think that because an inexact boundary is no boundary, the use of a word must be everywhere bounded by rules. Again the analogy with games is very instructive here. Even in games with broad and definite rules, such as baseball, the game is still a game, still baseball, even with those areas of the game that are not governed by rules. For instance, there is no rule on how fast or slow you can pitch. A home run is a ball that goes over the fence—but there is no exact measure here—an inch over the fence is as good as a mile. Also, there is no time clock in baseball, and so on. Thus a game can get on quite well without exact rules and without a rule to cover every case. Why must the rules for the use of a word be exact? What about words like *nearly, roughly,* or *almost*—or expressions like *sort of, in a way, just missed*? What about the word *vague* itself? Does there have to be an exact use for *vague* or *ambiguous*? What about *not being sure, confused,* or *having a bad feeling* about a situation? Wittgenstein points out that many of these uses, to make any sense at all, must be vague or fuzzy. If we examine language in practice, exact boundaries in definition begin to look more like a requirement than actual fact.

We often think that in order to say that we know something or for an idea to be counted as knowledge rather than as a guess or an opinion then the idea must be exact and it must be possible to express the idea exactly. It may seem to us to be impossible that someone knows something but cannot express it in precise terms. In other words, it may be thought that imprecise knowledge is not knowledge at all. Wittgenstein wants us to see that the various forms of language often mislead us in this regard. As he says at remark 78, in this context we are most often thinking of factual reports—such as the height of Mont Blanc. Usually, we say that if someone knows a fact it is something exact, and knowing it means he can repeat that fact exactly. We might allow that there are certain situations where it makes sense to say "I know a certain fact but I can't say it," as when someone is keeping a secret. But that fact is still something precise and in other circumstances perfectly expressible. It wouldn't make sense for someone to say that he knew a particular measurement—such as the height of Mont Blanc—but that it was inexpressible. Again there is a general belief that facts and truths are precise, and clarity of expression follows from that precision. The idea at work here is that meaning demands crystalline clarity.

But Wittgenstein wants to think about how language functions in other cases where meaning is possible yet crystalline clarity is lacking. Think about saying how a clarinet sounds, or of describing the aroma of coffee, or the taste of wine—or describing how you felt on a beautiful summer day or the first time you fell in love. Here we must use images or metaphors, and precision no longer seems to be a requirement. This is the stuff of poetry. For Wittgenstein, the fact that our language operates like this is what is important. If language is meaningful as it is, then apparently the logic of language is not able to be captured in the exact formal system Wittgenstein envisioned in the *Tractatus*. Not every concept admits of exact description or can be given a precise definition. If I say "put the book on the table," I need not break the meaning down into so many millimeters from the edge, what particular angle to place, and so on. Of course, I could do this, but the point is that the idea "put the book on the table" is meaningful in all its imprecision. Of course we might wonder at why our language is like this, how it came to be imprecise yet functional, why human beings speak like this, and so on. But such questions are not relevant to Wittgenstein's project. It might be possible to explain these things, but this would be an empirical investigation, not a philosophical or a logical one. Again, we must keep in mind that Wittgenstein's investigation focuses solely on the logic of language.

Since grammar is a description of the use of words, we must consider whether every description has to be exact in order to be a description. In general, we should expect that since what grammar describes is inherently "fuzzy," then grammar itself should be equally fuzzy. But since grammar is an abstraction and essentially logical, the tendency is to search for the rigid, logical purity in grammar that we believe must exist in anything logical. But again, does a description have to be exact to be a good description? If I tell someone I just drove through a dense fog on a mountain road, is this description no good unless I can give the height of the mountain and the parts per million of water droplets in the air? Must I include how far I drove and the incline of the road? Certainly, a photograph is a great description of someone. But what about a sketch or a caricature? Can't we recognize someone from either of these inexact descriptions just as well?

When we try to grasp or understand something, we might think in scientific terms and so we might compare understanding to a kind of measuring, and we think of measurement as something exact. We think of defining a geometric figure such as a triangle by the degrees of the angles or defining an element by the atomic number or we identify a cell by the number of chromosomes, and so on. Certainly, there are cases when exact measurement is the most preferable—as in surgery. But Wittgenstein cautions us that we must be careful not to misunderstand the idea of exact measurement. We often confuse exactness in the result of our measurement with exactness of the tool we used to measure. I may want to survey a piece of property and, for whatever reason, I need the most exact measurement possible. Let us suppose I want to use a meter stick for this purpose—again the reason doesn't matter. But since I need exact measurement, I believe an ordinary meter stick from the hardware store won't do. So, I order one from a catalog that supplies science labs. In order that its dimensions won't be affected by changes in temperature, I could even pay a phenomenal amount of money and get a platinum meter stick made to the exact dimensions of the standard meter bar in Paris. Now, I believe, my measurements will be exact.

Besides this scenario's bordering on the ludicrous, there are a number of problems here. One is the idea of "exactly a meter." A meter is a convention used as a standard of measurement. We have tried to define this standard in as precise a way as is possible, but at some point the requirement for precision will have to stop. We have to realize that even if we take every precaution to prevent any alteration in the standard meter bar, ultimately it is a chunk of matter and so some change is inevitable. So the requirement of ideal mathematical precision as far as the meter bar is concerned will never be met. If you have a definition that you set as a standard, it is a fundamental misunderstanding of the idea of a standard to try to compare the standard to something more perfect. If you do so, that which you originally had as a standard loses its status as a standard, and the new, more perfect example that you are seeking must be the standard. But what would make this new thing—whatever it is—into a more perfect example of your standard? To what are you comparing it? Aren't you imagining something more perfect beyond even the present example? Here we see that we are involved in an infinite regress—an endless loop with no point. The only way to stop it is not to start it.

The idea of a meter is exact enough. It appears inexact when we think of defining it in a vacuum—that is, apart from the job it is supposed to do. The concepts of *length* or *measurement* are understood in conjunction with concepts such as *determining a length* or *taking a measurement*. It is difficult to make sense of *length* without understanding it in conjunction with measuring the length of something. *Meter* is part of a system of measuring length or distance. A meter has a particular fundamental role in that system, and apart from that system it would be difficult to define.

Since a meter is a convention or our creation that springs from the need to measure, it would be wrong to think of a meter as a previously existing abstract perfect entity. We must also realize measurements must be made to determine results. I could take my million-dollar meter stick out to the land I have to survey, but I would have to lay the perfect stick end over end to get my measurement. In actual practice this procedure will probably produce imperfect results. Again we should notice that use or actual practice is key to the accuracy of measurement; the accuracy of the tool by itself is insufficient.

In the case of measuring land, if we needed a superaccurate measurement, it would probably make more sense to get a surveyor to measure the land with precise optical equipment. But here again we should not think that the measurement of the land—say listed in a deed—is discovering an object in the way measuring to drill for water ends in finding water or in the way that using sonar ends in finding a sunken ship. When we measure a parcel of land as accurately as possible, we may have a variety of purposes, e.g., we want to know where to put a foundation or a pool or a fence—or we just want to know where our property ends. Measuring our property doesn't produce anything new, but it does give us a new way of describing our property. Measuring here is a tool needed to accomplish a particular task; it is not an end in itself. It is also important to realize that as with any tool the accuracy or precision of the tool does not guarantee the accuracy of the results. The tool needs to be put into practice in order to produce any results, and it is the use that determines the accuracy of the tool. Again, even the most accurate meter stick imaginable is not much good for measuring your property. I can spend five thousand dollars on a camera and still take very bad pictures—a great musical instrument does not guarantee a great musician.

The overall logical idea that Wittgenstein is addressing is the ineffectiveness of trying to define concepts in a vacuum. The belief among many philosophers throughout history, the early Wittgenstein included, is that truth about the world can only be achieved by refining our conceptual tools such as logic. For Wittgenstein this approach generated many false pictures because concepts were being defined and refined apart from their use and then applied to reality. When the concept or theory and reality didn't match up, very often reality was twisted to fit the theory or our ordinary experience was relegated to "appearance." I think Wittgenstein would count his theory of logical atomism in the *Tractatus* as an example of just such a false picture generated by a logical requirement. That the logical atoms or "objects" weren't observed or apparently played no part in the world of our experience didn't matter. Logic dictated that they must be there. Once we drop the logical preconditions as unnecessary, we can see that the "objects" become irrelevant. In general, Wittgenstein wants to caution us against thinking of, for example, a concept such as measurement as an independent entity or length as the object measured. Both length and measurement are part of a conceptual apparatus. *Measuring* is an operation or a calculation, and *length* is a result. Both are defined as part of an actual practice and not as abstractions. Wittgenstein wants to show us that when we let use dictate the meaning, the truth will emerge and false philosophical theories will be avoided.

Our discussion of measuring above has produced some results that may be applied to an analysis of grammar. Grammar describes how we use a word. As with measuring, we think that by sharpening our definition, we get a clearer understanding of the meaning of a word. The clearer the boundary—the clearer the distinction, we think, the clearer the meaning, and so the more I can know about whatever it is. In part this is true. The better our concepts are, or the more logical we are, the more likely we are to find the truth. But as with measuring we should not confuse the tool or the method with the result. Again, just as I cannot define a method of measuring in a vacuum—measuring is part of a system that is only meaningful when understood as part of a practice—so, too, I cannot define a word in a vacuum and thereby search for its precise definition. I have to look at the employment of the word and see how we use it in order to understand its meaning. If I try to "freeze" the picture of, say, *game* by drawing a very sharp boundary around what I call games, then very likely I have missed out on the actual employment of the word and so its meaning. In the same way, my very accurate meter stick did not produce great results when I tried to use it to measure a large, rough area—the tool was unsuited to its purpose. In grammar, we can draw a sharp boundary around the use of a word for a particular purpose—but in ordinary language, in most cases, no such boundary is drawn.

Although we must come back to this later, the basic fault here lies in thinking the use of a word is dictated by something other than the way we ordinarily speak and write. Meaning often seems like something the mind can peer at through introspection in abstraction from language and the use of a word. To speak of words and their meaning outside the context of language really makes no sense. It is language that is meaningful, and words are a part of language.

In measuring, the tool—the meter stick—must be put to some use in order to talk about the measure of something. What would the tool be otherwise—an art object? By using the tool we can tell someone where to put the property line, compare dimensions, etc. It is similar with grammar. As a tool, if used correctly, it tells us where the words go or fit in the language. Grammar is the instrument or lens through which we look at language.

In this context Wittgenstein raises an important issue—one that we will have to explore more completely later on. Outside of or in a context other than its use it is hard to say what a tool really is. Think of the difficulty that archeologists have when they uncover an unfamiliar artifact. Again let us say we somehow completely removed or disassociated a meter stick from measuring. Imagine that we have forgotten the metric system or, better, have no system of measuring. Now, is this object still a meter stick? Does it still tell us that whatever it happens to be lying next to is one meter long? It no longer gives us this information because it has been removed from the system that made it a standard of length or made the numbers on the stick meaningful. In other words, outside of its original system, the question "*What* is x?" makes no sense. The answer to the question as to how we know what something is, its *essence*, is an idea in philosophy that has a long and tangled history. Clearly, for Wittgenstein the answer to the question as to the essence of x is found in the grammar of the language.[2] Let us save a deeper discussion of this issue for later. For now it is important to note that Wittgenstein illuminates the connection between grammar, concept or meaning, and essence. That is, there is a relationship between use, meaning, and knowing what something is. In the history of philosophy, this has been seen as an especially tricky relationship. Philosophers have long noted that my concept of x is (somehow) equivalent to my knowing what x is. In fact it is difficult to think of a philosopher that doesn't have something to say on this topic. A forest or two was probably needed for the books that have tried to elucidate that parenthetical *somehow*. For now let us note that Wittgenstein addresses this relationship as well and is anxious to clear up philosophical difficulties in this area.

At remark 75 Wittgenstein continues with the theme we have discussed above regarding meaning and precision. As we have noted, philosophers have long embraced the requirement that my knowledge of something, e.g., what a *game* is, in order to be true should be exact. When the use is not exact, it may appear as if an unformulated or nebulous definition is lurking in my mind. Looked at in this way it appears that I know something but just can't say it—can't get it clear. It could look as if there is some sort of psychological or epistemological malfunction gumming up the works. The solution then may seem to lie in introspection, or with a psychological or philosophical theory. But maybe, Wittgenstein suggests, this is simply the wrong way of looking at the problem or our misconception of the operation of language, in this case that meaning requires precision, has created a problem that doesn't really exist. Wittgenstein says:

> Isn't my knowledge, my concept of a game, completely expressed in the explanations I could give? That is in my describing examples of various kinds of game; shewing how all sorts of other games can be

constructed on the analogy of these; saying that I should scarcely include this or this among games; and so on[3] (PI 75).

And in the following remark:

> If someone were to draw a sharp boundary I could not acknowledge it as the one that I too always wanted to draw, or had drawn in my mind. For I did not want to draw one at all. His concept then can be said to be not the same as mine, but akin to it[4] (PI 76).

Here we see the connection between knowing what some x is and my concept of x—for example, *game*. Wittgenstein says that my knowledge or concept of *game* is shown in the examples and explanations that I can give about games. But as we saw above being able to explain or give examples of games involves the use of the word *game*. Hence when I am giving explanations about games I am describing the use of the word *game*, or I am explaining the grammar of the word *game*—at least as far as I understand it. Again, as we see in the second passage this might be thought of as drawing a boundary. Someone might want to use a great deal of precision in a particular use. But Wittgenstein insists that no such boundary needs to be drawn. Again Wittgenstein sees the concept *game* more like a fiber constructed of variously intertwined threads. He sees the two concepts mentioned above—one with a sharp boundary and one without such a boundary as interrelated—two concepts of the same thing with similarities and differences.

There are a few important ideas here, but we should take particular note of the relationship between *concept, grammar, meaning*, and *essence*. Though we will have to return to this later, just as knowing what something is means having a concept of that thing—it is apparent that having a concept entails a description of the use of a word. In other words the concept, essence, and meaning of *game* mean the grammar of the word *game*.

What Wittgenstein says here is quite complex and not without controversy. As we might expect, there are a number of issues that have been discussed in the literature that hover around what Wittgenstein says about grammar, meaning, essence, and concepts.[5] I would like to explore some of these issues in a general—not so much to settle them but so that the reader can navigate his or her way through them when they come up while exploring the text.

We should note from these passages that, as with the idea of measuring discussed above, two concepts that are dissimilar are not distinguished as "right" or "wrong." Certainly we make value judgments about certain ideas—slavery, for example, would be considered wrong, and many of our scientific ideas, like the Ptolemaic picture of the solar system, have turned out to be wrong. And of course we can generate many fictitious ideas that are false and indulge in ideas that are simply contradictory. What Wittgenstein wants us to realize is that none of these critiques of various ideas take place in a vacuum. Concepts, for Wittgenstein, stand or fall based on use. Whether a particular idea is meaningful or what it means depends on is its use. Measurements might be right or wrong or my ruler might be wrong—but we should not think of a method of measurement as right or wrong in the same way. Constructing the standard meter and defining the concept of length is not right or wrong, in the sense of being contrary to or in accord with the facts of nature. True, if things grew and shrunk in size at random intervals, then the concept of *determining the length* would lose its meaning and would probably be discarded. But a meter is a conventional method of measurement that doesn't correspond to anything in nature. I may take some unit of measurement from a natural occurrence—just as I might use a river as a natural boundary for a state or piece of property—but this need not be so. In other words, I may use a ruler incorrectly, and so the piece of wood I wanted to cut squarely is out of square, but this is not the fault of the ruler. But let us say I claim to have invented a ruler, a rod with Greek letters on it set at what appears to be random intervals. Certainly this object cannot be used in conjunction with our idea of *determining a length*. Again we would not say that this rod was out of sync with any facts of nature, but it would certainly be of little use in its intended application—we couldn't make sense out of it as a method of measurement.

The idea that concepts are neither right nor wrong in the sense of either corresponding or not to the facts of nature can be confusing or even objectionable when we think of the concepts of natural science—such as species or a law of nature. If botanists catalog a species of plant, say roses, they have delineated what a rose is and what we mean by *rose*. Surely this is done on the basis of scientific investigation, and so we would think that this concept is derived from or corresponds to the facts of nature. However, Wittgenstein wants to point out that this is a very narrow understanding of "concept" and "meaning" that restricts these ideas to classification. But the use of any word goes well beyond simple classification. Think here of expressions like "rose-colored glasses" or "he came out smelling like a rose." The concepts employed here are related to the botanical classification of *rose*, but extend well beyond simply classifying a rose.

We might imagine or know of a group of people who think that oak trees have evil spirits in them or whatever, and since there are no evil spirits we say this idea is wrong. But if we just examined the idea of "oaks are trees with evil spirits" as such, it is so far neither true nor false since we are not asserting that such a thing is real. A mathematician could discuss, for example, the concept of a thousand-sided polygon without being able to imagine anything connected with it or to provide an actual example of such a thing. Or we might discuss the concept of a *golden mountain* by noting it is constructed out of the concepts *gold* and *mountain*, but we have not thereby made any claim that the thing exists and so as of yet truth or falsity is not an issue. So logically speaking a concept by itself, like a method of measurement, e.g., a ruler, doesn't assert anything. Just as with method of measurement, a word must be used in order to assert something. The grammar of the word x doesn't assert any facts—unless you count "I will call such and such an x" an assertion. The grammar of *game* describes the use we make of the word—it is not the use of the word. The sentence, "Today's game was cancelled because of rain," can be true or false, but when we discuss the grammar of the word *game* we are in the realm of logic, not empirical facts.

Again, we might say that the concept *an oak is a tree with evil spirits* is wrong because there are no such things as oak trees with evil spirits. But the existence or nonexistence of something, for Wittgenstein, is an empirical question, not a conceptual one. Scientists do of course discard concepts such as *phlogiston* or the *ether* that was supposed to pervade the universe because it was shown that there is no such thing. But sometimes we keep a concept such as Ptolemaic astronomy even though the picture it presents us with is not correct because it is still possible to navigate on the ocean using Ptolemy's idea. Be that as it may, Wittgenstein's interests are conceptual or grammatical and therefore philosophical. The issue here with the oak tree and the evil spirits might focus on compatibility of the grammar of "evil spirits" with that of "oak tree," and certainly on this level we might say the concept doesn't work for us. The concepts of evil spirit and material object would be hard for us to reconcile. The language associated with trees—height or color or leaves or soil quality—does not fit the language of nonspatial and nontemporal entities such as spirits. It is perfectly plausible, however, that there are some people even in the West who would relish such irreconcilable differences, and there might be those, certainly, for whom the concept of evil spirits in oak trees presents no problem at all. There may be people who talk of the size, shape, and color of spirits because, say, it is important to their beliefs or society. The role this idea plays in their society may of course be nothing like the role it plays in ours. The problems we have with the relationship of the material to the spiritual and to the physical never occur to them. However, whether any or all of this is so is an empirical or sociological issue and not of concern to Wittgenstein. Nothing logical would be gained in an imaginary consideration of the beliefs of tribe x, except to point out that a particular context must be added for certain concepts to be understood as meaningful or perhaps to set up a language game that throws light on the nature of our own language—as we have seen. Again, the above idea might be highly useful in a scientific investigation. However, Wittgenstein's focus is the logic of language and the problems of philosophy, not science or anthropology.

The above ideas have sometimes opened up Wittgenstein to charges of relativism—ethical, cultural, scientific—and so on. Most often philosophers argue that if concepts are interrelated and elastic and neither true nor false in themselves, then there is no absolutely correct or "privileged" viewpoint. If all conceptual systems are equal, then some philosophers argue this means that truth is impossible to attain and skepticism is the only reasonable position to maintain.

If relativism means that language has various structures and that words are used in a variety of ways and that our descriptions of this—our grammar—is equally multifaceted and mutable, then it is hard to disagree with the assessment that Wittgenstein's ideas lead to relativism. These are the simple facts of language. But we must be very cautious here. Wittgenstein is making no scientific or, directly at least, ethical pronouncements. To discuss or examine how certain concepts of physics function is not to do physics. In doing so we have produced no facts or scientific results, nor have we propounded or disproved any scientific theory. To be sure the scientist may fall victim to conceptual confusion and faulty logic. Certain concepts such as *force* or *cause*, if they become variously mangled, may lead to faulty theories. For example, thinking of *force* as something mechanical led to theoretical problems with gravity such as accounting for the action of this force over huge distances and the initial rejection of Einstein's geometric concept of gravity in the General Theory of Relativity. Understanding that the concept *force* may be seen in a variety of ways other than mechanically may help clear the way for General Relativity, but it does not produce the theory or confirm it. We might try to argue for relativism in science by noting that all theories as theories are of equal value—they are all equally intended to be tools or instruments for understanding the natural world. However, it would be ludicrous to say that all theories are equal in application. This would be saying the theory of bodily humors is as effective in treating and understanding disease as the germ theory.

Clearly, it does not follow from the flexibility of our conceptual apparatus that truth is impossible to attain. On the contrary, it is this very flexibility that makes scientific progress possible. Imagine if the concepts of *time, space, matter, force,* and so on were unalterable or could have only precisely one meaning at any given time. It is often the case that only through challenging accepted notions that progress can be made, as happened when Einstein challenged the Newtonian notion of absolute space and absolute time. I think it might be nearer the mark to say that for Wittgenstein a rigid conceptual structure offers a false picture of language and so is a barrier to the truth, while a flexible conceptual structure reflects the way language actually operates and allows the truth to emerge.

When considering Wittgenstein's analysis of language and its relation to various types of relativism, the case with ethics is similar to science, but it is very complex and must be treated more fully later. For now we can say that unlike in *Tractatus*, there is no mention of what we might call ethics in the *Investigations*. In the *Tractatus*, Wittgenstein counts ethics as part of the unsayable but manages to have quite a lot to say about it—as many commentators have noted. The *Investigations* corrects this defect. As with science, Wittgenstein makes no ethical pronouncements in the *Investigations*. No ethical theories are specifically supported or discarded—and the same may be said for ethical or unethical actions. Our ethical concepts may be clarified, but as with science, clarifying ethics concepts might be beneficial or even necessary to ethics but is not in itself an ethical action. Clarifying ideas such as love or friendship may make you a better human being—if you apply them. But analysis alone won't produce a friend or love interest—unless of course you meet someone nice in philosophy class.

Thus, as we can see, Wittgenstein in the *Investigations* examines many ideas fundamental to the concept of language he developed in the *Tractatus*—that the essence of language is understood by exposing some underlying common element and that an essential component of language is a system of strict logical rules, made plain and refined through symbolic logic. Against the first notion, he proposes in the *Investigations* that the examination of language reveals language to be a series of interrelated structures. Against the second, he wants to show that using language is not like operating a rule-governed logic. Language is not everywhere bounded by rules. Uncovering the rules of language—its grammar—is a descriptive process that must be as flexible and multifaceted as that which it describes. Our grammar does not produce ideal objects that support our vague and ambiguous language. The vagaries—in the sense of use being flexible and words having multiple uses—are an essential part of language.

A further notion in this regard that can cause misconceptions, to which Wittgenstein and we will return to discuss at length, is that we can literally see what is common to a group of objects and this becomes the common element that forms the basis of meaning. It may seem as if Wittgenstein is belaboring this point. But actually he is examining another source or picture that generates the same misconception of the operation of language. Up to this point, Wittgenstein has been focusing on the idealization of grammar from a logical point of view. The picture of language in the *Tractatus* developed from a commitment on the nature of meaning and thought, which we have described as "logical atomism." However, it has been the case in philosophy that a similar approach to language has been derived from an empirical viewpoint. So, for example, the meaning of the word *tree* is thought to be derived from the empirical examination of various trees.

Wittgenstein wants to show that the idea of "seeing what is common" should not be assumed to have a particular meaning—there are a number of uses for this phrase, and not all of them could necessarily be covered by literally seeing something, as we might suppose. At remarks 72–74, Wittgenstein compares this idea to showing someone a series of color samples and telling him that what the samples have in common is what is called *blue*. This would supposedly serve as a definition of *blue*, which means the person would now be able to use the word *blue*—point to blue objects, comment on the blue sky, fetch a blue marker, etc. We might think that this definition has created a general mental color sample for the person that the person uses as a guide or reference for the correct use of the word *blue*. We might compare this to a catalog or chart used by a clerk in a store. The chart has, for example, the name and number of a car part on one side and a picture of it on the other so that when someone orders a part the clerk knows which one to get. The chart has a well-defined use in the clerk's work. But what would a "general mental color sample" be like? I certainly could use a color sample to buy paint. But how would a "general color sample" work? Do we know of any such thing? Again, this is not an empirical or psychological question for Wittgenstein, but a logical one. He wants to see if any use or meaning can be made out of "general color sample." The sample would have to be somehow general because there are so many different shades of blue. But here we have something of a contradiction—a color sample of a shade of blue that can't be any particular color. It is difficult to see how anyone could possibly make use of such an object—the idea is meaningless and wrecks the notion that the use of the word *blue* is carried on through some sort of general mental sample. Thinking of the meaning of *blue* as some sort of generalized image fails to account for what we mean by *blue*.

Again Wittgenstein is not trying to answer the psychological question of how the mind works when we learn the use of a word or mean something. We would of course expect something to be happening in the eyes and the brain when we "make sense." However, Wittgenstein wants us to note that a mental event that may be a concomitant to meaning cannot account for the use of a word. Grammar describes the use of a word in language, and there is where the word has meaning. When grammar gets tangled up in psychology we lose the thread of how the word actually operates in language. In the above example, although we may have defined the word *blue* by pointing to various samples of the color, it is clear that whether someone understands the word is not shown by noting something in the person's nervous system. Nor can we say that a person's having a psychological experience is sufficient for demonstrating fluency with a concept. The key to understanding the meaning of a word is being able to use it as we all do. What shows whether a person knows the meaning of the word *blue* is that they can point to a color sample of blue, pick out a blue object, and so on. There of course may be some psychology involved here, but if our interest is meaning then, for Wittgenstein, the psychology can be bypassed.

Again, a philosophical investigation, for Wittgenstein, is a grammatical one. Such an investigation does not aim at penetrating phenomena but is directed at the possibilities of phenomena—as he indicates in remark 90.[6] In other words it may look as if Wittgenstein is interested in our experiences in an empirical or scientific sense. However, with regard to experience he is interested in examining the logic of our language regarding experience—the possibility of making sense. Wittgenstein's project is to examine the various kinds of statements that we make about phenomena. Some scholars take these ideas regarding phenomena as evidence of a Kantian strain is Wittgenstein's thinking. Discussing the relationship between Kant and Wittgenstein would be too involved for our purposes here, though we will look at this a little bit in the final chapter. For those versed in modern thought, the interjection of the word *phenomena* of course brings Kant to mind, and Wittgenstein is certainly discussing the limits of language in a way that is similar to Kant's discussion of the limits of reason. But, as Rudolf Haller notes, Kant's intricate epistemology and his interests in grounding science in that epistemology are foreign to the *Investigations*.[7] It is the psychological and epistemological aspects of Kant's work that is apt to cause the most confusion if applied to the *Investigations*. As we have noted, Wittgenstein is not building any kind of theoretical apparatus. Wittgenstein's focus is language and the clearing away of misunderstanding caused by our failure to understand the intricate workings of language.

When Wittgenstein speaks here of the "possibilities of phenomena," I would suggest that this is merely to indicate that his investigation is not directed toward the natural world in a scientific way, but that he is interested in our forms of expression—the language we use and the description of that language. Through grammar we can form many different descriptions of the language of things and events— there are many possibilities in this regard. Some descriptions will be nearer to our actual usage than others. It is Wittgenstein's intent to note inaccurate pictures and try to dispose of them. This has no bearing on the things themselves. It changes nothing, really, but leaves everything the same. However, we let go of certain illusions conjured up by the complexities of language.

NOTES

1. PI 128.
2. PI 370–371, 373.
3. PI 75.
4. PI 76.
5. Cf. Garth Hallett, *Companion*, 28-34.
6. Cf. PI 90.
7. Cf. Rudolf Haller, *Questions on Wittgenstein* (Lincoln: University of Nebraska Press, 1988), 44–56.

4

Grammar and Philosophy

Talk of grammar and the rules for the use of words raises some philosophical issues centering on knowing, understanding, intending, and
of course meaning—to name a few.[1] Traditionally in philosophy,
questions of meaning have generally involved a wide range of puzzles
involving epistemology, psychology, and even metaphysics. Even a
cursory study of, for example, a Platonic dialogue illustrates how
problems and questions naturally arise when meaning is under consideration. To illustrate these issues and attempt to unravel them,
Wittgenstein constructs a language game at remark 143, which we
will examine in some detail. Again this section of the *Investigations*
for about a hundred or so remarks has received a great deal of scrutiny,
generally under the rubric of "rule-following." As usual Wittgenstein
himself made no such demarcation in the text, but these remarks do
seem to follow a thread, and at remark 244 Wittgenstein does begin a
"new topic"—also much discussed—the "private language argument"
(discussion, analysis, whatever).

Hearkening back to our initial discussion of language games and
Wittgenstein's use of the term, I think we should bear in mind that
the language game we will be discussing is intended as a heuristic or
diagnostic devise—not a theory on learning or the psychology of learning or understanding. In other words, Wittgenstein discusses a number
of psychological concepts in this section, and his remarks might strike
the reader as indicating the development of a theory on education or
something of that sort. However, as usual, Wittgenstein's focus is the
logic of language, and here the particular focus is the status of rules.
The status of rules in language is important since, as we have noted,
language certainly appears to be a rule-governed activity.

The language game is the following—we attempt to get a pupil to continue the series of numbers in decimal notation 1,2,3,4 . . ., etc. What we want to know here is when can we say the pupil has understood the series? The possibility of getting him to understand depends on his being able to continue the series independently in the way that we all do it. If we cannot get him to do this then we cannot say that he understands. The key idea here is possibility. We remember what we said previously about a grammatical investigation being about the "possibilities of phenomena." Here we are imagining a language game with the word *understanding* and trying from this to get a clear picture of its use. Clearly the word *understanding* in this case only applies if we have certain reactions from the learner—if he *does* or can do certain things. Notice we are not looking at this psychologically or necessarily from any experience that we have had. We are taking the ordinary word *understanding* and constructing a set of circumstances for its employment. We note that "getting someone to understand" includes the possibility of getting him to do such and such, and "not understanding"—for whatever reason—means he will do certain things.

It is important to note that so much of what Wittgenstein says here about *understanding* depends on the circumstances and the kind of case we have created. This point may appear very trivial, but a great deal is shown here. Notice that we have not altered the meaning of *understanding* in this language game in any way, but that its nature as an instrument is revealed. That is, in other circumstances other activities may count as understanding. Think of understanding a musical theme, for example. A person who *understands* a piece of music may play it differently—or react to it differently than would someone for whom it meant nothing. Compare understanding a game. Someone who understands cricket or baseball could, say, manage a team, whereas the casual observer could not. We will explore this in greater depth shortly.

Another important point that Wittgenstein shows us here is the absence of psychology in this language game. We often think of understanding as meaning "something going on the mind." The person who understands certainly has something going on in his or her mind. But this idea sometimes misleads us into thinking that the various things "that go on in our minds" are what accounts for the meaning of *understanding*. As we will see, the idea that mental events are the substance behind meaning often sends us off on philosophical wild goose chases.

Part of the difficulty with concepts such as *understanding* is the tendency to treat the concept as being the same as the "mechanism" of understanding. In other words we want to define *understanding* by locating what causes understanding—be it something neurological, psychological, or metaphysical. This practice has been common in philosophy. It is an ancient dictum in philosophy that we know what a thing is by what it does. In many respects this idea would be hard to deny. Things naturally belonging to a group share many characteristic activities and attributes. Hence, knowing the "inner workings" of something may seem like the best way to define it, for by knowing the inner workings of something—its design—we can clearly know and predict what it does. Thus it seems natural to define a car engine as an "internal combustion engine," or a human being as "a rational animal." We might say that concepts that are based on what things do seem to have a great deal of predictive power. If I know a car engine is an internal combustion engine, then I know from this definition that the engine burns fuel internally in order to run the drive mechanism. I seem to know everything about the idea once I grasp it. I may not know everything about this particular engine or internal combustion engines in general, but I know what, to a large degree, it makes sense to say and what it doesn't make sense to say—or at least this definition guides me to what follows and what doesn't. For example, I know the engine is not powered by water or electricity—I know that there will be ignition and exhaust—and that certain laws of physics will apply, and so on. Hence the concept is compared to a blueprint or design that exists independently and dictates what we say. There is, of course, a similarity here to Platonic ideas regarding concepts and language.

There are, however, a number of problems with this model. First, if we follow all the threads, we can see that such a model tends to divorce meaning and language. The meaning of a word in this model depends on or is compared to a design or blueprint that somehow exists separately from language in an idealized reality. As usual this "somehow" should throw up a red flag. Explaining what is meant by these separate ideas or blueprints is notoriously problematic for ancient thought. However, Wittgenstein wants to show that the meaning of a word is adequately explained by a description of its use. The meaning of a word is not something that accompanies a word that can be appealed to as a basis for understanding the word—without appealing to language. As we will see, Wittgenstein takes great pains to examine this idea and show that thinking of meaning as found anywhere but in language is unnecessary.

A related problem with the Platonic model described above is that it tends to divorce concepts and meaning from their application. It appears from this model that ideas exist and are meaningful independently from any actual use or application. Hence this model presents us with a theory of ideas in which the idea may be seen as a set of rules—e.g., an internal combustion engine must do x, y, z—but we can supposedly grasp these rules apart from their application or use. The idea is simply there and the person understands it—perhaps through introspection. Wittgenstein wants to show that understanding a rule requires the possibility of applying the rule.

Finally, there is in the Platonic model a tendency to confuse the concept with the thing. If we imagine the concept as equal to the perfect design or blueprint of the thing, it may seem to have more reality than the thing itself. Since the concept is the perfect paradigm of the thing, the Platonic model suggests that we properly need only to consult the concept of x in order to know x. With a concept such as an internal combustion engine, this model might not cause a great deal of confusion. If we had a perfect design and a perfect blueprint or model of an engine and the engine was a perfect copy of the blueprint, then the blueprint would be as good as the real thing for understanding the workings of the engine.

But there are problems with applying this idea as a general model for concepts and especially for applying this model to something like *understanding*. First, this approach assumes that the concept acts like a model or design. This presumably means something like, as we noted above, the concept of, say, understanding is the same as the mechanism for "understanding." But is knowing the "design" or apparatus of the understanding sufficient to allow me to use the word correctly? Does it allow me to know, for example, whether someone understands something? If this were the case then in order to know whether a person understood something I would have to peer into his or her mind and see if the mechanism is in operation. Clearly, this is usually not done. We must examine this problem in depth, but we can say that Wittgenstein wants to show that the concept *understanding* and hence the meaning of the word does not function as a blueprint for the mechanism of understanding. Rather, it is a tool with a variety of uses. The meaning of *understanding* depends a great deal on its application and circumstances of its use.

It is equally important to note that in the same way that the design of the engine is not the engine, the concept of *understanding* is not the same as understanding. Again the concept or grammar of *understanding* is a description of the use of the word. Grammar describes the language we use about something—it is not a description of the object, but a description of what we say about an object. Grammar or language is of course not the object itself. It may seem odd to draw this distinction or to insist that this distinction must be made. But it is important to note grammar's descriptive role. As we shall see, it is important to have certain concepts in order to do certain things. If I know nothing of engine design, I can hardly design an engine. However, we must bear in mind the need for putting the concepts into actual practice in order to accomplish any task. Having the concepts alone is insufficient to do something. The great similarity between the design and, e.g., the actual engine, and the fact that we can use the design to understand the engine, may blind us to the need for concepts to be understood only in their application. The difficulty created here is that the concept in this model seems to operate independently of any application—that the concept is the same thing as the object except that is a mental version and acquires meaning simply through this transference—simply by being in the mind. The concept as a copy of the thing may seem to run and work just like the real object—only in some idealized form. This model suggests that the concept simply mirrors the object. But as we shall see Wittgenstein wants to show that if we try to model the operation of concepts along these lines, then we cannot account for meaning. For now we should realize that a picture, mental or otherwise, by itself does not impart meaning. If a picture was the same as meaning, then looking at the writings of a foreign language or hieroglyphics should be sufficient for understanding them—but we know that this is not true.

If we return to the language game at remark 143, we can analyze these ideas in greater depth. Again let us recall that we are trying to find out the meaning of *understanding*. In this particular language game, I am trying to get a student to understand the expansion of a series of numbers and after several attempts he can continue the series independently. Now I might say that he understands the series. But of what did this understanding consist? When did I stop explaining how to continue the series? Clearly, when there was a particular reaction on the part of the student: being able to continue the series independently. Certainly this would be an unobjectionable use of *understanding*. That is, using the word *understanding* in this context would be well understood by speakers of the language.

Recalling that the purpose of this language game is to focus on the nature of rules in relation to meaning, two things must be noted here. The idea that "understanding the series" means or is restricted to the idea that the student consciously followed a rule and therefore understanding means picturing this rule or having it before his mind and following it step by step is not quite correct. We can see the defects of this idea if we think of something simple like counting. Must someone really have the notation +1 before his mind as he counts? Would we say he is not really counting unless he had this rule before him? Think of learning to add and subtract using apples—"two apples and two apples equal four apples"—must we always count using pictures or objects? This idea treats the rule as an icon or a sign, such as one that says *exit*. If we know a door leads to the outside, would we stop to check the sign before we used the door to escape a fire? If the sign were gone would we be unable to know how to leave a burning building or be unable to leave?

Let us compare concepts to rules for a moment. As we said, the concept *game*, for Wittgenstein, is the grammar of the word *game*, which consists of the rules for the use of the word and so the means through which we know the meaning of the word. But should we think of our concepts as rules in the above sense; that is, as an icon—as something once stated or displayed that directs our behavior? I think we can say that this model disregards the importance of the application of the rule and assumes this application is contained in the image or the statement of the rule. No matter how well constructed a sign or an icon, if we just consider the image then the application hangs in the air. If we see an arrow pointing to the left we go left. But this assumes a great deal of convention and practice. If we were walking through the pyramids in Egypt and came to a fork in the path and saw some hieroglyphs that included a snake pointed to the left, would we assume that we should go left? It might mean that there are snakes to the left or there is danger to the left—it might be the sign for the rest room for all we know. Clearly signs are conventional and don't contain their own application. The key thing about rule is its application. Hence *understanding* in this case depends on correctly applying the rule. It is a mistake to think that understanding means grasping a rule if this does not include its application. Thus to clearly understand a concept means understanding its application.

The other error in this regard that Wittgenstein wants us to note is that of confusing the accompaniments of understanding with the understanding itself. There may be a host of experiences, feelings, or even thoughts that accompany the understanding of something. These events are, of course, not the understanding itself, but, again, we are taken with the idea that understanding is something mental—a state or a process, and so we look for something to fit the bill. But feeling like you know how to fly a plane is not the same as knowing how to fly. Would you get on a plane with a pilot who said, "I certainly *feel* as if I could fly this plane"? Or if we gave him a drug that we knew reproduced the feelings of knowing how to fly, would we then get on the plane?

But are the processes which I have described here understanding? "B understands the principle of the series" surely doesn't mean simply: the formula "a(n) = ..." occurs to B. For it is perfectly imaginable that the formula should occur to him and that he should nevertheless not understand. "He understands" must have more in it than: the formula occurs to him. And equally, more than any of those more or less characteristic accompaniments or manifestations of understanding.[2]

In other words, Wittgenstein is telling us, if we look at the normal use of *understanding* we see that although a formula may occur to someone who is trying to understand, this trivializes or oversimplifies the concept *understanding* and masks the totality of what really occurs. Imagine encountering a tough problem in physics, let us say understanding the theory of General Relativity. Would it be sufficient to understand the theory if you merely pictured the equations of General Relativity: $G_{ab} = 8\pi T_{ab}$? This explanation is inadequate to capture what we mean by understanding—what happens when someone understands. Clearly if a rule or formula—even the correct formula for, say, developing a series—occurred to someone and yet he did nothing or was unable to develop the series in question, we cannot say that he understands. Of course, understanding may have something to do with knowing rules or formulas, and it is natural to assume that understanding is in one way like a process, in one way like a disposition, in another way like a state. Language permits all these constructions. We say, "So-and-so is in a certain state of mind" or "he is mulling it over," or "figuring it out," or "he is inclined to agree with you." Again, as we noted Wittgenstein wants to point out that there is no inherent boundary to the concept of *understanding*—a family of cases can apply. The word does not carry its meaning with it, but the circumstances dictate the use and so the meaning. As we have seen, Wittgenstein invents various language games—"primitive" or "simplistic" ideas of how a word works—to illustrate this and help us sort out illusions created by the flexibility of language. Here Wittgenstein asks us to consider the language game involved in getting someone to understand a simple mathematical series. He wants us to question the temptation to leap at an accompaniment of *understanding* as a complete description of what we mean by understanding.

It is important to realize that the language of understanding—"I have had this experience while understanding," "Now I can go on," "That's easy!" "I see the formula for this series," "The answer is on the tip of my tongue," "I realized in a flash that the answer was six," and so on are not the same as understanding but contain common expressions for understanding. These expressions can mislead us into thinking understanding is a type of process, inspiration, etc. Again the primitive or basic language game is used to show us what counts for us as understanding. In a sense the very primitiveness of the language game helps to illustrate our problem. The lack of complexity in this description of understanding—its simplicity—allows us to substitute mistaken explanations of *understanding* for an accurate one. Again this is the problem with our grammar or our concepts—they represent snapshots or pictures of the use of a word, which can be incorrect and so lead us astray.

> Thus what I wanted to say was: when he suddenly knew how to go on, when he understood the principle, then possibly he had a special experience—and if he is asked: "What was it? What took place when you suddenly grasped the principle?" perhaps he will describe it much as we have described it above—but for us it is the circumstances under which he had such an experience that justify him in saying in such and such a case that he understands, that he knows how to go on.[3]

Again, a crucial point is that without a context *understanding* makes little sense. It is within the employment of a word that you find its meaning—that you find the logic of language in operation—not in reference to any occurrence, mental or otherwise. Meaning is not found in anything external to language. Thus the word does not function independently but acts like a tool. We will continue discussing this idea as we move along: the description of inner experience—the language of inner experience—fails to capture *understanding* and in fact leads us into the difficulties of skepticism and behaviorism, as we will see.

Wittgenstein looks at another language game, that of reading, beginning at remark 156, in order to throw more light on *understanding*. Many of the same issues pop up. Although reading is a very complex activity, we take a simple case here in order to illustrate the type of difficulties we encounter when examining this idea. First, we look at the characteristic actions of an experienced reader so that we might see the word in its everyday employment. Various activities might accompany his reading of a newspaper, such as his eyes skimming the page, but we generally don't count these as marks of his having read the paper, for an actor in a play might make the same motions, but actually be looking at a blank piece of paper. Generally, if we want to know whether our reader has actually read the paper, we ask him questions about what was on the page.

Now compare this to a beginning reader—he starts and stops as he reads, sounds out the words, mispronounces the words then corrects himself and so on. Now if we think of the example of the beginning reader as standing in for all of reading then we might be inclined to think of reading as being the result of a particular mental process. Since we are dealing with a "subset" of reading it becomes easier to think of reading as a process. One of the problems with the beginning reader is that it might be difficult here to tell whether the person has actually read and understood what is being read the way an experienced reader would. The person stops, starts, stammers, and so on while looking at a printed page, and we have no clear indication that the person has read what he is looking at. Now in order to answer the question of whether the person has read, we might want to literally peer in to his head as he is reading in order to "see" if he is actually "absorbing" the text. Of course, no such problem occurs when we look at the experienced reader. When we normally talk about reading we don't wish to peer into people's minds to find out what they read. Again, we just ask them. We know nothing, in the ordinary case, of any mental mechanism. But the case of the beginning reader seems to cry out for just such an explanation. We theorize or speculate about various mental mechanisms that are supposed to explain the reading, to distinguish between reading and not reading. However, if it weren't for the "primitive case" no such mechanism would be required. Again, in a normal case we should simply ask, "What did you read?" Thus the incomplete picture leads us astray. The point is that if we want to know about reading—what really counts for reading, we should stick to the plain, old, ordinary language game of *reading*. That is, use the word as we normally do.

When we think of determining the difference between reading and not reading, some people might think that if we could somehow look at the nervous system very carefully, then we could make the distinction between reading and not reading with precision.[4] But doing so will not solve our problem. In fact our problem will become a good deal worse, for now presumably other uses of "reading" would not be legitimate. If we assume for a moment that the nervous system model is absolutely true, then a teacher, for example, could not be sure whether a student had read a particular work by asking him questions about it. If this model were correct then we would be forever skeptical about answers the student gave—we would always be stuck with the skeptical doubts, such as he might be lying or cheating in some way. The only way to "know" would be through a neurological work up that revealed, for example, the "right" neural connections—whatever these happen to be.

Perhaps to solve our difficulty we would invent a device for students to wear that continually monitored their nervous system—it would reveal the neurological connections as they are made. So now when a class is supposed to be reading the teacher can check this device and see that they are reading instead of daydreaming.

Apart from being science fiction (at this point), again this doesn't solve our problem. We have just made it more surreal. Wouldn't we have many of the same concerns regarding whether some students have actually been reading? What do we do in the case of partial or incomplete neural connections? What happens if a clever student figures out how to "beat" or reprogram the machine? It seems as if we need a machine to check the machine. Neuroscience will not tell us any more than our ordinary concept of reading—and in fact may tell us a good deal less. In general we know nothing about neural mechanism in connection with our concepts of reading and understanding—yet our ordinary concepts work perfectly well—if we let them. We should note that even with the addition of a neurological perspective, the concepts involved are on par, in a sense, with our ordinary concepts of reading. That is, there are in both cases certain criteria of application that are applied in order to distinguish reading from not-reading. The addition of a brain-scanning device merely shifts the criteria. It does not resolve problems inherent with any usage. Since the boundaries for concepts are flexible, there are no rigid guidelines for any application. There will always be gray areas. It is important to note that Wittgenstein is not denying the existence of any or all neurological processes that may have bearing on our understanding. We will examine this idea in depth later. But for now it is important to see how small a part the idea of a mental process plays when we examine the meaning of *understanding*.

Sometimes when reading the *Investigations* it is difficult to keep in focus that Wittgenstein's object is language and its workings. Because of his interest in psychological concepts such as *understanding* it often appears as if he is saying something about psychology—that he has a psychological theory. Wittgenstein repeatedly denies this. But the focus on psychology and the absence of any pronouncement on what the understanding is has led some people to argue that Wittgenstein is a skeptic or perhaps a behaviorist. His insistence that the actions of a person and the circumstances surrounding psychological concepts are crucial to psychological concepts is taken by some to mean that Wittgenstein holds that psychology equals psychological behavior. The lack of any definite psychological theory and Wittgenstein's focus on the flexibility of concepts has led some writers to argue that this shows that truth is impossible in psychology and that Wittgenstein is advancing some sort of skepticism. Wittgenstein specifically denies the charge of behaviorism, which we will take up later.

The charge of skepticism is a bit trickier, and there is a good deal of literature on this issue.[5] First, "skepticism" in philosophy usually means something like supporting statements such as "there are no absolute truths" or "there are no final answers" for any questions other than logical or mathematical ones. The reasons for this position are various, but the argument for skepticism that Wittgenstein probably was most familiar with is the empirical or sense-data argument. In this theory, what I know is based on sense experience and that experience is "local"—restricted to only here and now. Therefore, what we know is open to change—nothing that we see right here and now will necessarily be the same five minutes from now. Further, it is sometimes argued that sense experience is generated within the person who has the experience—there are no perceptions outside of a perceiver. Hence my sense data are "inner" or private and so the connection between my sense data and the sense data of others is in doubt. If this is the case any idea of absolute truths goes out the window because a consensus between all "experiencers" is hardly a given. Clearly, without the possibility of consistency and agreement in our observations, it is hard to see how we could achieve something like scientific law—a statement that holds good for all observers. This problem is much deeper, but hopefully the above description will suffice as a basic outline of the problem. Wittgenstein takes up this idea in depth in his famous discussion of sensations and private language to which we will turn shortly. I think he wants to show that the skeptical position we have just outlined rests on a misunderstanding of the language of sensations.

But some see another form of skepticism lurking here that is far subtler and related to what we said about relativism. It may seem as if Wittgenstein is saying that since the meaning of e.g., *understanding* shifts or changes with circumstances, then there is really no such thing as understanding, that we must be forever thwarted in our attempt to "nail down" what the understanding is. Thus we can never truly know what understanding is. There are a couple of errors lurking here. First, since as we have noted above that the concept and object are not the same thing, then examining the concept of understanding is not a scientific examination into understanding on a psychological level. This statement may seem paradoxical because we think that expanding our concept of, e.g., *understanding*, is precisely what the scientist is doing. Isn't it precisely the job of science to increase our knowledge? Of course there is no denying this. But the scientist's interest in the concept of understanding is far different from Wittgenstein's. Wittgenstein's interest is restricted to logic—he wants to see how the concept functions and separate out incorrect pictures of the way the concept works. However, the laboratory here is language—not nature. Again, Wittgenstein denies that he is doing science. An examination of the concept of understanding makes no scientific pronouncements beyond protecting us from false accounts generated by misunderstanding the workings of language. But this does not mean falsifying a scientific theory in the sense of presenting counterexamples, and so on—rather, it is discarding false pictures of the operation of a concept. It may be argued that this adds little to our store of knowledge because this process, as Wittgenstein says, discovers no new truths and leaves everything as it is. But we should not interpret this as indicating that no new knowledge is possible. Rather, we are not even attempting to augment our concepts, empirically speaking.

It is true that our language of *understanding* is flexible and shifting. But we must be careful in making statements about what follows from this. Fundamentally this is a fact of language, not a fact of psychology. In other words, it does not follow that e.g., my brain or nervous system must possess or exhibit something to account for the flexibility of the language of *understanding*. It may be possible to mean various things by *understanding* but this in and of itself has no effect on my ability to understand. The grammar of a word considered by itself represents a possibility—the various ways in which a word may be used. The meaning of *house building* in itself does not get you a house—it is a description of how the words are used. The same would be said of the grammar of *understanding*. In order to understand you must do what the grammar describes. Considering the grammar of understanding is only a logical description of the use of the word. Again grammar is not empirical science, but logic. Yes, we may not have "nailed down" the psychology of understanding yet—or a host of other things. But the flexibility of language does not preclude this. In other words, just because there are various meanings to *understanding* or *matter* or *energy*, this does not in and of itself mean that no scientific truth regarding these concepts can be found. Wittgenstein has no intention of denying the possibility of scientific truth. Clearly, we have managed to learn a few things over the years. The word *sick* may mean a lot of things. But we certainly know that bacteria and viruses make us sick in the sense of physically ill. Should the flexibility of our concepts cause the doctors to give up trying to make us well? Wittgenstein is not doing science, but he is interested in discarding illusions created by an incorrect picture of language. But it does not follow from this that we can never be right.[6] In fact, we might want to consider that scientific progress might be impossible without this flexibility of our language.

Thus, I think, Wittgenstein has been falsely accused of supporting various scientific or psychological theories. As we noted, Wittgenstein has sometimes been charged with behaviorism because of his insistence on the necessity of considering the activities and circumstances surrounding the use of a word as vital to its meaning. Wittgenstein is certainly interested in the mechanistic interpretation of thought and ideas, and he explicitly discusses and denies the charge of behaviorism.[7] There might be various reasons for his interest in this area. As usual, Wittgenstein does not offer an extensive specific treatment of the source of the problem he is addressing. Again, Wittgenstein most likely avoids an extensive discussion of sources because he thinks the problems of philosophy are generated by language, not a particular philosopher—thus who said what when is of no interest. Be that as it may, if you have never framed the difficulty of thought and behaviorism in the way Wittgenstein is discussing it—and this is certainly possible, especially if you have read extensively in philosophy—then you may find Wittgenstein's treatment of the topic opaque. It may be helpful or of interest to note that Wittgenstein was an avid reader of William James—both *The Varieties of Religious Experience* and *The Principles of Psychology*. James was very much an empiricist. Although this would be quite complex to sort out, part of the genesis of Wittgenstein's interest in this topic could also be Freud. Wittgenstein read a good deal of Freud, and apparently for a while described himself as a "follower" of Freud.[8] But this appellation seems to have been temporary. Freud may not have been, strictly speaking, a mechanist or a behaviorist, but he held that many of the processes of the mind take place on the unconscious level in a deterministic way; that is, apart from the free intervention of the individual.

Probably the strongest statement of behaviorism and the mechanistic view of human psychology is that the human brain is basically a sophisticated computer. One of the foremost proponents of this idea was Alan Turing. Turing was a mathematician and an early computer scientist who was instrumental in breaking the Nazi code during WWII. It is interesting to note that Alan Turing was one of Wittgenstein's students. One of Turing's more interesting ideas was that of the so-called *Turing test*. The test is designed to examine the circumstances under which we are able to distinguish human intelligence from machine or "artificial" intelligence. The idea is quite complex, but basically it describes a situation in which a person is in a room looking at a computer screen and attached to the screen is a keyboard. Now we tell this person that his screen is linked to someone else sitting at another screen and that he might communicate with this other person by typing at the keyboard. The contention is that if he types in, say, questions and gets always typical responses—"Hi. How are you?" "Hi there. I'm fine. How are you?" then there would be no way to tell whether there was a person or a machine at the other end.

Turing described his "test" in an article that appeared in 1950, and since this section of the *Investigations* was probably completed by 1945 it is not possible that Wittgenstein is responding to these specific considerations. Wittgenstein does very briefly raise the issue of whether a machine can think at remarks 350–360—to which we will turn momentarily. Though it would be rash to suggest that Wittgenstein is considering the complexities of artificial intelligence, I think he is addressing certain general considerations connected with the concepts and the language of thought. It is possible that Turing raised some of these considerations with Wittgenstein at Cambridge. It is perhaps more likel; that Wittgenstein had some influence on Turing. Though fascinating, whatever the case may be, a full treatment of this topic is beyond the scope of this book.

To return to the Turing test, for now we will bypass the technical issues of whether and how such a computer simulation is possible (there are currently some very sophisticated versions of programs of this type). The general issue is the distinction between man and machine, and Turing was definitely of the opinion that there would ultimately be a machine that would pass his test. We might say that for Turing the difference between human and artificial intelligence was only a matter of degree, not a matter of kind. He thought that by the end of the last century technology would have improved sufficiently that machines would routinely pass the Turing test. This has not happened to date. However, the empirical question is not at issue here. Rather, we should discuss the basic philosophical idea behind Turing's hypothesis. It would seem that the basic philosophical idea might be that what we call humanity is nothing more than a series of responses to conditions and circumstances framed in a particular language. To be human means to use a particular language as we all do. Looked at in this way the idea seems to have a relationship to the way Wittgenstein discusses language as we noted above. Wittgenstein does stress the importance of behavior and circumstances for language and therefore meaning. But the question here is not so much the essence of language but the meaning of *human*. Just as we were trying to distinguish "reading" from "nonreading" in the above discussion, the question here is how we distinguish "human" from "nonhuman." Of course normally this presents little problem. We routinely distinguish between human and nonhumans. It is only when we "invent" a borderline case or a primitive language game such as that found in the Turing test that difficulties surface. Our humanity seems to be in jeopardy because we can imagine a frightful future with robots that are smarter but look like us and may perhaps replace us—or some such. However, when we consider the circumstances of the Turing test, a context has been given for *human, thought,* and *language* that oversimplifies the complexities involved. Perhaps in these circumstances it makes sense to use language as a test of humanity—in other cases no such considerations would arise. To restrict "human" to "language use" would be a primitive use of *human*. It makes the mistake of trying to locate the use of a word in one, single, definite process or activity—a special determining factor—as we saw above with *reading* and *understanding*. The words *human* or *thought* do not need to be tied to a specific action or set of actions to be meaningful. There is no reason to draw such sharp boundaries around these concepts. "Being human" hardly means performing only a restricted set of activities as if we must act according to a set script in order to be human—as if there were only one universally accepted, predetermined set of criteria or a checklist for humanity.

So many questions arise when discussing human nature—but fundamentally we should ask ourselves the reasons for settling on specific criteria for a definition. Certainly any definition or the grammar of a word includes criteria for deciding how a word should be used. But we must use care in understanding what criteria are actually employed. As with *understanding* or *reading* we should wonder why we should be so ready to accept the idea that the characteristic activities of humanity, such as language use, are best understood as "inner" or mechanical processes. When we consider the concept of humanity used in the Turing test, we should question the limited scope of the concept. Why accept the limited version of humanity that seems so at odds with ordinary usage? Weren't we human to begin with? Why must there be a specific test for humanity, or a method to distinguish man from machine? As we said, ordinarily, this presents no problem. People are easily distinguished from telephones, cars, or toasters. But when we create a specific, limited framework that excludes so much of what ordinarily counts as human, as we find in the Turing test, then a host of philosophical questions present themselves. "Humanity" seems to lose its meaning in some sort of fuzzy gray area. These questions seem to vanish as soon as we give up the notion that *human* means only a limited set of activities, such as language use—as if human or inhuman existed solely within these prescribed, artificial boundaries. "Humanity" is something far more complex. These words are simply tools and their use depends on circumstances, etc. This does not mean that only one set of circumstances truly determines the use. Again we have not tried to answer the question about what counts as human. I think we can only say that the circumstances of the Turing test, because they are so primitive, seem more to cloud the issue than settle it.[9] Again, I would not say that Wittgenstein wants to settle the issue of artificial intelligence. Rather, if we follow what he says about *thinking, understanding,* and *consciousness,* then we can see that it is a mistake to pin these words on any process—neural, mechanical, or otherwise. Neither could humanity be reduced to these or any other simple set of activities.

The upshot is that Wittgenstein is clearly interested in the topics of philosophy, and his work touches many traditional areas of the philosophical endeavor—from meaning to human nature. His ideas have profound consequences for all these philosophical topics—but not from advancing any theories. Rather, Wittgenstein's investigation is logical or grammatical. Clarifying philosophical concepts can help us to rid ourselves of misleading pictures and so reveal the truth in these areas.

NOTES

1. Cf. PI 138ff.
2. PI 152.
3. PI 155.
4. PI 158.
5. For an excellent overview of the controversy cf. P. M. S. Hacker, *Wittgenstein: Connections and Controversies* (Oxford: Clarendon Press, 2001), 268-309.
6. PI 305–306.
7. PI 307–308.
8. Ludwig Wittgenstein, *Lectures and Conversations on Aesthetics, Psychology and Religious Belief,* ed. Cyril Barrett (University of California Press, 1967), 41–52.
9. PI 418–419.

5

The Grammar of Mathematics

At around remark 211 Wittgenstein begins a specific discussion on rule-following that has connections to mathematics in a number of places. In the time prior to putting together drafts of the *Investigations*—around 1944—Wittgenstein was engaged in a concentrated study of mathematics. Many of the passages in this *section* of the *Investigations* appear in the *Remarks on the Foundations of Mathematics*.[1] Wittgenstein's interest in mathematics deserves its own treatment, but there are some clear similarities to what Wittgenstein is addressing in other parts of the *Investigations* to what he says on math. In general Wittgenstein's investigations into mathematics are conceptual or logical, not mathematical. That is, just as Wittgenstein is not producing any scientific theories in the *Investigations*, so, too, his mathematical investigations produce no mathematical theorems. However, he is anxious to rid mathematical concepts of any psychological or metaphysical justifications for their truth or usefulness. We can see a relationship here to the investigation of psychological concepts discussed above. In general Wittgenstein rejects the notion that our psychological vocabulary is meaningful because it refers to an inner process of some sort or an external logical system. Rather, meaning is found solely within the language itself. In the same way, he argued that math should appeal to nothing outside itself. Again, this is quite a large topic which we can only sketch.

To fully appreciate what Wittgenstein says here, we should draw some connections lurking in what was said above. We discussed some ideas connected with behaviorism and the mechanical nature of thought. Let us try to be a little clear about mechanism and draw out some consequences of this idea. We often think of a machine as operating according to a fixed plan or a design, and consequently we think that all the actions of a machine are predetermined by this design and are therefore predictable. Often this mechanical notion, as we saw above, is applied to the nature of ideas. Sometimes ideas are thought to be like designs or formulas, and therefore everything that follows from an idea is predetermined, as is the case with the blueprint or design of a machine. Just as, we think, all the possible actions of a machine are exhausted by an examination of the design, so too, everything we need to know about something is contained in the idea of that thing. Whatever we want to know about something, then, is merely a matter of unraveling the idea of the thing.

It may seem to be the same with a scientific law, such as the law of gravity. We might think that the law sets everything in the universe up on some sort of railroad tracks, and all the motions of each particle follow the law and then the particles fall precisely into a predetermined position.

But there is a very subtle flaw with the above description of a scientific law, which is important to see because of the close connection that is often noted between the nature of scientific law and the nature of ideas. The above description tends to impart a causal or ordering power to the law. It is important to note and bear in mind for the discussion that follows that really the law determines nothing in the sense that it doesn't cause anything to happen. A law—such as Newton's law of gravity—is really only a tool for making predictions about, say, the path of heavenly bodies, if we know some of the data involved. The "force" of gravity—or whatever it is—acts between massive bodies in a way that can be described by Newton's inverse square law. We might say that the force causes the planets to behave in such a way, but not the law. Hence the law on its own determines very little about the actual motion of particles, etc.; that is, until we put it into practice by, e.g., using the law to calculate the orbit or position of a planet.

As we said, many theories of ideas in philosophy have connected the nature of ideas with the nature of scientific law. Thus, the concept *humanity*, for example, can be compared to the rule or rules that define the human species. If this is true for all ideas, then an idea, like a scientific law, can seem like a machine in which all the possibilities of "movement" are given in its structure. That is, just as the design of the machine restricts the actions of a machine, so too, what can be said or done with *humanity* is restricted by the concept. The concept tells us what human beings are and what they do. It seems, then, that the concept tells us what is possible for human beings.

We should examine the notion that a law, design, or idea "restricts the possibilities with regard to x" a little more closely, following Wittgenstein's remark at 194. For example, we say that a machine has a particular possibility of movement. We can think of a variety of machines, but a simple one such as a lever constructed for moving a stone will suffice. We want to ask about the possibility of movement for the lever and, of course, the actual lever may move in a variety of ways—up and down, side to side—it may even break or not move at all. All these things are possible. But this is not what we are after—we want to know something like all the inherent limitations in the design because we are looking for the laws associated with the design. We are looking for the essence of the motion, and so we wish to idealize the machine and think of it in the abstract as something super-rigid. Because of this need to idealize the design, the "possibilities of movement" become ideal as well and function as a limiting factor in the design. The fact that the design specifies just these and no other possibilities of motion is what gives the design its ideal character. Once we have looked at the machine in an abstract ideal state and delineated the possibility of motion in this sense, then we think we will know everything that follows from the design and so we know everything that can happen with the machine. It now appears as if we have captured the essence of the machine. Just as there is no possibility that two plus two can equal anything other than four, in the same way the lever can only rise to a specified height, and so on. These restrictions or "possibilities of movement" look like something inherent in the design.

But Wittgenstein wants us to note that "possibility" described in this way, as the limiting factor of a design, is a superfluous notion. Notice that when possibility is discussed in this way, it is nothing like what we would ordinarily associate with what could possibly happen with our machine. We have created some sort of "superpossibility." It cannot be seen or calculated, but it must be there. It is an ineffable "something." It is not the movement of the machine, but a ghost or shadow of the movement.

For Wittgenstein, we have just talked ourselves into a metaphysical entity—possibility—a substance that can neither be felt, seen, or described; a substance of no use to the machine or ultimately to us, yet it must somehow be there. A notion of this type can even acquire a kind of superimportance. We might think this "possibility" directs the machine, and since it cannot be found in the blueprint or the machine, but only in our language, that philosophy should replace engineering.

But as Wittgenstein says, "the waves subside" as soon as we look at how the phrase "the possibility of movement" is used. This metaphysical idea of possibility developed out of our need to idealize the design in order to uncover its lawlike "essence." Of course the possibility of motion is not a shadow of motion but is dictated by the placement of, for example, the gears, levers, rods, and pulleys—the laws of mechanics and physics and so forth. Apart from this, some sort of metapossibility adds nothing to our understanding of the machine. In the same way, as we will see, the "mathematical impossibility" that two plus two cannot equal three is not a metaphysical or natural barrier but simply a function of the logic of mathematics.

A rule or a concept can appear in much the same guise and suffer from a similar misunderstanding. The steps to be taken given by a formula may appear as a shadowy accompaniment of the formula like the "possibility" of movement for the machine. As an example, think of the recipe for a cake. The recipe is a list of instructions. A good deal else must happen in order for us to get from the list of instructions to the baked cake, to do with time, temperature, and chemistry, to name a few things.

Of course no cne would expect to find all these "extras" in the recipe, or make these "extras" dependent on the recipe or formula in any way. After all, the cake is not in the recipe but is a result of applying the recipe. However, it often happens when philosophers discuss the nature of ideas, particularly with regard to mathematics, the idea and the consequences of the idea are often identified. That is, all results must be "hardwired" somehow to certain basic principles. In mathematics, this idea has led to a search for the absolute foundations of mathematics. For example, a math teacher tells a student to add a column of numbers and multiply the result by two. Obviously, there are numerous other things the student might do in order to arrive at the same number—he may multiply by four and then divide by two, or multiply by eight and divide by four, and so on. Clearly all these results are connected, and they are all equally true. But the question that has occupied philosophers of mathematics is the nature of this connection and truth. What gives mathematics its absolute certainty? What are the foundations of mathematics? Is all this consistency to be found in the mathematical idea itself? Are all the possible moves to be made in the above example somehow present in the original rule—add the numbers and multiply by two—in the way that we thought the "possibilities of movement" are somehow present in the design of the machine? Or is there some other source? There is, of course, another possibility—perhaps there are no "foundations of mathematics" in the traditional sense.

Wittgenstein spent much of his working life, since before the *Tractatus*, trying to answer the question as to the foundations of mathematics. As I said, this work occupied so much of Wittgenstein's working life that it clearly deserves a separate treatment. However, for our purposes here and now we can say that in the end, I think, Wittgenstein came to believe that mathematics has no foundations in the way that he once thought. There is no "superstructure" that supports mathematics. In what follows we shall explore a little of what Wittgenstein says on this subject as it relates to the *Investigations*.

During his lifetime, Wittgenstein became embroiled in a controversy between two different approaches to the foundations of mathematics called intuitionism and logicism. Logicism is the thesis that all mathematical statements are statements of logic and logic is the foundation of mathematics. The work of Frege and Russell was dedicated to showing how mathematics is derived from logic. A large part of Wittgenstein's *Tractatus* intended to refine and further this idea. Logicism was embraced by a number of mathematicians in Russell and Wittgenstein's circle at Cambridge. Intuitionism, which we will discuss shortly, offers a challenge to the logicism of Russell and Frege, and some commentators have argued that this was a primary reason for Wittgenstein's return to Cambridge and philosophy in 1929. Apparently Frank Ramsey, a Cambridge mathematician, had discussions with Wittgenstein on the controversy between logicism and intuitionism while the latter was a schoolteacher in Austria after WWI following the publication of the *Tractatus*. Wittgenstein also heard L. E. J. Brouwer, the founder of intuitionism, lecture in Vienna just prior to his return to Cambridge. A number of scholars have pointed to this event as the turning point in Wittgenstein's later career, prompting his renewed interest in philosophy. The story goes that after the lecture Wittgenstein was quite animated and expressed the idea that he might still do good work in philosophy again.

While intuitionist mathematics and its debate with other schools of thought would take us well beyond the present volume, some information on the topic is important. I think Wittgenstein was very much concerned with the ideas of intuitionism, but I do not think he subscribed to any of them. In fact, from what I understand on the topic, I would argue that Wittgenstein is sharply critical of intuitionism.

The intuitionist program is in part designed to rid mathematics of any metaphysical speculations. On this point I think Wittgenstein and the intuitionists would agree. To pursue this agenda, intuitionists claim that mathematics is based on an immediate "intuition" of the natural numbers. According to intuitionism, the natural numbers 1, 2, 3, . . . can be empirically—albeit mentally—grasped and verified as true, and they are known to everyone. Anything else said in

mathematics is a mental construct—a finite set of operations following this fundamental intuition—that can be, again, empirically verified by introspection. In order for a statement to be mathematically
"meaningful" there must be a means of calculating whatever statement is made. Thus Intuitionists deny the law of the excluded middle.
In order to see this, let's look at an example of what appears to be a
valid mathematical statement: x is the greatest prime number such
that x - 2 is also prime.[2] A lot of numbers satisfy these requirements: 3,
5, 7, 13, etc., but we are looking for the greatest number that satisfies
the statement. Now if we think of the set of natural numbers as really
existing in the Platonic sense, we might think, according to the law
of the excluded middle, that either such a thing must exist or it must
not. Either such a thing will be found if the set of primes is finite—or it
will not be found if it is not. One case or the other must be true. However, since no method is given of determining which case is true—we
only have the supposition that either one or the other must be the case
based on the law of the excluded middle—then intuitionists reject the
above statement as a valid mathematical proposition.

Part of this Wittgenstein would agree with: a mathematical statement requires a mathematical proof in order for it to be accepted as
true. We cannot assume the statement must be true based on the law
of the excluded middle or any other logical law. Demonstration is necessary, and we will have more to say on this in the final chapter. However, one idea here that I think would be particularly bothersome to
Wittgenstein is that a mathematical idea is a mental construct that is
"intuited" and verified by introspection, that the rules for the application of the formula are known because the formula has "appeared" in
the mind. In other words, according to the intuitionists, the intuition
of the number line 1, 2, 3 . . . is sufficient to understand what these
symbols mean and what follows from them. On this model, it appears
as if you can simply see introspectively how the rule or formula is
meant, you just grasp it. True, as we saw before when someone understands a rule it seems to make sense to say that he has grasped or
intuited something. The difficulty is how we understand the concept
of *grasping*. One tendency Wittgenstein is addressing here is that we
often want to describe what is being grasped about a rule in terms
similar to the shadow of "possibility" discussed above—as an accompanying mental phenomena. In other words, we "intuit" or mentally
inspect a formula and because all that follows from a formula, that
is, what it means and how it is to be used, is not present in what we
see introspectively, we then want to say that what follows from the
formula is something that accompanies or surrounds the formula. Of

course, since the object under discussion is "mental" we want to locate these accompaniments in the "mental" as well—traditionally, in a psychological act of intending or meaning.

But this is where we have taken a wrong turn. What I think Wittgenstein wants to show is that what is grasped is not some psychological accompaniments of a rule but the practice of using a rule—or at any rate that this is what we mean when we say "he has understood" or that "he now knows the rule." We say a person has learned to calculate x formula not by finding the intuited something, but when he has calculated as we all do. He is justified in saying he knows how to go on in certain circumstances—not because of any mental process. Thus a "mental construct" is not required to follow a rule—this is an unnecessary intermediate step. Knowing how to use or apply the rule is what is important.

When we make the mistake of thinking of a rule as a mental construct that we grasp by introspection, then we need to explain how this would occur, and at this point we are often led down several philosophically blind alleys involving words such as *meaning* and *intending*. The mistake is failing to distinguish between the logically determined and causally determined where meaning is concerned, and this tendency gives rise to epistemologies of various types, such as psychologism.[3] In what follows, I will try to explore this idea in some depth.

Say I want someone to develop a series, and so I give him the formula for the series, and I explain what I mean or intend for him to do. He then goes and does what he has been told to do. If we don't try to explain what happened here with any more depth, then this scenario presents little problem. However, if we ask what psychological or mental occurrence is responsible for his grasping the rule, then we might think that what happened here is that the student had a mental construct come before his mind and that this construct is responsible for his behavior—that the construct guides him in how he is to follow the rule. We may think of this as the explanation of *meaning* or *intending*: my conveying the meaning of the formula or intending him to act in such a way means that this mental construct came before his mind as the result of my instruction. But it would be natural here to ask how did this occur and how is the mental construct involved in determining what the student is supposed to do? Notice we have entered the realm of the psychological or epistemological, and now we need a theory to explain what happened. We have interpreted understanding the rule or meaning and intending as grasping a mental construct, and thereby we have painted ourselves into the corner of a room where only psychology or epistemology will count as understanding what has happened.

Now we must explain how the mental construct determines the actions of the student. Again we have limited our inquiry to the "mental" or "inner," and so we seek to explain this by appealing to some sort of inner guidance or intuition. Since the mental construct is somehow the determining factor in the student's ability to follow the rule, we must discover (or invent) the mental mechanisms that accomplish this task.

We think that the steps to be taken have to be predetermined by the formula or construct. Again this means more than the answer is found in an analysis of the equation. We have made intuiting the formula responsible for the student's behavior. So it seems we are mired in a mechanical or causal explanation of meaning, intending, or understanding. The idea of the series that is supposed to be developed appears, says Wittgenstein, as if the expansion of the series were set on rails stretching out to infinity, negating all choice.[4] It is as if following a rule was like being given the order to "move out" by a drill sergeant of whom I am terrified. I do it blindly, without thinking, without choice or reasons.[5]

But is this really a good understanding of the way we operate with rules? If I give someone the formula $y = x + 3$ and tell him $x = 2$, must he involuntarily write 5 if he had understood the formula? Couldn't he write 3 + 2, 10 - 5, or 2 x 2 + 1 or any number of other constructions and still be correct? Or perhaps nothing occurs to him. Isn't it possible to understand a rule—let us say a very complicated one—and still get the answer wrong? In other words, even if it were true that all the steps were determined by the rule and we had this picture of the answers as set in stone, does this help clarify "understanding the rule"? One must still get the answers or write them down—one must do what the rule specifies— that is, apply it successfully. Correct application is what determines the meaning of "grasping the rule." Without at least something like the above set of circumstances, the fact that the rule occurs to an individual means little. Again, someone might know the rule and still not know how to apply it. I may tell someone who is learning to drive to apply the brake when he sees a stop sign. He may successfully repeat the rule to me, but it is not much good if he doesn't know what the brake is.

If it is the case that applying the rule is crucial to grasping the rule, then the causal and mechanical explanation of grasping a rule becomes superfluous. This psychologically oriented explanation held that understanding a rule or a formula was grasping a mental construct that was somehow connected to the steps that needed to be taken to accomplish the task. This construct determined how someone was to proceed in the presence of the rule. But here, as we have mentioned, we have substituted an ineffective causal explanation where a logical one is required. The mere statement of a rule does not contain its application, and it is the application that is of paramount importance. That the results of the equation or formula are predetermined, even if this were the case, does not guarantee that they will be applied by our learner—that he will do the correct thing—unless we include the notion that the rule forces its application on us. But it doesn't follow from a series being written in stone that it is forced on someone. Even though the English alphabet is something that is "predetermined," it doesn't follow from this that a learner will automatically remember it correctly and be able to recite it properly. Unless he is able to do this we cannot say that he knows the alphabet. If we agree that the rule does not contain its own application then we are inclined to posit some psychological apparatus to explain why we follow a rule in a particular way. But clearly following or understanding a rule means adopting a particular practice—doing something as we all do it. And the concept of my "meaning" the rule or "intending" that the student should follow it is clearly explained as getting the student to adopt a particular practice. Psychology or epistemology need not enter into the picture in order to explain *meaning, intending,* or *grasping a rule.* And here we are just brought around in a circle to the mental construct. Its connection to following a rule is an "unnecessary shuffle."

Again the important consideration is the logical one—understanding how the phrase *following a rule* is used in our everyday lives. What counts is doing what we all do under these circumstances. After all, a rule is simply a rule—"drive on the right" or "drive on the left." Following a rule is seen in what we do under these circumstances. The idea of a rule being dependent on a mental construct adds nothing at all here and screens the real problem from view.

We started this discussion with mathematical concerns—specifically intuitionism. We noted that a key idea in intuitionism is that a formula or mathematical theorem is similar to the mental construct as we described it above—in the sense that we determine the correctness of the formula through a type of introspection. I think what Wittgenstein is trying to show here is that this is an unnecessary step. A formula need not be thought of as a mental construct in order to operate as a formula or a rule. However, we should also note that there is something correct in what the intuitionist says: a formula need not be thought of as metaphysically expanded to be of any use. It may be that Wittgenstein is trying to show the inconsistencies of both classical mathematics and intuitionism. As was mentioned, philosophers have been searching for foundational concepts in mathematics, the ultimate ideas from which everything else may be deduced. These ideas have often seemed to many thinkers to be something like ultimate metaphysical rules, and the law of contradiction and the law of the excluded middle have always been candidates for such "super-rules." But if we deny these ideas this metaphysical status, mathematics remains unaffected. It loses nothing in generality or consistency. We would simply carry on calculating as before. Although we will return to the idea of contradiction when we examine Moore's paradox later, unfortunately a more complete treatment of this deep and fascinating topic is beyond the scope of what we are doing here.

To finish this section and transition to the next we should look at Wittgenstein's remark 237. Here Wittgenstein asks us to imagine the following situation: there is a line on a page and someone has a compass (the kind you use in geometry—not the kind that points north) with which he traces the line with the point, following it as if it were a rule. While the person traces the line with the point, he very deliberately studies the line and opens and closes the compass, making a figure with the pencil end. Since there is nothing we see that guides him in this process, and since we see no regularity in what he does, we can't learn his method of drawing the figure. Here we might say that the line intimates to him the way to go or that he is following an inner voice. In either case, clearly the line can't function in the way a rule ordinarily does.

But can we say that it is a rule but it is a rule only for him? Does it make sense to say that there can be private rules? Here we have raised an issue that Wittgenstein spends a good deal of time and an issue that has received a good deal of intention: the so-called private language argument (discussion, analysis, whatever). Some commentators think this question is interesting in its own right—i.e., can there be a private language? But I think the discussion follows the above thread and has an impact on questions that vexed Wittgenstein since his teenage years when he was an avid reader of Schopenhauer: skepticism and solipsism. We should recall that these ideas figure very prominently in the *Tractatus*.

NOTES

1. Ludwig Wittgenstein, *Remarks on the Foundations of Mathematics*, eds. G. H. von Wright, R. Rhees, G. E. M. Anscombe, trans. G. E. M Anscombe (Cambridge, MA: The MIT Press, 1978), 413-422.

2. Cf. A. Heyting, *Intuitionism: An Introduction* (Amsterdam: North-Holland Publishing Co., 1971), 2-12.

3. Cf. PI 204ff.

4. PI 218-219.

5. PI 212.

6

The Grammar of Experience

Wittgenstein was very familiar with the problems generated by empiricism. Austrian philosophy in general has a much more empirical bent then other philosophies in the German-speaking world.[1] Philosophers whom Wittgenstein certainly knew or read, e.g., Mach and the Vienna Circle, testify to the interest in empiricism in Austrian intellectual circles. Wittgenstein's connection to Russell and Moore and the latter's interest in empiricism is well documented. Moore and Russell were known for advocating a sense-data theory of knowledge as an antidote to the Hegelian metaphysics that dominated philosophy in the early part of the twentieth century. Science and mathematics were far from immune to empiricism as well.

Empiricism comes in many guises, but most forms of the theory hold some form of the so-called sense-data theory of ideas, which states that ideas are derived from sense experience. Exactly how sense experience "becomes" an idea is a matter of controversy. This theory, stated in its simplest form and propounded by Hume who was following Locke, states that an idea, say *red*, is a faded copy of the original sense impression. Complex ideas such as *snowball* can be analyzed into its simpler components—round, white, cold, hard, and so on.

As is well known, this seemingly innocent idea creates a host of problems. As we noted above, the major difficulty is that any experience occurs within the person that has the experience. There is no perception outside a perceiver. If my ideas are based on experience and my experience is completely internal, then I can never be sure that my knowledge and my experience is exactly the same as anyone else's. It is conceivable, under this model, that two people looking at something red are each having a different experience. If my idea of red is based on my experience, then what I know about red and what I mean when I say *red* is unique to me. The world—the only world I can know—is my world. The same must be said for each individual. Objective truth, then, is an illusion. Solipsism—the idea that my reality is the only reality—would seem to follow from the above considerations.

Looking at the text of the *Tractatus* it looks like Wittgenstein had come to something of the same conclusion.

> For what the solipsist means is quite correct; only it can't be said, but makes itself manifest. The world is my world: this is manifest in the fact that the limits of language (of that language which I alone can understand) mean the limits of my world.[2]

This section of the *Tractatus* has vexed many excellent scholars, so it would be rash to try to offer a final word here, and to attempt to do so would take us too far afield. But let us for a moment go back to an original premise of the *Tractatus*: words function as the names of *objects*. Now *objects* in the *Tractatus* are the ultimate simple constituents of the world. Since they are utterly simple they cannot be described—they can only be named. A complex thing is composed of objects and that complex can be described by stringing names together in a way that pictures the object. These propositions so formed "mirror" or picture the state of affairs.

Now let us make an (extremely large) assumption, for the sake of argument. Let us assume that "Tractarian" objects are roughly analogous to sense data in the manner described above. Since language is meaningful through naming objects, it would follow that limits of language would be the limits of my experience or the limits of the world. Only language about that which I could experience would be meaningful. Thus the solipsist would be correct—each individual can be certain only of his or her own experiences—that is the only thing that can be meaningful or be meaningfully talked about. Each person possesses a private language. Only solipsism as a theory cannot be said—it is not a direct statement about objects. It neither pictures nor names anything. Solipsism is a general statement about what can be known, and such statements cannot be said, but they can be shown.

Against this idea, I would have to point out that the "objects" of the *Tractatus* are usually thought of as metaphysical entities in the manner of Leibnizian monads—not as any type of sense data. However, at least on the surface, the above reading of the section on solipsism in the *Tractatus* is consistent with the text and to my mind makes it less puzzling. And if this reading is accurate, we would have a clearer focus for what is referred to as the private language argument (discussion, analysis, whatever). The so-called private language argument is a well-known, well-commented on, and controversial section of the *Investigations*. As I said above, I think this section can be understood fruitfully as following from the discussion on the nature of rules. If grammar is a description of the rules for the use of words, can we make sense out of the idea of a private rule or a private language? This question is important for Wittgenstein because as we have noted, philosophy often sees meaning as a psychological or inner phenomenon—but so much of what we call psychology is hidden from others. If meaning then is some sort of psychological phenomenon then doesn't it follow that only I can know what I truly mean when I say something? If so, then this model could tend toward a solipsistic view of meaning and concepts. If the above description of the Tractatarian view of objects is correct, then perhaps the section on "private language" would be more than a general statement on language and meaning, or a discussion on the language of sense-experience. Rather, as with the earlier discussion of naming, we have a further reworking of the themes of the *Tractatus*. Just as Wittgenstein now sees the picture theory of meaning as incomplete, so Wittgenstein is no longer satisfied with the idea that solipsism is right but cannot be said. He no longer sees meaning as founded on words acting as names for the constituent objects of experience, and so Wittgenstein in the *Investigations* is consistent in rejecting the skepticism and solipsism that follows from this position.

At any rate, we should examine the so called private language argument. We ended our discussion on the nature of rules with the question of whether a rule can be a rule just for an individual. We might imagine such a thing, but the circumstances required to make sense out of a private rule—as we saw with Wittgenstein's example of the person "being guided" by a line in drawing with a compass—leave us with a situation that is unlike following a rule. We would have to conclude that the person is not guided by a rule but by something inner which we could not follow. Imagine the chaos that would ensue if traffic were privately interpreted by each individual driver.

I think we can see that, in general, if language were in any way a system of rules, then it would make sense to say that these rules cannot be private either. The rules for the use of a word can be no more "inner" than the rules for, say, developing a mathematical series. We will examine this in depth as we move along. Let us return to considering the problem of the privacy of experience or sense data. We should note that even if it were granted that language is a public phenomenon, the language of sensation could be quite confusing in this regard because sensation appears to be something unique to the individual. But even if we assume that sensations are in some way unique to each perceiver, this does not mean that the language of sensation is equally unique. Thinking in this way results from a misconception of how the language of sensation operates. Wittgenstein wants to show that words about sensation do not become meaningful by referring to an inner experience. The rules for the language of sensation are just as public as any other rules we ordinarily use. In addition it is generally the case that the language of sensation is not meaningful because it refers to sensation. Again, we might think that words acquire meaning through reference to an object. But as we have seen, Wittgenstein goes to great lengths to show that reference or naming is an inadequate explanation of meaning. Reference or naming is certainly a use for a word, but usually one use among many, and it is only in use that we find an explanation of meaning.

As we saw above, the confusions generated by the language of sensation and the notions of the privacy of sensations usually begin quite innocently and are often wrapped up with questions of certainty. Hence, we seem here to touch on the question of what an individual can know or be sure of. Let us try to trace Wittgenstein's analysis of the development of these problems and their solution. Wittgenstein starts a long discussion of this topic at remark 246. A sensation such as pain can seem very mysterious. On the one hand there is hardly a sensation that is more direct or immediate. However, like our innermost thoughts, the experience of pain can be hidden from others to the degree that it might be said that only an individual can know for sure that he or she is in pain. We might think that since no other person can have my experience, then no other person can ever know with certainty what an individual is feeling. Clearly this situation is related to the problem of solipsism discussed above—I am certain only of the reality of my own mental states and experience. Sometimes this problem in philosophy comes under the heading of "the problem of other minds."

In one way the idea that I am unaware of the "inner" experience of others is simply not correct. We often are quite sure and quite correct when say someone else is in pain. There are certain circumstances when we might think someone might be faking it—as when a child wants to stay home from school. But there are a host of circumstances in which knowing someone is in pain presents no problem, such as when we see someone miss a nail with a hammer and hit his thumb. However, our problem is not an empirical one—e.g., devising a test to find out whether someone is faking an illness on a particular occasion. Our problem is a philosophical one. We wish to know if experiences are by nature private, and we wish to know what follows from this. If sensations are essentially private, then we must remain skeptical about the sensations of others. If I know about sensations only from my own experience, I have no right to transfer these experiences to others, and I must remain skeptical about someone else's inner experience.

This problem can become very deep and complex. So much of what we regard as human—thoughts, emotions, feelings, etc., without a doubt goes on inside us. In fact it can be argued that this inner experience defines us as human. So when we examine this problem our very humanity can seem to be at stake. If I am skeptical about the existence of thoughts, feelings, and emotions in another, then I must be in doubt about the very qualities on which humanity depends. Perhaps if these psychological attributes are truly private, I can only be certain of my own humanity. This puts me the awkward position of having to decide whether someone else or some group fits the bill. We see how quickly this idea of the privacy of my experiences puts humanity up for grabs. The flip side of this position is behaviorism. Instead of skepticism about other's inner states, we might just deny them altogether and claim there is nothing to a human being other than behavior. This removes the problem by removing the source—there is no "inner life." Behaviorism argues it is all illusion or metaphor.

I think Wittgenstein wants to show that neither approach appears to be a completely satisfactory understanding of what we might call psychological or inner experience. To deny or remain skeptical about the thoughts, feelings, and emotions of others is unwarranted. As we saw above, in many cases this situation ordinarily presents no problem at all. One individual certainly knows when someone else is, for example, depressed or happy or hopeful. And it is easy enough to distinguish being, say, depressed, from merely behaving that way. If we tell someone to simply act as if they are afraid, we don't suppose that they are really afraid of anything. Something is really going on inside a person who is really afraid. So it would seem to be unwarranted to leap to the conclusion that all psychology is nothing more than behavior. However, we cannot so lightly dismiss such entrenched philosophical problems and theories.

Wittgenstein wants to say that our problems with experience, empiricism, and the difficulties generated by these theories are very often grammatical. What happens is that we become enmeshed in a particular way of looking at things, and a particular way of speaking becomes the norm. This process very often takes grammatical fictions and turns them into theoretical entities. The solution is to take the blinders off.

First, we must understand the part that language and grammar play in our philosophical problems with experience. The statement, "Sensations are private," is generally not used in philosophical contexts as an empirical proposition; that is, we have not found out, say, after a series of scientific experiments, that sensations are private. In fact Wittgenstein wants to show, as we will see, that this statement will fail as an empirical proposition. This statement attempts to say something in general about the nature of sensations—what sensations can and can't be. Thus whatever else we might say about this statement, clearly it is about the meaning of "sensations": it shows how we want to restrict the use of the word *sensation*. Thus this is a grammatical or conceptual remark.

Wittgenstein compares this statement to similar statements, such as "Every rod has a length," or "One plays patience (solitaire) by oneself."[3] Someone who is familiar with Kant might recognize the above statements as examples of a priori or analytic propositions. Wittgenstein is familiar with these ideas, but he does not identify a grammatical remark in precisely these terms, and I do think Wittgenstein wants to make a distinction here between these other ideas and what he is trying to say. Wittgenstein is not interested in science or the epistemological foundations of science in a Kantian sense. Hence it is probably best to avoid the language of a priori propositions and analytic propositions. Again Wittgenstein's focus is language and the logic of language, and in this sense a grammatical proposition could be considered a logical truth. The statement, "Every rod has a length" does not really tell us anything about rods—it offers no information or news in the same sense as an empirical statement, e.g., "this rod measures one foot long." One could hardly go up to someone and say "Every rod has a length, you know—pass it on." This could only be information to someone unfamiliar with these concepts. But here you would not be informing the person of a fact—such as the rod is six feet long—but you would be explaining the meaning of *rod* and *length*. In a grammatical explanation, we are saying that the words *rod* and *length* are always connected or that it would not be meaningful to speak of rods as not having length or possibly having length. In other words, we are saying the circumstances in which it would make sense to say "this rod may or may not have a length" are lacking—the phrase does not have a use.

So if we ask about the meaning of a proposition we must ask about its use. In what circumstances is it useful? The proposition "Every rod has a length" is not of much use except in explaining the meanings of the terms involved. The same could be said about "One plays solitaire alone." The only circumstance in which this statement has much use is in explaining the meaning of *solitaire*. Hence, Wittgenstein wants us to focus on these statements as grammatical remarks: statements about the meanings of words.

Thus "sensations are private" as a statement about sensations can be seen to function in a similar manner. The statement restricts the use of word *sensation* to that which is private. This statement tries to direct us to talk about sensations in a particular way. Now we must ask whether this is legitimate. In other words, it seems to tell us that there are no circumstances in which it makes sense to say that sensations are public. We must find out whether this is so.

This method of proceeding is apt to cause some confusion, particularly for those students familiar with traditional philosophical approaches. We think of epistemology as being about the mind, the senses, and how these faculties function and interact to create concepts, and so on—at this point we want to say that philosophy and science meet.

But remember Wittgenstein is not doing science or psychology. He is making no empirical claim. Wittgenstein is examining this statement about sensations as it is used in the language. The idea of the privacy of sensation is examined to rid us of possible confusions it might cause—so that we might see things in the right light.

"All sensations are private" does not make an empirical claim about sensations, although it appears to. As a statement, it appears to make a general claim about sensations—restricting the word *sensation* to that which is private. This statement would appear to be obviously true. As we said above, sensations are internal, and we may choose whether to communicate them in most instances. But is this "obviously true statement" one that we should regard as an extraordinary or essential fact about sensations? If we look at it, the use of this statement is extremely limited. It does not state fact comparable to the fact contained in a statement such as, "I had a headache yesterday." As we noted, "Sensations are private" is not the result of a scientific discovery. It is certainly not presented or supported as such, as would a statement such as, "Studies have proven that constricted blood vessels in the neck cause migraines." There is in fact no causal link suggested at all. This statement would hardly be considered a news item—"Flash—Sensations are Private—Film at 11." As with "Every rod has a length," no information is communicated here, except possibly to someone who does not know English—or the meaning of *sensation*. We might pinch such a person and say, "That is what we mean in English by 'the sensation of pain,' and by the way only you feel it." But it would be very strange indeed to have to add the codicil "only you feel it" for someone who was familiar even in the most elementary way with the meaning of *sensation*. Perhaps we might try to explain this to a child who somehow thought that other people could feel their pains or hear their thoughts: "Only you can feel your sorrow, etc." In this case, the statement "sensations are private" has the role of a starting point for future dialogue—e.g., learning the "language game" of sensations.

If we examine the statement, we note that "all sensations are private" has very little use. It serves only to circumscribe the use of a word—and it may even have missed the mark at doing that. Like "every rod has a length," we might conclude that the statement is nonsensical—that it is not really about anything factual or about anything at all because no other use than a possible explanation of the meaning of sensations presents itself. For Wittgenstein, this will turn out to be a key feature of a grammatical remark and something that we must return to later.

Here, when we are attempting to address the nature of sensation, the statement, "All sensations are private" is presented as a kind of superfact—an idea that must attach to any statement about sensations. Really what is being said as far as the meaning of *sensation* is concerned is that any statement that seemed to negate the privacy of sensations must be considered meaningless and be removed from circulation.

But why should we choose to explain the grammar of sensations in this manner? Why would we want to make this restriction? What could be gained?

As to the origin of this idea that "sensations are private," at remark 246 Wittgenstein suggests that this restriction arises because of a confusion regarding the use of the word *know* in this context. This difficulty is also related to the problem of certainty. As we noted above, it is often said that I alone can know if I have a sensation such as pain. Framed this way the question about sensation becomes a question about knowledge. And now we have a mystery: how is it that I know (or perceive) my own sensations, and how do I know whether someone else has the same sensations as I have? The decisive step in the conjuring trick has been made, but it has passed by unnoticed.[4] Our question equates sensations and knowledge, and we are off and running trying to answer our question before we have verified whether this identification makes sense. Our difficulty is profound. We now want to "know" whether someone else has the same as we have, but we can't see how we are supposed to know this, for we want to know what is inside someone else's mind, which is completely hidden from our scrutiny. After all, sensations are private.

We must note that this model has to explain how we know our own feelings or sensations, and it seems quite simple. I know them by introspection. I can look inside his mind and "see" them. And, of course, if this is how I am aware of my sensations, then of course it makes sense to say that my sensations are private. Only I can introspectively examine my mind.

Notice how complex this is becoming. Now we have invoked the concept of *seeing*. Of course there are expressions such as, "I see what you are saying," which means, "I know what you mean." We use the word *see* in many contexts to mean *understand* when nothing visual has occurred. But when we talk about knowing our feelings or sensations by *seeing* them through introspection, what exactly do we mean? What is it exactly that has been seen, and how is this seeing accomplished?

It is easy to imagine circumstances in which we might say, "I see that he is in pain." But let us focus on the logic of language for a moment and look at the circumstances in which there would be a use for "I see (understand, know) that *I* am in pain." Certainly these circumstances would have to be out of the ordinary. There would have to be a situation in which it made sense to say, "I now realize that I am in pain." Are there circumstances in which a person might be confused about whether he was feeling a pain? What type of confusion could there be here? Can we imagine a situation in which a person knows someone is in pain but doesn't know who and only later realizes that it is he? Perhaps someone might say this when anesthesia has just worn off or perhaps when he is "under the influence." Maybe you have felt listless and fatigued lately and finally realize you are suffering from a depression. Again this would be a very specific circumstance, and something generally more complex than pain.

But in general sensations do not occur because you come to know them or saw them as if you had discovered the answer to a question. You simply have them. I use criteria to evaluate someone's moods or feelings or sensations. If I have known someone for awhile, I can tell when he is sad or isn't feeling well by noticing certain characteristic activities. But I do not need to do this for myself.

If we do "look inside our minds" introspectively, what would we *see*? We can, of course, try to pay great attention to our pains—really focus on them and become intensely aware of our pains, which pretty much means having intense pain. But even if we did this, in what sense would this mean that what I experienced was something known or knowable only to me—or in Wittgenstein's terms, Why would this mean that the grammar of sensation must include privacy? Wittgenstein examines this question at a number of places, but let us consider the remarks at PI 258–261 and 270. As usual, let us look at what it would mean to define sensations privately; that is, let us look at circumstances in which it makes sense to say we had done so.

Let us say I had a particular sensation and I wish to identify that sensation for some purpose. So every time I have this sensation I write the letter S on the calendar on the day I have the sensation. This could apparently be called a privately defined sign; it is certainly not a definition for anyone else. If you said no more about S other than "I have this particular sensation that I identify as S, then no one would know what you are talking about—if you are talking about anything at all. Notice I have not said here that this sensation is a tingle in my elbow or ache in my wrist that I call S. That would not be private. This identification is limited to a bare name that I supposedly can apply when the sensation reoccurs. But what is this sensation? There is no grammar of S and so no description of the sensation. If this is the case, then we literally can't say how it feels or what it is like—we can't call it an ache or a burning sensation, and so on. This sensation, like a Tractarian object, cannot be described but only named. So how can I recognize it when it returns? This might seem perplexing at first, but if you think about it, how can you recognize something that has absolutely no description? A bare name offers us no criterion of identity—that is, no way of picking something out. If you reported a missing person to the police and told them the person's name but could not describe the person, that person would be impossible to find. Sure, they could round up everyone by that name, but since you don't know what the person looks like then which one is the person you are looking for? If this bare name was the only criterion of identity, then there is no way of telling if the right person is found or even if a mistake has been made. There is no right or wrong here. It would be very peculiar to say anyone at all had sensation S.

With our sensation S we might think that we could simply appeal to our memories and then say this is simply the same pain that I had the day before. But this recourse has two mistakes. Since we only have the bare name S as that which identifies this sensation, then what are we checking against what? There has to be something objective we can check our memories against. We can check galley proofs against the original manuscript and see if a typesetter has made a mistake. But we can't check the galleys against a copy of the galleys to see if there is a mistake in the typesetting. With our sensation S there is no objective criterion of identity. I can say I am comparing today's impression to my memory of yesterday's sensation, but how am I to say that my memory is right? Do I need an earlier memory? Clearly there is an infinite (and unprofitable) regress involved here.[5] The recourse to "the same" is no better. To say one pain is "the same" as another assumes the meaning of *the same*. When we say two things are the same we have, if we use these words as they are ordinarily used, if not overtly, then tacitly, assumed a method of comparison. If no such method of comparison exists, then we are right in asking "the same what?" or "how are they the same"? In the use of S as we have described it no such method of comparison exists.

Now let us say I attach to my forehead a detector of some sort that is plugged into a machine, and every time I have this sensation I wish to call S a dial reads +8. Now that I have an objective criterion of identity, my problems dissolve.[6] It no longer matters if my memories deceive me regarding this sensation because I can check their accuracy. Now S might be given a definition (but not a terribly useful one) and I can legitimately call S the name of a sensation. However, we must note that this definition is no longer private. The point Wittgenstein makes is that the idea of a private definition does not accomplish what we wanted. It does not identify the sensation or give S any meaning.

We wanted to say that sensations are private and can be defined by introspection, but when we tried to apply this model we found nothing useful. The sensation that we wished to have private access to turned out to be a nonentity—what Wittgenstein refers to as a "private object."

Wittgenstein discusses the "private object" in a number of passages, but one of the most well-known is the "beetle in the box" at remark 293. Again, he is addressing the grammatical model of understanding the meaning of a word for a sensation such as *pain* though introspection—or from one's own case. This model could be compared to the following scenario—Let us say everyone had a box and in this box was something called a *beetle*. No one is allowed to look in anyone else's box, and each person knows what *beetle* means only by looking in his own box. Notice that the thing in the box becomes irrelevant. It could be anything or nothing or something that constantly shifts its appearance. The consequence is that although *beetle* appears to be defined privately, by each individual referring to what is in his box, the word is actually meaningless. If this word is supposed to refer to something it fails to do so because in actual practice it refers to nothing. Again each person defines the word *beetle* by looking in his own box, and this object might as well be constantly changing. The possibility exists that for any individual, the word *beetle* is fixed at one moment as he looks into the box, but when he closes the box the object could change and there would be no way for anyone, even him, to know this. When he opens the box again a new "definition" must be given. The thing in the box really becomes irrelevant—an unknowable object—and the word *beetle* meaningless. Thus, if we think we can define sensation privately, then the sensation, like the beetle, becomes the "private object"—something that is unknowable for anyone. Thus what we thought was so important becomes a non-entity. That which we thought we could know so clearly by introspection becomes a myth.

As we noted above, sometimes Wittgenstein's insistence on objective criteria in the use of a word for experience, combined with his inveighing against introspection, has lead some critics to the conclusion that he was denying that there was any mental or psychological component to our sensation and so advocating behaviorism. For example, pain must be reduced to pain behavior. But Wittgenstein explicitly denies this (PI 305–308). Clearly, *pain* cannot be defined by introspection. The assumption that a sensation can be defined as an inner object that the mind can "see" internally bears no fruit, as we saw above. But when we see, for example, someone crying in pain, when we have an objective element, then the word *pain* gains a foothold. However, Wittgenstein is clear that this analysis does not reduce the meaning of pain to pain-behavior or deny that an individual feels pain. It makes as little sense to say that pain is merely pain behavior as it does to say pain is an inner object.[7] Wittgenstein is merely denying a grammar of sensation that is modeled on "knowing" or upon "object and designation" or "naming." Again, sensations are felt, not known.

Hence when considering my sensations and concluding that only I can know that I have an experience and I end up being skeptical about the experiences of others, it is the use of *know* here that causes the difficulty. We have a "classic" case of taking a word, in this case *know*, in its ordinary employment and transferring it to a context that causes a number of philosophical problems. It makes sense to say I know someone else is in pain, but not to say that I know I am in pain. We do not know our sensations; we merely have them.

The idea that our words for sensations refer primarily to an inner experience to which I alone have access is based on a faulty assumption about the grammar of sensations and the grammar of *know*. We assume the grammar of sensation must be connected with the realm of experience in general—it must be like knowing an object. We then misconstrue the grammar of sensation so that it is aligned with the grammar of experiencing an object. Doing so creates a private object. But once we give up trying to use the grammar of *know* to understand sensation, this difficulty goes away. *Sensation* does not mean something private.

Hence "a private language of sensation" will not work—or we can say it is a fiction created from the flexibility of language. Generally, Wittgenstein shows us that when the grammar of our ideas does not work, but we are unable or unwilling to let the idea go, then we must use a theory to fill in the gaps—in this case sense-data theory or the like comes to the rescue. In other words, Wittgenstein shows that there is no logical connection between sensing and knowing. The grammar of *sensation* cannot be modeled on knowing. Yet a theory is often used to make a connection when logic fails. Sense-data theory tries to make this connection between sensation and knowledge. In this model sensations are held to "morph" into an object of knowledge—a sense experience becomes an idea. This theory assumes that sensations are present before the mind and this assumed inner reality of sensations allows us, we think, to construe "I see a red patch" as "I know a red patch"—the sensation, through the "magic" of the theory, transforms into an idea—an object of knowledge. "It" is after all, we think, before my mind. Wittgenstein does not want to deny that we have sensations. He does want to deny that *know* is correctly used here or that we can make sense of *sensation* as meaning an object "before one's mind," as if there was something here that we could mentally observe. The statement "I know my sensation" has no practical use in ordinary circumstances. This statement does not report a fact, as in, "I have a pain in my foot." That you are aware of your sensations is something which you hardly need to communicate to anyone in ordinary circumstances. "I know my sensation" is a grammatical remark that incorrectly construes our own sensations to be objects of knowledge. *Pain* does not mean something that I have identified in myself by means of introspection. It is something I feel. I do use criteria to identify someone else's feelings. Hence, I know when someone else is in pain. But "I am in pain" is not something I become aware of through an analytical process. The pain I feel is not an object of knowledge.

Once we correctly understand the grammar of *know* and *sensations*, we notice that skepticism does not necessarily follow from the language of sensation. If I do construe the language of sensation on the model of referring to an object, then skepticism is the result. This model turns sensation into something that I mistakenly believe that I inwardly "observe," and so a sensation becomes a private object, and I become skeptical of the sensations of others. But if we drop this model we see that there is no problem, beyond the ordinary (someone faking, etc.), in knowing that others have experiences. Mostly our language of sensation must make use of outer criteria. There are characteristic activities and circumstances that are part of the grammar of our sensations. We might want to imagine a stone having pains, for example, but this would include a host of mental gyrations. Our difficulties disappear when we see someone groaning in a hospital bed. No mental gyrations, psychology, or any type of theorizing is required to definitively state the person is in pain.

Wittgenstein wants to extend this analysis to other concepts in the psychological arena, such as thinking, intending, and willing.

Before we continue we should note that so far we have connected the *Investigations* to a number of major philosophical ideas, such as behaviorism, solipsism, and skepticism. Yet it is often difficult to see that the *Investigations* is "about" these (or any) philosophical problems. As we noted in the beginning Wittgenstein never announces anything like "I'm attacking the problem of . . ." Although this must wait for a fuller treatment in the final section of the book, I think there is a deep philosophical background to the *Investigations* that is not unlike that of the *Tractatus*.

Briefly, although there is no social theory of language presented in the *Investigations*—remember that there are no theories of any sort—we can no doubt conclude from the preceding discussion, among others, that language is a social, not a private or inner phenomenon. It is part of our lives. As such it shows a good deal about us, namely what forms of expression we are inclined to accept or to find attractive. Clearly, as we saw above, there is no logical necessity in thinking that experience is private, and that therefore skepticism or even solipsism is the natural state of human beings. We don't have to think of ourselves as social atoms, cut off from other people, but we have expended a great deal of (misguided, Wittgenstein wants to show) philosophical energy in defending this very idea. Why this is so Wittgenstein does not speculate, but that it is so is clear. That many of the ideas we have discussed are the source of much misery is also clear—it was not idle chatter when Wittgenstein spoke of "the darkness of this time" in the preface to the book. I think much of the "point" of the *Investigations* is that if we rid ourselves of these muddled conceptions of language, then we have gone a long way to curing many of our social ills. It might be difficult to connect ideas such as skepticism regarding other minds or solipsism to the various problems that plague our society.

But as Kant would point out, and I hope most people would agree, it is a fundamental moral fault to think of oneself as deserving all the freedoms, rights, and privileges accorded to human beings while being willing to deny these same rights to others, say a minority. I think we can see how the aforementioned skeptic or solipsist may find themselves on the leading edge of just such a position, arguing in effect "I'm sure I am human because I have clear introspective access to my mental states, but I have no such knowledge of anyone else. In fact, if someone looks or acts differently maybe they are somehow inferior." For Wittgenstein, the danger is that these forms of expression may have become embedded in our language, guiding what we say and ultimately what we do. This critique of our language goes much deeper than ridding ourselves of some offensive words. The culprit is the desire or attractiveness of certain forms of expression. If we can show that they go nowhere perhaps they will lose their appeal. After all, we generally hold them because we think they have so much theoretical justification—nonscience in a symbiotic relationship with nonsense.[8] We will have more to say on this in the final chapter.

NOTES

1. Cf. Barry Smith, *Austrian Philosophy: The Legacy of Franz Brentano* (Chicago: Open Court Publishing, 1994).
2. TLP 5.62.
3. PI 251.
4. PI 308.
5. PI 265.
6. PI 270.
7. PI 304.
8. Cf. von Wright, *Wittgenstein*, 208-209.

7

The Grammar of Psychology

We have so far given an introductory overview of the major themes in the remarks up to roughly remark 316—close to half the remarks in part I. Much of the rest of the *Investigations* discusses psychological concepts, and many discussions in part II also address these topics. Here we must briefly address the construction of the work. As we noted in the beginning, there is a great deal of overlapping material between the last section of part I and part II. There is also something of a controversy as to whether what we have as part II really is intended as a separate section or was meant to be worked into the last section of part I.

Part II of the work is something of an anomaly. Apparently, Wittgenstein conceived of the *Investigations* in many different formats, but he never settled on a final presentation of the book. It seems that there were supposed to be two volumes or two parts. However the second part might have been intended to be on mathematics. It also could have been Wittgenstein's intention to include a second part or volume on psychology. For some reason, Wittgenstein seems to have left no clear indication as to what was to be published or how.

Wittgenstein's literary executors placed the book in its present format, but why they chose this particular presentation is not exactly clear. Two of the three, Rhees and Anscombe, are of the opinion, expressed in the editor's preface, that Wittgenstein would have suppressed the last thirty pages or so of part I and worked the material in part II into its place. Unfortunately they do not explain in the preface why they think this is so. It does leave us with something of a contradiction—they put certain material in a separate part II but they don't think there really is a part II. G. H. von Wright, the third literary executor, was of the opinion that Wittgenstein's thought was taking off in a new direction. What we have as part II, he thinks, is part of a new phase, with the book *Zettel* being a new transitional work—or part of a trilogy.[1] Perhaps this disagreement between the executors was settled by breaking the work up into two parts, with Rhees and Anscombe publishing a dissent in the preface. However, von Wright, who published a lengthy study on the composition of the *Investigations*, does not say anything other than he disagrees with Rhees and Anscombe on the idea that the work as is forms a unit.

It would be well beyond the scope of my book to try to settle this problem. Speaking for myself, I would say that von Wright's assessment of Wittgenstein's work has usually proved to be uncannily accurate. However, at present, I am more impressed by the continuity between the two parts of the *Investigations*. It seems to me that Wittgenstein developed a method for attacking philosophical problems, which he explains in the beginning of part I, and the end of part I and all of part II is spent in applying that method to the problems of psychology. When von Wright talks about a new direction, I don't think he means a change to the degree that took place in the period between the *Tractatus* and the *Investigations*, i.e., something involving a complete discontinuity. However, this must remain a speculation. In any case I would not argue for this type of discontinuity between parts II and I. We will explore this topic at greater length when we get to part II.

At about remark 318 Wittgenstein embarks on a discussion of what we might call mental phenomena or mental processes. These include thinking, intending, understanding, willing, expecting, wishing, and others. Some of the discussion seems new, while some seems to circle back to previous ideas. This method of treatment can be quite dizzying at times, but it is consistent with Wittgenstein's claim in his preface: that is how he proceeded. He was continually approaching a set of problems from different angles and making new "sketches" of the problems and their solutions. As I indicated above, I think for the most part what we have covered so far is outlining Wittgenstein's "grammatical" method of investigating the problems of philosophy. This method reveals that misunderstanding the function of words often leads us down the blind alley of bad theorizing. Wittgenstein's solution is to bring the words back to their original home by showing how an incorrect picture fails in its application and seeing how our question subsides when words are returned to their original language game.

When discussing these psychological concepts (thinking, willing, intending, and so on), Wittgenstein focuses on the tendency to identify thinking, for example, with an inner mental process. Thinking is supposed to be the mental process that accompanies, say, speaking, writing, or calculating. The words we say or write or the calculations on the paper are supposed to be seen as the results or signs of this process. Traditional philosophy usually holds that the process in the mind is the important thing—the real thinking—while the answer we derive from calculating that we write down on the paper is just a sign or a symbol. But if the manipulation of the mathematical symbols and getting an answer is not calculating, but calculating is a process going on in my mind, then this process is notoriously very hard to get a hold of. As with sensation, when we try to locate this "process" through introspection we seem to come up with nothing or with many conflicting results. Where once we could have simply said "I am thinking of the answer," or some such, now we have to construe *thinking* as referring to a mental process that we can't seem to nail down.

In the same way it is tempting to think that when we use language, or when we read a printed page and grasp its meaning, that this is the result of a psychological process. The words we read seem unimportant—it is the thought process that gives words their life. After all, a sign in a foreign language or a series of hieroglyphs is dead to us. Nothing occurs in our minds when we look at them. Once their meaning has been explained to us we understand them. Hence it is natural to think that meaning is essentially a psychological or mental process.

Words in this picture or model of meaning are like the pieces in chess. Their size and shape—their configurations—are arbitrary and irrelevant to the game. One can play with painted stones as long as one can make the important distinctions, and these distinctions are made by the rules. These rules are not painted on the piece necessarily—we who know the rules remember them or have a grasp of them. These rules then are inner mental phenomena—these rules are what is important: I know this is the king and it can move this way and that, and so on. The real matter of chess takes place in the mind—learning openings and endings, strategy and tactics. Very talented players only need an algebraic notation to play and can play entirely in their imaginations. The pieces are just lumps of plastic or metal or whatever—they are nothing without the mind. The mental processes of playing are what is important.

When this model is applied to language, words are taken as unimportant on their own, and a mental process is required to supply "meaning." But what can be said about this mental process? What exactly is "supplied" by the mind that accounts for meaning? We talk of mental processes, but the use of the phrase is unclear. Do we mean something that accompanies a word? Do we mean the mental events surrounding language—feelings or images and so forth that are present or swim before our minds as we "mean" something? Perhaps this process is an action performed by the soul? Maybe we are at a loss and conclude that these mental processes just are strange, but at some point in the future psychology will sort them out. After all, psychology as a science is in its infancy. In the years to come it will have advanced enough to answer these questions.

But Wittgenstein wants to show that advances in science will not solve the problem of mental processes because our problem here is grammatical, not empirical. Our search for mental processes as outlined above is a fool's errand. Our language has tricked us into thinking that words are meaningful only when they express thoughts or refer to something inner. The model is that words are signs of or point to something within us. Because we are stuck with these and other pictures, we have been led to a further picture of the inner mental phenomenon that lies "behind" thought. This phenomenon, we think, is what constitutes the actual thinking. When we can't get a hold of it we resort to theory to explain it, compounding the problem. Wittgenstein wants to show that if we look at how psychological words are used, the need for a mental phenomenon as a support will disappear.

As with many other problems discussed in the *Investigations*, this one too may have its origin in the *Tractatus*. In that book a thought was considered to be the result of picturing facts to ourselves.[2] Propositions are pictures of facts, and thought is considered to be a proposition with sense.[3] Thus it would seem that thought or thinking is essential to meaning or sense. If this analysis is correct, then, it is possible that Wittgenstein partially succumbed to something he was trying to rid logic of: psychologism—the idea that inference or making a deduction is a psychological process. In the *Tractatus* Wittgenstein shows that inference is a logical, not psychological, process. However, it would appear that psychology or epistemology is necessary for meaning. It is an insight of the *Tractatus* that the propositions of language stand in perfect logical order just as they are.[4] It would seem though that for Wittgenstein in the *Tractatus* this was insufficient for meaning. A proposition must be thought to be meaningful. Apparently the *Investigations* is aimed at correcting this idea. Meaning is not seen as something psychological but is found in the use of words. Wittgenstein sees that we no longer need a psychological process that forms the basis of language in order to account for meaning.

Wittgenstein wants to examine this problem in depth. The problem is usually generated when we consider "meaning" or "intending." There is a phenomenon that we can identify as meaning something or intending someone to understand what is said in a particular way. A few examples should serve to illustrate this. A parent tells the babysitter to teach the children a game. The babysitter teaches them gambling with dice. The parent says, "Wait a minute. That is not what I meant."[5] Or an artist paints a picture and someone looks for a variety of symbols in it and declares that the painting is about the "futility of all created existence." However, the artist says, "I meant the painting to represent nothing of the sort. I meant it only to be a pretty picture."

Given these circumstances, meaning or intending does seem to be something divorced from its expression. What is meant seems to be something inner and something other than the expression. But do these examples and this interpretation give us a fair picture of meaning or intending? It seems to steer us once again toward the private object—something "inner" that is part of the meaning but is itself not capable of an exact description. Let us look at the following text.

> "But when I imagine something, something certainly *happens*!" Well something happens—and then I make a noise. What for? Presumably in order to tell what happens.—But how is the *telling* done? When are we said to *tell* anything?—What is the language game of telling?

> I should like to say: you regard it as too much of a matter of course that one can tell anything to anyone. That is to say: we are so much accustomed to communication through language, in conversation that it looks to us as if the whole point of communication lay in this: someone else grasps the sense of my words—which is something mental: he as it were takes it into his own mind. If he then does something further with it as well, that is no part of the immediate purpose of language.

> One would like to say "Telling brings it about that he knows that I am in pain; it produces the mental phenomenon, everything else is inessential to the telling." As for what this queer mental phenomenon is—there is time enough for that. Mental processes just are queer. It as if one said: "The clock tells us the time. *What* time is, is not yet settled. And as for what one tells the time *for*—that doesn't come in here."[6] (PI 363)

In other words, if communication depends on this so-called mental phenomenon, it is strange that it seems to play such an insignificant part in our actual everyday communication and everything else—gestures, tone of voice, circumstances, and so on that seem to be so prevalent in our language—is reduced to inessential.

Wittgenstein's example of time here is significant. Time is a frequent scientific and philosophical mystery. Let us say for a moment that clocks might be looked at in two ways. In one way they are conventional instruments like any measuring apparatus—like a ruler, for instance. We have broken up the day into twenty-four segments called hours that roughly get us from one sunrise to the next. This idea has all sorts of uses—it is mostly good as an objective marker for scheduling or coordinating events in a variety of ways. I say to someone, "Meet me at six o'clock," or "The game starts at 7:30," or "I saw him jog by and then again an hour later," and so on. Telling the time here is hardly mysterious. It's something we learn to do when we are children.

But let us suppose for a moment that the clock reports to us and lets us know "the time"—since the idea of time is based on the rotation of the earth, then the clock is reporting some objective fact such as the position of the earth. But even if this were true, notice how irrelevant this fact is to telling the time. Of course, time might be thought of in many other ways—such as an a priori form of experience, as Kant would have it—but how is it that the clock "tells" us this? A "form of experience" would not enter into what is meant by telling the time. In reality the clock does not report on any physical or metaphysical phenomenon. Strictly speaking, a clock "reports" on nothing at all. A clock represents a handy method of measurement, but a measure in the sense of a means of agreement or a medium—not as if it necessarily measures anything particular. In a similar way paper money is a medium of exchange. Beyond its value as paper and as a medium of exchange, a dollar bill is worthless.

Thus, if we drop the idea that the clock reports something or informs us of something—about the status of this strange object time—we are less inclined to see telling the time as a mystery. If we try to figure out what it is that the clock reports to us we are in fact making time into a very mysterious object. Notice, however, that if we look at what clocks are used for, we do not need to settle the question of the essence of time. This does not mean that the question never comes up in other circumstances. But here, paying attention to the actual use relieves us of the difficulty posed by time.

The same might be said for meaning and a host of other psychological concepts. Our difficulties arise from assuming that our words are meaningful only because they "tell" of or report on a psychological state. Let us try to think about how some of these psychological words are ordinarily used. If I say my arm hurts, this is not a report of an inner state or a mental process that I have discovered and am now describing. Or if I ask, "Do you want to go to the ballgame?," I am not expressing a mental phenomenon and neither do I want you to look inside yourself and try to locate something similar. You may turn the question over in your mind to see if you have the time or to see if you do want to go. But this is not looking for some sort of mental occurrence: images, sensations, or what have you. It would make as much sense (probably more) to take your pulse and see if it is racing and then conclude that you were really excited about the game and wanted to go after all.

The language of inner experience as it is used above—as referring to an "inner" occurrence—tends to turn inner or psychological experience into a private object. To model our psychological language on reference—my words only are meaningful if they refer to an inner state—tends to make what you are talking about irrelevant. If someone says "let me think about it" and this is supposed to mean something like the person is attempting to observe an inner phenomenon, then how am I supposed to know what, if anything, he is doing? Worse still, as we saw with the language of sensation, if thinking about something means "trying to observe inner phenomena," then it really is impossible for the individual to know what he or she is thinking about.

This last sentence may seem puzzling, but it is important. After all, don't we always know exactly what we are thinking about? Well, we must use caution because even in this case our language can play tricks on us. Suppose someone said that he or she was "thinking about" the last number in the expansion of pi. Now this might possibly mean something like the person was wondering if there is a last number or wondering what it might be. But we know it cannot mean that he or she knows exactly the last number in the expansion of pi since pi repeats indefinitely. Remember when we discovered that trying to understand the meaning of "having a sensation" based on the model of "knowing an object" we found it couldn't be done. We found that there was nothing to know. We have pains, and this is not a process of knowledge or understanding.

Something similar is at work here. If we want to construe "thinking" as meaning only "a process going on in my mind," we will find that this is a very inadequate definition of *thinking*. The very thing that we want to understand will disappear from view—this "process" has no objective content and so it becomes like "the beetle in the box." We want to try to describe or talk about something—"the inner process"—but we have inadvertently tossed away all of our tools for describing something: the language of description. There is no way to consistently identify this process, but this is exactly what we want to do by naming or referring to this process as *thinking*. As we saw a word cannot be defined privately as if it refers to something only you can know. And it is no answer to say I do the same here as everyone else does, for we have no idea what it is that we are supposed to call "the same." To say what I am doing now (whatever it is) is thinking and this must be the same for everyone else is absurd. There is absolutely no way to tell what is happening in everyone else's mind. We should note, of course, that this statement offers an idea similar to what is expressed in solipsism: my thoughts are all thoughts.

If we look at a text that follows the one above on, calculation this idea might become clearer:

> Is a sum in the head less real than a sum on paper?—Perhaps one is inclined to say some such thing; but one can get oneself to say the opposite as well by telling oneself: paper, ink, etc. are only logical constructions out of our sense-data.
>
> "I have done the multiplication . . . in my head"—do I perhaps not believe such statement?—But was it really a multiplication? It was not merely "A" multiplication, but *this* one—in the head. This is the point at which I go wrong. For now I want to say: it was some mental process *corresponding* to the multiplication on paper. So it would make sense to say: "*This* process in the mind corresponds to *this* process on paper." And it would make sense to talk about a method of projection according to which the image of the sign was a representation of the sign itself.[7]

There is, of course, no real difference between doing a calculation in one's head and doing it on paper. But since calculation seems to be a thought process, we want to say there is a thought process accompanying the calculation on paper and that this is the *real* calculation. But what would this duplication achieve? Does it make the answer more correct to say that there is a thought process behind it? Would we say a person isn't thinking because he is using a pencil and paper or his fingers to calculate? Isn't calculating in your head and calculating on paper following the same set of rules? If the calculation in your head and the one on paper are the same, then it makes no sense to say one corresponds to the other—this is simply redundant. If we take a simple sign, such as a stop sign, and we make an image of this sign—say we take a picture of the sign—there is little point in offering a method to translate between the two signs. Which would be called the image, and which would be the real sign?

In general a calculation on paper is not the sign or a representation of a mental process. What would be the point of saying the calculation on paper represented the real calculation in the head? The calculation on the paper is not merely the image or representation of a "real" calculation. If I write 2 + 2 = 4 this is an equation with a result, not a drawing or a picture of math, much less a drawing or picture of a mental process.

When we treat the equation on the paper as an image of the real calculation, this might be because we are tempted to think that the image carries with it its own application, as when we are presented with an image we must do certain things or certain things are called to mind. It may be that we think the image alone is sufficient to explain what we are to do with it.

Notice that if we take this description literally it carries with it a mechanical understanding of meaning or signs. Let us consider a simple sign: an arrow pointing to the left. Presumably this tells someone to go to the left. But let us further assume that this sign is never used in our culture or has not been explained to an observer. How is the sign supposed to tell someone to go to the left? The sign must somehow transfer or impart this application to my mind, and through this activity or something like it, I will be able to follow the direction of the arrow.[8] Presumably looking at the sign informs someone of what they are to do. But how could it accomplish that? We might say that my mind absorbs it—but absorbs what? My explanation of this process appears empirical or causal, yet nothing empirical or causal presents itself. We certainly see nothing else connected with the arrow. So in order for the sign to accomplish the desired result I must supply a theory—a myth of meaning: something happens in my mind or occurs to me that causes me to act in such a way. But we would try in vain to find something inner that accounts for the meaning here as we have seen in numerous examples above. Basically the inner object is private, and it is difficult or impossible to make sense out of a word or sign when its meaning is something peculiar to the individual. Meaning is public, and the inner object is not. An image on its own does not suffice for meaning. But we can prescribe a use for an image, and now our difficulties dissolve.

If one accepts the tradition of classical epistemology that stresses the spirituality of the intellect, one might object to Wittgenstein's critique. For in the classical model, it is precisely the abstractive power of the intellect that gives meaning to a sign or a word. Curiously enough, the classical thinker would likely agree with Wittgenstein that an image or a representation is not the same thing as an idea. A concept is that through which we understand. But the classical thinker bases his argument for the spirituality of the intellect on precisely this fact. Since an image is particular and meaning is universal, imagination and memory are insufficient to form an abstract idea that would be required for meaning. For the classical thinker, material characteristics—size, shape, weight, color—individuate and so must be abstracted from in order to reach the universality necessary for meaning. Hence an abstract idea such as mathematics, it is argued, is nonmaterial. Hence the mind which considers this idea must be nonmaterial as well.

Whatever we may think of this argument (or whatever Wittgenstein may have thought of it—as usual he doesn't mention this idea directly) it is clear that for the classical thinker it is precisely the "mental process" of abstraction that is responsible for meaning. The classical thinker wants to insist that this psychological apparatus is necessary for meaning. On one level this is precisely what Wittgenstein wants to deny. Meaning is not primarily a psychological process. But as we have said, Wittgenstein just as clearly does not want to deny that meaning takes place in the mind—or that we know the meaning of a word. But there is a particular picture here that Wittgenstein finds objectionable: that meaning is a "hocus pocus" performed by the soul.[9] If we go back to the arrow pointing left, we note that the fact that we go left when we see this sign need not be understood as the result of psychology, much less spirituality. Even if the abstraction model were correct, it is impossible to "generalize" a sign without the system of rules that support the sign. If we looked at the hieroglyph for "go left," the mind cannot intuit the meaning of the sign without knowing its underlying grammar. And indeed even Plato would agree that the idea of anything would be equivalent to its essence, which, among other things, might be described as the set of rules that govern inclusion in a particular class. For Plato, it is this essence or form that dictates the meaning of the sign for the idea.

However, for Wittgenstein, to explain the meaning of a word or sign we must attend to its grammar, the language game to which it belongs. Meaning does not depend on anything external to language. Meaning takes place within the set of circumstances and activities of a language, and outside of this sphere words may mean anything or nothing at all.

To explain meaning psychologically—by a mental process of intuiting the application of a sign in abstraction from knowing its grammar, among other difficulties—assumes that there must be a causal explanation to the meaning of a sign. This model suggests that to produce the appropriate response for a sign (go left) there must be something going on in the eyes or the nervous system or the soul. Although the response to the sign, the behavior, is important—it seems to be the whole point of the sign—as we have seen, this is a logical, not a causal, requirement of meaning. To understand the meaning of a word is a problem of logic, not science. Words make no sense without their characteristic activities and circumstances. Examining the nervous system of someone while they "mean" something might settle a psychological issue, but not a grammatical one. As we have said, if we consider the meaning of a word so intimately connected with the nervous system, such as *pain*, when I say "he is in pain," this does not mean I have an insight into his nervous system. Again our psychological language is not meaningful by referring to inner states. We learned to use our psychological vocabulary not by studying psychology, but when we learned language.[10] Hence, once we see that the arrow we referred to above "points" because of the use we make of it, not because of any psychological activity, many of our problems dissolve. When we rid ourselves of the idea that the language of psychology requires a psychological explanation, then the search for the mysterious mental processes behind e.g., *meaning* and *calculation* can be abandoned. *Calculating* does not mean a process occurring in the mind, unless of course you mean what we ordinarily call calculating: manipulating the symbols involved, checking sums, following the rules, looking up formulas, and so on. *Calculating* takes place according to a system of rules governing signs, a technique that we learn or even invent. We have instituted a use for numerals, operators, and so on that allows us to communicate using these signs, investigate their use, and accomplish a plethora of tasks. A calculation on paper can certainly be said to follow the rules for calculating and to accomplish the same tasks. This is something that we can check. If we write 2+2=?, and someone writes 6 or a letter or a squiggle consistently, we say that he can't understand how to calculate. If he eventually does this and other examples correctly, then we say he is calculating and perhaps that before he was trying or learning to calculate. Now he can measure, count change, balance his checkbook, and so forth.

Thus the calculation on the paper is as much an example of calculating as anything else—this includes using an abacus, slide rule, pocket calculator, or computer. Sometimes we want to object to saying that the computer calculates because we believe saying so robs us of our humanity. We want to say that our ability to do mathematics is part of what makes us unique and uniquely human. But how could the use of a word or a sign rob us of anything? How could it take anything from us? It could only do so if we allow it. Wittgenstein's analysis is not an attempt to completely bypass psychology, for clearly something is going on "in the pupil's head" when he or she is calculating, but he is trying to show what is important in the meaning of *calculate*. If we ignore the use of *calculating* and what counts as *calculating* and insist on explaining the meaning of the word by reference to an inner object, then we have created a mysterious mental phenomenon. The temptation is to solve the mystery with a psychological theory that our language seems to allow but for which there is no support in our everyday lives and hence little purpose.

Here again we might encounter a difficulty in regard to certain classical philosophical ideas. When we want to know what something is—be it meaning or calculating or understanding or thinking, for the classical thinker, we are asking for the essence of that thing or its nature. Essence is explained in different ways by different thinkers in the classical tradition, and a quick review would probably do disservice to the idea. But all seem to agree that any natural object possesses certain properties and characteristics by nature and these properties serve to define or delimit membership in the species. So man is by nature rational and has the capacity for symbolic communication, abstract thought, etc., and is defined as a rational animal. Thus when Wittgenstein proposes a grammatical investigation into calculating or thinking, it may appear to run counter to the classical notion, which tends to view an investigation into the nature of something along scientific lines.

But again Wittgenstein's focus is language, not science. As even the classical theories would admit, the meaning of the essence or nature of man defines the word *man*. That is, the species or nature of man delimits that which is called a man. This word is extended to include that which is a member of the species and so has properties x, y, and z. In one sense Wittgenstein would not disagree. The meaning of a word does tell us what something is, or as Wittgenstein puts it "Essence is expressed by grammar" and "Grammar tells us what kind of object anything is."[11] Although Wittgenstein is not doing science, it is clear that if we want to know what something is we must look to what the word means and so, for Wittgenstein, we must look to how it is used. The question as to what understanding is asks for us to give an account of what counts for understanding. As we have seen, this entails an account of the grammar of *understanding*—of how *understanding* is used.

Hence, both the classical thinker and Wittgenstein agree that the question of essence must attend to meaning. The difference for Wittgenstein is that meaning is in language and its use. Thought is not something behind language as an accompaniment, but language itself is the vehicle for thought (cf. 329). Meaning is found in the circumstances and activities—the form of life—associated with the language game in which the word has its home. Meaning is not found in reference to an idea or essence in the classical sense. The classical thinker may feel "cheated" because he may think he is looking for truth in the scientific sense, whereas Wittgenstein is "only" talking about words. But Wittgenstein's point is that the question as to what something is cannot ignore meaning and so cannot ignore language and its use. The more profound the investigation the more profound is the need for its language to be meaningful.

We must remember that Wittgenstein's investigation into the grammar of our psychological concepts attempts to tell us what we are speaking about; it is an odyssey of clarification. Again, his efforts are against the bewitchment of our thinking that occurs because the vagaries of language have gone on unchecked. Philosophers have talked of mental processes and inner states, thoughts, meanings, and the like without considering the traps set by language.

As we said, in the last 200 or so remarks of part I Wittgenstein extends this analysis to a number of psychological concepts including consciousness, intending, meaning, thinking, expecting, wishing, and willing. Previous topics sometimes pop up briefly, and there sometimes seems to be less of a "flow" to this last section, perhaps reinforces the notion that the second half of part I was still "under construction" at Wittgenstein's death.

Still prevalent is a focus on the need to distinguish the actual use of a word from the substitution of that which might accompany the use of a word for an explanation of meaning or as part of a psychological theory that explains psychological language. Thus Wittgenstein wants to point out in this last section of part I that we must see how *consciousness*, *expecting*, or *willing* are used and not confuse the feeling or inner experience which can accompany these words for the meaning of the word. This is how language can trick us.

Let us take a look at the following remarks as examples of this:

Do I observe myself, then and perceive that I am conscious? And why talk about observation at all? Why not simply say "I perceive I am conscious"?—But what are the words "I perceive" for here?—Why not say "I am conscious"?—But don't the words "I perceive" shew that I am attending to my consciousness?—which is ordinarily not the case.—If so then the sentence "I perceive that I am conscious does not say that I am conscious, but my attention is disposed in such and such a way. But isn't it a particular experience that occasions my saying "I am conscious again"?—What experience? In what situations do we say it?[12]

Is my having consciousness a fact of experience?—But doesn't one say that a man has consciousness, and that a tree or a stone does not?—What would it be like if it were otherwise?—Would human beings all be unconscious?—No; not in the ordinary sense of the word. But I, for instance, should not have consciousness—as I now in fact have it.[13]

Notice that this last sentence does not answer the question of whether we are conscious by appealing to anything inner, by arguing or showing how consciousness is unique to human beings. This is because the question looks like a "scientific" one that demands we produce "something" to settle it. But the question is really grammatical—it asks us to tell what counts as consciousness.

We are first presented with the question of whether having consciousness is a fact of experience. But why would this come up? Presumably because we want to identify something within us that we can attend to or observe, something called consciousness. After all, consciousness is real—it is something that I have—something within me. But although we may say "I perceive I am conscious" and the language here sets us up to expect the perception of something, this is certainly a strange way of speaking. We might just as easily say, "I am conscious." But it would be very peculiar circumstances that would justify an expression of this sort. We might say it as we were being awakened from anesthesia. The doctor asks "Are you awake?," and you respond "Yes, I am conscious." "Yes, I am perceiving my consciousness" is redundant. If you are not conscious then who is doing the perceiving? As Wittgenstein says, the statement that "I am perceiving my consciousness" is not ordinarily used to indicate that "I am conscious," but that I am attending to my consciousness in a particular way. Only it is difficult to think of circumstances that would make it necessary to attend to your consciousness. Ordinarily, the experience here is nothing more than that of consciousness—you see, hear, feel, etc.

Thus, would we say that consciousness is a fact of experience—an empirical fact? Is it a matter of discovery? Haven't we found out though careful observation that, for example, people have consciousness and stones do not? We certainly say that people are conscious and stones are not. The question certainly makes it seem that this is something that could be settled empirically, but what would it mean to say that we have found out that stones are not conscious? Would it mean something like that we have spoken to them and got no response on many occasions, and so we have inductively concluded that stones are not conscious? Likewise have we "found out" that other people or we ourselves are conscious, again over a period of time? If it is a discovery that stones are not conscious but we are, then the opposite would have to be thinkable. There must have been some unknowns regarding this question at some point. What would it mean to say that stones were possibly conscious and we were not? What circumstances would we have to obtain for this to make sense? If this were the case then we would not suddenly become unconscious but "consciousness" as we know it would not apply to us. It would make no sense to say that human beings are conscious. If the activities of a stone are what counts for consciousness, then this word could not apply to human beings.

It may be hard to see how this analysis settles the question of consciousness because it is hard to see the question as grammatical rather than empirical. The question as to what counts as consciousness does not ordinarily arise. We say of a living, awake, responding person that he is conscious. The question does pop up when we are doing philosophy and looking for the nature of consciousness. Here we often want to identify something that we have and can identify what counts for consciousness: an experience, an observation, a feeling—anything at all. It must be a unique something, and to point out this uniqueness we stand ready to deny consciousness to trees, stones, furniture, etc. But ordinarily no one would want to put it there in the first place. ("My wastebasket is mocking me," "The doorknob hates me.") The word just doesn't apply, and so there is nothing to deny and really nothing to look for. To make it apply I would have to twist our language in such a way so that to give consciousness to an inanimate object I would have to deny it to human beings and, of course, this is ludicrous. The interesting point, to which we will have to return, is that even though our language clearly allows constructions of this sort, it is strange that we resort to them.

In the final sections of part I on psychological concepts, Wittgenstein enters into what might be a new discussion or a technique of analysis of these issues. Here he compares understanding a sentence to understanding a theme in music.

> Understanding a sentence is much more akin to understanding a theme in music than one may think. What I mean is that understanding a sentence lies nearer than one thinks to what is ordinarily called a musical theme. Why is just this the pattern of variation in loudness and tempo? One would like to say "Because I know what it's all about." But what is it all about? I should not be able to say. In order to "explain" I could only compare it with something that has the same rhythm (I mean the same pattern). (One says "Don't you see, this is as if a conclusion were being drawn" or "This is as it were a parenthesis" etc. How does one justify such comparisons?—There are very different kinds of justification here.[14]

We might not be acquainted with what Wittgenstein means by understanding a theme in music. Wittgenstein is not explaining the grand theme behind an orchestral work such as "redemption" or "man's inhumanity to man," and so on. But we might think of a passage from our favorite classical composer and ask how we would explain the theme to someone. It may be helpful to think of looking at the written score (assuming you know how to read music) and then telling someone how it should be played. Wittgenstein was famous for being able to whistle concertos and the like, pausing only to note a nuance or an important passage. Think about how you would explain the passage to someone in this manner. There would of course be many possible variations in how the music might be played—let us imagine something like this: you would say to someone "This section would be loud, followed by soft one, then this bit here would be loud and rapid, and this part is very soft and trails away." Now suppose the person you are explaining it to asks why it should be played like that. What would you tell him? "Because I understand it" is all well and good but unhelpful because he wants to understand it too. "Well, that's what the score says" doesn't help much either. It would not be much of an explanation of a complex mathematical proof to say "Just look at the page."

Notice that it would be equally difficult for the student if we said something like "Well, this just feels right to me" or "This way it is beautiful." This would offer no information or at least nothing that is necessarily reproducible for the student. How is he supposed to understand what "feels" right to you? Nothing has been explained to the student that is of any use. He can hardly go off and say "I will now play this piece so it feels right to the teacher" (although a great deal of education probably seems like this).

The only way we could explain the passage would be through a comparison with something of the same pattern and rhythm. The above "theme" might be explained in terms of an argument. You might say something like "Think of it terms of an argument: a loud domineering boss yelling at his secretary. He yells and she says something meekly in her defense, but he just comes back more aggressively, and so in the end she sort of gives up."

Admittedly, this explanation lacks a certain sophistication (but the theme was not that sophisticated). However, at least it points to what is required—something reproducible or public that the student can do something with. Explanations that turn toward the inner are of little use as we saw in Wittgenstein's earlier discussion of meaning. But the above explanation with the boss and the secretary worked because it reproduced the pattern of the theme.

But what has this to do with the understanding of a sentence? I think Wittgenstein wants to point out that when we wish to explain meaning, then we have come to the operation of language and we have hit rock bottom. If, for example, a theme in music is to "say" something or be explained it can only mean something or be explained in the way that language can be explained. "A" may be translated into "B" if you find something about "B" that works in the same way. To put a musical theme into language in the sense outlined above—to explain it—means finding a pattern in language that does the same thing. Thus we might say the fundamental logical operations of language—its grammar—are basic to meaning on any level. I think Wittgenstein would want to say that the meaning of music is not something accompanying the music or somehow behind it. I think Wittgenstein wants to guard against a psychology of music or a myth of meaning in regard to music, as he did with psychological language.

What can confuse us here is that when we talk of the meaning of a word, painting, or piece of music, we are not always talking about its sense, but its significance, or importance, or how it moves us. We choose words for their "color" or "liveliness" or "familiarity" or even "shock value." This often gives sentences their "weight" or "depth" or a piece of writing its "character" or "flavor." The danger here is in thinking that this significance or meaning is something imparted to us by these words and that understanding the meaning is to an extent an interpretation or translation of the "color," "flavor," etc., of the language. Again, we can tend toward psychologizing meaning.

But really we have two related uses of *meaning* that should be distinguished. There is of course the meaning to a poem in the sense of the definition of the words. But there is also the meaning of the poem or its parts in the sense that it's "uplifting" or "deep" or "sentimental" and this is achieved by the choice of words and so on. But notice that when we want to explain meaning in this sense we resort to language of similar construction or grammar: color, flavor, lively, weighty, intensity, moving, charged, etc. Hence meaning in either sense cannot be *understood* without a grammar for the words. Understanding a sentence here is not an interpretation or a translation of an indefinite something in a sentence but finding other words or phrases with the same pattern and rhythm that accomplish the same thing with more familiarity.

We can say, of course, that we "understand," for example, the "color" of a word or the "depth" of a sentence. Poets struggle over the right word in a line of a poem, and the choice can make all the difference in the mood or tone of a poem and so its significance. But here the struggle is not over the meaning of a word. They know what the word means but struggle over its character—its "feel." When a painter wants a particular color for a section of a painting he is not operating on the question of what is called "yellow ochre" or "cobalt blue."

Rather, he wants to create a particular impression or the like. Clearly then this is a different though related concept of understanding, and the two should not be confused (cf. PI 532). Though Wittgenstein amplifies this idea in part II, here we can say that judging "this is called *blue*" depends on the grammar of *blue*, while judging that *blue* would be the best color in this part of the picture is a grammatically different sense of "judgment." The confusion between the two ideas often leads us to favoring the latter as a model for judging or knowing—we look for a psychological picture of judgment. Thus we take all judging for a type of intuiting or interpretation. The reverse is also the case. When we want to make fine distinctions of taste, for example, we want to think that this can be treated logically. When we want to describe the genuineness in a person's facial expression and find that we "know" the expression is sincere, we may have trouble describing what makes the expression sincere—"where" is the sincerity in the expression? Again when we fail at exactly locating the sincerity in the expression—that "something" that defines or is responsible for the sincerity—we might feel the lack of something to point to, or the lack of a vocabulary. But really neither is missing. We cannot "point" to the sincerity or describe it as if it were something separate from the facial expression—the facial expression, that which is open to everyone, is all we can point to or describe. Our vocabulary is intact. It is not a fault of our words that we cannot "point" to the sincerity. There is nothing specific to point to. We have here a complex form of life that is difficult to master. Knowing that this particular face is "sincere" in this sense is not a problem of logic. We know what sincerity means—what we want to know here is if this person is really sincere. In other words here we want to be sure we are not being fooled. This is judging the individual case—or applying the concept—and this cannot be done with the same 100 percent certainty we have with logic. Thus Wittgenstein wants to distinguish judging in the sense of taste from judging from the standpoint of logic. There are different but related senses of meaning at work here. What Wittgenstein wants to guard against is seeing meaning in the logical or grammatical sense as meaning in the interpretative sense.

But what has this to do with psychological concepts? The modern tendency is to explain psychological concepts by an appeal to that which accompanies the psychological. Let us take the case of expectation, which Wittgenstein treats at various places.[15] Someone fires a shot and I expect to hear the report—a loud bang. How should I understand *expectation* here? Expectation here might look like a psychological state in which there is a gap that the report fills in—again the tendency here is to seek a mechanical explanation for a psychological state. Expectation in this model might be seen as a mechanism, like a trap that anticipates what is to spring it—in the way that a mousetrap is set up for a mouse. Expecting something like a report would be like the trap waiting to be sprung, and this is accomplished by the report. The report fulfills or satisfics the expectation. This might be accompanied by many feelings such as hesitancy, fear, the pulse races, and so on. Thus we seem to have a perfect picture of a psychological mechanism and accompaniments that would seem to explain *expectation*.

But what is it like to wish or hope for or expect something? As always we should ask how these words are used. If a friend is due at any moment and you are anxious about his getting there you might be very agitated or even annoyed, pace the room, call his phone, try to distract yourself, and so on. Now imagine doing all this when no one is expected. Well, you might have a case of the fidgets, or nervous anxiety, but it would not be a case of "expecting" anything. Why? It is not because you now lack any of the mental accompaniments, but the circumstances have changed—no one is coming and nothing is supposed to happen—you are not waiting for anyone or anything in particular. No one could say of you that you are expecting something, except to perhaps indicate that you were suffering from a nervous disorder—"He believes something will happen—but we know it won't." The important thing is that what counts as expecting is that which counts as expecting for everyone. This is where we find the meaning of *expectation*.

Now what has this to do with the previous discussion? It is in the language of expecting that we see what expectation is and what is expected. To explain a psychological concept of expecting, we note its patterns and rhythms in its surroundings. We should recall here Wittgenstein's remark comparing understanding a sentence to understanding a musical theme. Understanding a musical theme, or putting it into words, requires expressions that mirror the patterns and rhythms of the music. So too, understanding a sentence requires capturing certain patterns and rhythms in order to draw out the significance of the sentence. The same might be said for the understanding of psychological states. Again the language of psychology is fundamental to this process—the way this language operates—and we note it must operate in particular circumstances embedded within the rhythm and patterns of life. The activities that a word lives within are not the accompaniments with the mental experience being what is essential; rather, it is the other way around. The "inner experiences" only make sense within that larger picture. The moods or feelings that accompany the psychological cannot explain the psychological any more than the "color" of a word explains the word. Again, there are two types of significance at work here. The feelings that accompany the psychological are of course significant, but these are not what explain our psychological language. In the same way the color or depth of a word is significant, but these don't explain the meaning of the word. Further, to explain the "moods" or "feelings" that accompany the psychological, the grammar of these words is required just as it is necessary to invoke grammar to explain the "color" of words. "Pointing" to the "feeling" doesn't occur—we could not "exhibit" an "inner" feeling to someone—except of course to tell them about it and so on. Thus "feeling" or an "atmosphere" is not what explains the psychology—we need the language. There is the understanding of a facial expression or gesture, as when we react to someone with pity or love, or we think of them as courageous or timid, etc., but this is a related concept of understanding to which we will return shortly.

As strange at it may sound, Wittgenstein wants to point out that it would not make sense to speak of someone as expecting or hoping or to even make sense of our own expecting or hoping without the grammar that attends these words. Can we hope or expect that someone would arrive and say nothing to ourselves, or pace, or wonder where he was? Could we not think of a person all day, and then when he arrives make sense of saying, "I really was hoping that you would come?" We of course could say it, but what use would the sentence have here? Perhaps to make the person feel better, to assure him he was not interrupting your day. It certainly could not be a report of a "mental state" or even what you did during the day, given these circumstances. It would be very odd if you picked up the phone when someone had called a wrong number, and you said, "I was waiting for your call." Again there is a language to hoping, expecting, thinking, intending, understanding, etc.—a certain set of activities and patterns in which what, e.g., hope is and what is hoped for is clearly seen. It is through this language, this grammar, that we explain and understand the psychological.

Again, the meaning of someone's actions is found in the actions, and because of the simplicity of this idea it often escapes our notice. But this is most important to the grammar of our psychological language, and so is important to our psychological concepts. So if we speak of gleaning anything from behavior or a facial expression or a posture, what we focus on is precisely those activities.

Let us look at the following text 536. This will serve to close our discussion of part I and introduce us to part II.

I say "I can think of this face (which gives an impression of timidity) as courageous too." We do not mean by this that I can imagine someone with this face perhaps saving someone's life (that, of course, is imaginable in connexion with any face). I am speaking of an aspect of the face itself. Nor do I mean that I can imagine that this man's face might change so that, in the ordinary sense, it looked courageous; though I may very well mean that there is a quite definite way in which it can change into a courageous face. The reinterpretation of a facial expression can be compared to the reinterpretation of a chord in music, when we hear it as a modulation first into this, then into that key.[16]

This passage echoes a much longer discussion on the same topic in part II. There Wittgenstein treats the idea of seeing something as something else in much greater depth. We will visit part II later, for now I want to relate this remark to the previous discussion.

A persistent problem that Wittgenstein has been circling is the relationship of the psychological to the empirical. As we have noted, there is frequently a question regarding the relationship between what is observed of a psychological state and what can be known about a psychological state. We have seen that the great flexibility of our language allows us to form many ideas or grammars for our psychological vocabulary. The great variety of ways we can account for meaning allows a great deal of confusion, and thus we resort to, for example, behaviorism or introspection as theories that explain or limit our psychological concepts. In these cases we might believe we are carrying on an empirical investigation, but in reality, Wittgenstein wants to say, we are very often being led around by the nose by our language.

As we will examine in greater depth when we come to part II, the concept of seeing itself is a source of confusion and this is evident in the above passage. When we say that we can see timidity or courage in a face, what is it that is seen? If we think of explaining the meaning of *seeing* on a purely visual level, it is difficult to note anything specific that is seen or referred to relative to timidity, as we mentioned above, other than the actual face and its expression. The discussion in part II centers on the notion that if we want to maintain this visual model for the meaning of *seeing* we are going to have to add something—and here we must add a psychological apparatus—to explain this *seeing*. The most developed psychological theory that explained our visual apprehension of the psychological is Gestalt theory, which Wittgenstein deals with extensively in part II. Here in part I he only hints at Gestalt concepts.

In the final sections of part I Wittgenstein returns to familiar paths in treating the visual apprehension of the psychological. Again, to understand how it happens that one sees timidity or courage in a face we should look at how the word *see* is used. When we talk of seeing emotion in someone's face, it is not a process of trying to associate this emotion with these particular features, as if it were a matter of guessing the person's emotions by trying this or that idea—like trying various hats on the person to see which one looks best. Let us look at what this model would be like in actual practice. Someone makes a face. Now I am not supposed to know what the face "says," so I try various possibilities—I try to connect courage or timidity or fear with the face. But what could I possibly be connecting or fitting here—what kind of object do I think that I am "fitting" on to the person's face? I have got nothing—other than the concept of fear or timidity, etc. But again this concept is nothing more than in certain circumstances these features are used to register this particular emotion. These types of facial expressions are part of the form of life we call fear, etc. Thus understanding an emotion in someone's face is not a question of recognizing a psychological object. Rather, it is a question of being familiar with the concept of that emotion. But this is nothing more than simply understanding the circumstances, activities, and expressions of that emotion.

In other words I do not "connect" the emotion to the face. Rather the person is showing, for example, his or her fear. His face is alive with the emotion, and I react to that emotion. This is the language game of the expression of emotion. The idea of "fitting" or "connecting" is superfluous and has led us astray. And the concept of *seeing* is certainly modified. When I say I *see* an emotion in someone's face I need not be referring to anything specific—neither a psychological process in me, nor a psychological process in the person I observe. We have noted the many layers of *seeing* and hopefully we have let go of a purely visual model for the meaning of *seeing*. Again language is of fundamental importance to the psychological on a number of different levels. Fundamentally it is through the grammar of our psychological concepts that we understand and communicate the psychological. The characteristic circumstances, activities, and behavior that are part of our psychological concepts are not superfluous. It seems paradoxical, but those things that we tend to count as important in a psychological discussion—the various accompanying inner feelings, processes, and so on—are actually superfluous when discussing the meaning of our psychological vocabulary. We can see that a purely visual model of *seeing* is ineffective in explaining *seeing* fear, etc., in a face.

Again, we want to model the meaning of *seeing* on something that happens solely in our sensory apparatus, and of course no one can deny that our vision requires a visual apparatus. Certainly our language accommodates us and even suggests that this might be the case—for don't the words we use for *sight* in essence, we think, point or refer to this "inner" apparatus? But this is where we make a wrong turn. Because we cannot find an actual use for these words in certain cases—such as *seeing* an emotion, we resort to bolstering our incorrect concepts with theories. However, these theories are supporting grammatical fictions. It is in part II that Wittgenstein focuses extensively on these ideas.

NOTES

1. Von Wright, *Wittgenstein*, 113-136.
2. TLP 2.1.
3. TLP 4.
4. TLP 5.5563.
5. PI, Prentice Hall ed., 33e.
6. PI 363.
7. PI 366.
8. Cf. PI 454.
9. Cf. PI 454.
10. Cf. PI 384.
11. PI 370, 372.
12. PI 417.
13. PI 418.
14. PI 527.
15. 16 cf. PI 444–5, 452–3, 581–2.
16. PI 536.

8

Part II

Part II of the *Investigations* has a different format than part I. The remarks in part II are not numbered and groups of remarks are collected in chapters, that is, a set of remarks that seem to be more or less connected. Speculation as to the reason for the difference and relationship between the two parts is a topic for a different work. For our purposes, as I mentioned above, part II appears to continue and amplify the discussion on psychological concepts in the last section of part I. Since the sections or "chapters" seem to form a unit, we should consider them individually.

Let us look at the opening text of section i:

> One can imagine an animal angry, frightened, unhappy, happy, startled. But hopeful? And why not? A dog believes his master is at the door. But can he also believe his master will come the day after tomorrow?—And what can he not do here?—How do I do it?—How am I supposed to answer this? Can only those hope who can talk? Only those who have mastered the use of a language. That is to say, the phenomena of hope are modes of this complicated form of life. (If a concept refers to human handwriting, it has no application to beings that do not write.) "Grief" describes a pattern which recurs, with different variations in the weave of our life. If a man's bodily expression of sorrow and of joy alternated, say with the ticking of a clock, here we should have the characteristic formation of the pattern of sorrow or the pattern of joy.[1]

Here we see many of the themes from the end of part I. Considering the question of whether an animal can hope reestablishes one of the key points from part I: *hoping* implies a complicated form of life. There are characteristics and activities that are essential to *hoping*. We want to lodge *hope* in the inner life of a person or an animal (what faculty or interior apparatus is the animal missing?) and so we are stuck with a number of conundrums (What apparatus is it that I have? How does it work and how can I find this out?). In many instances, this results in a continual skepticism as to whether someone or something has these emotions. We feel we should have to look inside the soul or nervous system to establish the truth here. Since this proves impossible, we are left wondering, not just about animals, but human beings as well. Our emotions become mysterious phenomena.

To counter this tendency we must look to the grammar of *hope*—or what Wittgenstein calls this complicated pattern of activities and circumstances that make up this form of life. This may make it seem as if we are ignoring the psychological—the mental—and only talking about a word. It may seem as if we are trying to reduce the psychological to language, and if language is merely a series of signs than connecting the psychological to language appears ridiculous. But I think we must take it as by now established that language is part of our lives—it is an instrument with a use. We must note that we do something with our words. We can think of, e.g., *complaining* as a state of mind, but it is far more complicated than that. Think of teaching the word *complain* to someone. We would probably have to explain many factors in order to teach someone this word. For example, we would probably use a typical situation of complaining: what led up to the complaint—we bought something and it didn't work—then we would explain what we do—we write a letter or call customer service or tell others not to buy the product and so on. There is a whole pattern of essential activities here, without which it makes no sense to talk of complaining and would be necessary in order to complain. It is the same with hope.

Wittgenstein wants us to realize that the question "What is hope?" is not a psychological but a grammatical question. It is about the use of the word *hope*. For Wittgenstein an actual psychological investigation would be an empirical or scientific one—perhaps something trying to uncover the cause of someone's neurosis. To understand the essence of the psychological, e.g., *hope*, we must see what the concept entails. Hoping includes a range and pattern of activities and circumstances.

We often look to explain psychological concepts such as *grief* or *hope* in terms of sensations—not like seeing or hearing, but as a type of feeling. But let us, for example, compare grief and hope to similar sensations. Grief is often associated with pain in a certain sense. We very often talk about the pain and grief associated with a loss. Of course pain is a sensation and to begin our analysis let us note that it makes sense to say someone felt pain for a second. But what about grief? Here this doesn't seem to work—momentary grief doesn't seem to make any sense. But if pain and grief are similar sensations, then what is the problem? Is grief perhaps so fine a sensation or too slippery that we can't get hold of it? Or perhaps our words are lacking—our psychological vocabulary is inadequate. But if this were the case why don't we just invent new words? Or fine-tune our senses by introspection.

Again, these strategies are doomed to failure because the concept is wrong to begin with. Grief cannot be reduced grammatically simply to a sensation. Rather, it is a complicated form of life. That there is a form of life to "pain" mostly escapes our notice because pain can be such an overwhelming and omnipresent sensation that we forget the importance of a pain behavior and so on for the concept *pain*. But, as we saw above, Wittgenstein was very careful to help us see past this limited view of the concept *pain*. Here in order to isolate the sensation of grief we might wish to "point" to the sensation: "Aren't you feeling grief now?" But of course the temporal question—"how are you feeling?"—does not answer the question as to what grief is—what *grief* means. As we have seen, the response "What I am feeling now is grief" could not settle the question as to the nature of grief. This is as useless as a botanist claiming, "What I think counts for the species 'oak tree' determines what an oak tree is." We would instantly reject unverifiable introspection as a model for scientific method in botany, physics, and chemistry. However, we seem to allow it when it comes to human nature, psychology, and so on. We cannot "get hold of" the sensation of grief because we have got our concepts mixed up. We are incorrectly modeling our concept of the supposed sensation of grief on the concept for the sensation of pain. Our failure to speak about the "sensation" of grief is not because of the inadequacy of our psychological vocabulary. Rather, it is a result of trying to force psychological language into an incorrect mold.

In section ii p. 149e, Wittgenstein continues to distinguish what is essential from what is inessential in meaning, focusing on the difficulties created by using models of meaning that incorporate ideas such as introspection, epistemology, and psychology. Here he amplifies an earlier discussion, the theme of which we might call "experiencing the meaning of a word." Again, the idea under scrutiny is that there is something that I can locate in my mind that occurs as I "mean" something—and this is what counts as meaning. In other words, I may have many experiences as I say a word, and if I want to use a psychological or epistemological model of meaning, I might tend to look in this direction for the psychological or mental "content" of meaning.

First, Wittgenstein wants us to note that a combination of words has a different sense than each of the words individually. Where this sense comes from, if we look outside the use, can seem like a bit of a mystery. It is tempting to think that when I say a sentence with a particular expression that it is the feeling behind the expression that imparts the meaning—that this is the psychological content of meaning. Wittgenstein will return to this topic, but here we can say that while the expression behind a sentence is important, it is not a separable atmosphere that accounts for meaning. Let us look at the following text:

> Experiencing a meaning and experiencing a mental image. "In both cases," we should like to say, "we are *experiencing* something, only something different. A different content is—proffered—is present—to consciousness."—What is the content of the experience of imagining? The answer is a picture, or a description. And what is the content of the experience of meaning? I don't know what I am supposed to say to this.—If there is any sense in the above remark, it is that the two concepts are related like those of "red" and "blue"; and that is wrong.[2]

In other words, there is a use for "the experience of a mental image." You could reproduce a mental image by drawing it or describing it. But now we want to "transfer" this language to the "experience" of meaning. This transfer seems possible because we think *experience* always means the same thing regardless of the context. But this assumes way too much. We would likely have a difficulty "putting our finger on" the experience of the meaning of a word. It may seem as if we have a problem with the faculty of experience—as if this faculty needs to be adjusted somehow. But the problem is, in fact, grammatical. To illustrate this, think of finding a use for "the experience of the meaning of a word." And now what would that be? No doubt when we say a word we may find that it is familiar or expressive, and we might have a particular feeling when we say a word, as when we tell someone that we love them. There may be many accompaniments for meaning. But why should these feelings be the meaning or even an experience of the meaning? If these feelings constitute an experience of meaning it should have something to do with meaning. One should be able to produce something verifiable to connect these feelings with what is meant. If I try to give this kind of content to this supposed experience of meaning, I might describe this experience in a variety of ways, but if I try to compare this experience to the experience of a mental image the comparison breaks down. We will find that the "experience of a mental image" and "the experience of meaning a word" mean very different things. I could draw a mental image on paper and this would represent my experience—I could say to someone "This is what I was thinking about"—or I could describe my image. Now consider what I would do if I wanted to describe the experience I had when I heard a word or phrase. Here I could tell someone the word or explain the meaning of the word and say, "I find this particular word very exciting," or whatnot. But what parts would the feeling and so forth play in explaining the meaning of the word here? What sense does "experiencing the meaning of a word" have? Again, saying I had a particular feeling as I pronounce a word does little to explain the use of a word—does little to explain what I mean by it. Hence this idea runs aground. I might have a particular experience when I say a word, but it is difficult to make sense out of the idea that this is an experience of the meaning. As we shall see, there are conflicting ideas of meaning at work here.

So, we may say that the sense of a sentence does not depend on the feelings, etc., that accompany it. True, the sense of a sentence is more than the sum of its parts, but the sense does not accompany a sentence. Rather, it is found in use.

Turning to the text in section iii, we see that Wittgenstein focuses on a similar idea. But instead of examining the idea that we can experience the meaning of a word, which leads to the incorrect notion that we can (or must) introspectively ascertain meaning, here Wittgenstein briefly looks at the notion that an image is the same as an idea.

Let us look at the following text from section iii:

> What makes my image of him into an image of *him*? Not its looking like him. The same question applies to the expression "I see him now vividly before me" as to the image. What makes this utterance into an utterance about *him*? Nothing in it or simultaneous with it ("behind it"). If you want to know whom he meant, ask him.[3]

The opening two sentences of the text perhaps at first seem paradoxical because it is precisely resemblance that we think is at the base of x being an image of y. Something is an image because it looks like that which it represents. The key idea here, though, is what is it that makes this image *my* image. In other words, if I imagine someone what do I need to have or do in order to determine that I have imagined that person? Clearly nothing further is required to make this image mine—nothing behind or betwixt or between the image makes it mine. Wittgenstein is again focusing on those tendencies that lead us into inventing psychological processes where none are required. I think of a friend or my mother or my child. Does this only become my image of that person if it meets certain criteria or passes certain tests? I am not here referring to the phenomenon of trying to remember, e.g., an address, phone number, or a song lyric—that is, of trying to remember something correctly. Rather, we want to test the idea that a mental image needs something else to identify it as one's own. If it were the case that some external or extra factor is needed for me to identify an image as my own then, as strange as it may sound, even the memory mistakes would be impossible to identify as yours. For what would identify the mistake as your mistake—some other external factor? And how would you know whether this was correct? Clearly we become involved in an infinite regress.

It would be strange to say, "First I think of something, then I have to find out whether I thought it." If this were the case then of course we would be open to the most horrendous skepticism. Again we would never know what we thought because we would first have a thought, then need another thought to check the first, and another thought to check the second, and so on into an infinite number of thoughts with nothing ever being decided. But this can be avoided by noting that "image" here does not depend on resemblance. The meaning of the phrase "I am imagining so and so" cannot be subjected to the same critique an art professor would make of a portrait: "That's not a very good likeness." We cannot say here "Well, draw your image and we will see whether you have imagined so and so."

Thus a picture cannot substitute for the idea here. Resemblance, or whatever, in an image of so and so cannot make the image into my image. The mistake is thinking the picture on its own must accomplish something—that the image in the mind carries something with it that makes it my image of x or my representation of x. Thinking this way makes my images, thoughts, and so on a source of skepticism, for I am now in the awkward position of having to justify the fact that this is my image. Paradoxically, with this model the image is unimportant and my imagining something is insufficient to make sense out of "I imagine x." For I must "get at" what "lies behind" the image—whatever it is that justifies it as an image. I have made this psychological object—whatever it is—the determining factor in this image being mine.

We can see that so much of what Wittgenstein has said before comes into play here. When I look for something adjacent to the image that identifies it as mine or that causes it to be an image, I am inventing a "myth of meaning" for the word *image* and bypassing the actual meaning of *image*. We think that by introspection we can see what identifies this as my image of x. We then look in vain for that which extends meaning to the image, and then begin to wrap the image in theoretical entities.

Clearly when I say that I just thought of x, all this "checking" did not occur—I did not identify an image and now I say, "I really thought of it."

Such a model literally cuts us off from ourselves. It makes us think that our thoughts or our imagination require criteria of identity. It seems as if what thoughts are mine depends on some as yet undiscovered other factors—although it is unclear who or what gets to determine which characteristics count and which don't. Presumably only the psychologist gets to tell which of my thoughts are genuinely mine and which come from "elsewhere." This model also cuts us from others, as Wittgenstein indicates in section iv:

> "I believe that he is suffering."—Do I also *believe* that he isn't an automaton? it would go against the grain to use the word in both connexions. Suppose I say of a friend: "He isn't an automaton."—What information is conveyed by this, and to whom would it be information? To a *human being* who meets him in ordinary circumstances? What information *could* it give him?[4]

To say of someone, "I believe he is suffering" might be a statement about his mental state when perhaps the person's depression or anguish is not obvious. There are circumstances where this would make sense. Perhaps at a funeral a person is putting on a good face, but inside he is feeling deep grief. Or perhaps you read an account of some tragedy in the paper, and you imagine that the people involved must feel awful. So a statement of this type might be considered an assumption or a guess about someone's feelings or emotions at a particular time. We would likely go up to the person at the funeral and say, "You must feel terrible—is there anything I can do?"

But if I say "I believe that my friend is not a robot," *belief* cannot mean the same thing. Clearly the circumstances for the question are not ordinarily present. We are not "of the opinion" that other people are human beings. What would make us doubt it? Under what circumstances would rendering an opinion on this matter be required?

Of course the planet could be taken over by aliens who are replacing people with robots. Then I suppose the question might make sense. Or we might be doing philosophy. If I think my statements about another person are of a nature that they always require justification, that there is something behind my words that I must perceive so that they are meaningful, then the result is a skepticism about "other minds," other's interior states, and so on. Because there is no limit or end to the need for justification here I can never be sure that I am right. What would tell me that I have perceived the correct something that lurks behind my words? The above model does not tell us. It is only if we accept the above model that the statement "I believe he is a human being" makes sense.

Let us suppose, as in the model above, that my ideas about someone are images or pictures and that which makes these images meaningful is something "behind" these images. The same problem we saw previously occurs: that which I want to know or speak about becomes irrelevant—it is logically excluded from my language. It is not the case that I simply think about or relate to the individual—"Here comes my friend. He looks depressed. I'll ask him what's the matter." If the above model is correct then this makes no sense. The meaning of my words is seen as something behind or surrounding my mental images. According to this model, the feelings, or whatever, behind my thoughts make them meaningful. Hence, really, what the person is feeling is not important, but my feelings are. I must identify my own feelings or "inner whatevers" to see if he's depressed. He could be sitting alone crying his eyes out and I have to search myself introspectively in order to determine whether he is depressed. How would I ever know anything about him on this model? To counter this tendency we must note that the phrase "He is depressed" says nothing about the observer. I don't need to ascertain anything about myself to use the word *depression* correctly. Likewise, as we have seen, *depression* does not solely refer to something going on "within" someone. When I note someone is depressed, this is not the result of peering into his or her mind or central nervous system. Here again, if we adopt this approach to understanding the psychological, skepticism would be the result.

However, as Wittgenstein says in section v, he is not completely denying the "inner." Psychology is not reduced simply to treating human behavior.

> Then psychology treats of behavior, not of the mind? What do psychologists record?—What do they observe? Isn't it the behavior of human beings, in particular their utterances? But *these* are not about behavior."I noticed he was out of humor." Is this a report about his behavior or his state of mind? ("The sky looks threatening": is this about the present or the future?) Both; not side-by-side, however, but about the one *via* the other.[5]

In other words, our psychological language, "He is depressed," etc., is not about behavior and so neither should our grammar, our description of the use of these words, try to force our psychological language into this mold. When I say that someone is depressed, I am neither referring solely to an inner state nor solely to particular actions and circumstances. But as we have seen it is only within the context of certain characteristic activities and circumstances that our language of psychology operates. To put it in a philosophical context, neither the Cartesian or behaviorist paradigms by themselves provide a correct context for psychological language.

In section vi on page 155, Wittgenstein returns to the notion that meaning is that which accompanies a word. Again, such an idea often causes confusion regarding our psychological language because we wish, understandably, until we consider the issue, to associate some mental event or occurrence with our psychological vocabulary. But, most often when we are doing philosophy, what we choose as a "mental event"—the feelings and so forth that accompany our psychological language—is mistakenly substituted as a referent for the meaning of a word. What is required instead is understanding the actual employment of the word. In section vi Wittgenstein says:

> How should we counter someone who told us that with *him* understanding was an inner process?—How should we counter him if he said that with him knowing how to play chess was an inner process?—We should say that when we want to know whether he can play chess we aren't interested in anything that goes on inside him.—And if he replies that this is in fact just what we are interested in, that is, we are interested in whether he can play chess—then we shall have to draw his attention to the criteria which would demonstrate his capacity, and on the other hand to the criteria for the "inner states."
>
> Even if someone had a particular capacity only when, and only as long as, he had a particular feeling, the feeling would not be the capacity.[6]

This passage gives a good overview of the material in part II. As we have seen, we might want to attach our psychological language to a mental process. The idea of a psychological process as a referent for our psychological vocabulary can be quite attractive. Here we perhaps model the psychological on the mechanical. We watch a machine, like an engine, at work and there are a number of steps or operations that the engine goes through in order to accomplish its result. The same might be said of a computer or a calculator. We think of the steps that the computer program takes and we see a clear analogy to our brains. Hence we assume thinking or understanding must be an analogous process. However, the comparison can be misleading on a number of levels. A mechanical view of thought can make it seem as if thinking is something that goes on in us quite apart from anything else—like a computer program running, only one that we don't see or know anything about. Thus thinking becomes something "hidden" or "behind" writing, speaking, doing a calculation, or playing chess. Thinking in this model is pictured as a brain or thought process running concurrently with these activities. But when we want to know whether someone can solve a math problem, speak French, or play chess we aren't interested in his inner feelings, experiences, processes, or what have you. If someone applied for a job as an accountant, would it be sufficient for him to say—"Well, I have that 'I can balance the books feeling' quite regularly"? Suppose your surgeon said, "I never studied surgery, but I feel as if I did."

As established, Wittgenstein clearly acknowledges that words can have a certain feeling attached to them just as a piece of music played in a certain way can give us a particular feeling. But this feeling cannot be separated from the music. It is necessary that you hear or play the musical phrase to get this feeling. This is not an "atmosphere" or an "aura" that accompanies the music; rather, it is how the music affects us. We need not appeal to something "accompanying" the music to explain its pleasing us, making us sad, and so on. So to, the fact that words move us or stimulate us need not be "caused" by something surrounding the word. Why appeal once again to this mysterious and unseen atmosphere, third party, or psychological middle man? Why does the feeling that a word gives have to be mediated by something "surrounding" the word? Again this is probably because we need something to feed or bolster the idea of the mental process—or the mechanical picture of thinking, understanding, and so on. Whether and what is happening in the brain when one thinks or understands is an empirical question. For Wittgenstein, the philosophical issue is that this model for our concepts cooks up a misleading picture of what is going on here. If we think our psychological language is meaningful because of some process going on behind it, and then we attempt an empirical investigation into this process, we are only chasing a linguistic dream.

We can create many captivating pictures with our language—many such dreams (and nightmares). Consider this text from section vii: p. 157e.

> The evolution of the higher animals and of man, and the awakening of consciousness at a particular level. The picture is something like this: Though the ether is filled with vibrations the world is dark. But one day man opens his seeing eye, and there is light.

What this language describes is a picture. What is to be done with the picture, how it is to be used, is still obscure. Quite clearly, however, it must be explored if we want to understand the sense of what we are saying. But the picture seems to spare us this work: it already points to a particular use. This is how it takes us in.[7]

The above picture is powerful because of the importance of the topic and the picture's generality; it seems scientific and explanatory in a very fundamental way. We seem to have captured very general facts of nature. This picture seems to be the encapsulation of the theory of evolution and the creation of human consciousness. The passage even echoes Genesis, but puts a more modern and therefore more "acceptable" spin on, "Let there be light." In this way the picture may become impervious to challenge and actually seeps into our everyday parlance—our everyday way of looking at human beings and our place in the world. The picture is not the gateway to investigation but seems to answer all our questions or, at least, to dictate the path of future inquiry.

But I think Wittgenstein would say that the investigation is only just beginning. We must establish a use for the picture. What does it describe? What does it teach us? How is this picture to be applied, and what fruit will it bear? The picture may in fact say nothing at all and have no use whatsoever. But even so I think it says a great deal about us. Why do we find this idea so appealing, and why are we so inclined to let this picture dictate our future actions, beliefs, and perhaps even our science?

We will return to these questions in the last chapter. For now I think we should note that the above picture has the character of a theory—a foundational statement about, say, human consciousness. However, it remains uninvestigated and so far useless. For a variety of reasons it is simply "received" and accepted. It is this that Wittgenstein wants to guard against.

Empiricism traditionally had been one of those grand unifying theories in philosophy. In empiricism ideas are supposed to be derived from sense experience, sensations, or sense-impressions. In the next few sections (with the exception of section x, which we will treat separately) and particularly in section xi, Wittgenstein seems to be focusing on some of the central claims of empiricism. This is not to say he has never raised this issue previously, but here he seems to be taking the discussion to a deeper level—particularly in his "seeing-as" discussion in section xi.

If there is a relationship between sense experience and ideas, then Wittgenstein would want to explore the relationship between the grammars of, e.g. *know* and *sensation*. As we have seen it may not be obvious that our inquiry is or should be grammatical. But again it is not the case, generally speaking, that sensation or knowledge gives us any great problem. We know this, but not that. We feel hot or cold or tired or we see colors and feel textures and so on. It is the concepts that give us trouble. It is when we consider our ideas of knowledge and sensation that our manifold difficulties arise. Most often, the relationship between sensation and knowledge confuses us, and so it is the logic or use of these concepts that must be explored. To accomplish this Wittgenstein begins with an example. In section viii on p. 158e[8] Wittgenstein asks us to consider a very slight movement of your finger and then investigate the phrase: "My kinesthetic sensations advise me of the movement and position of my limbs."

Here Wittgenstein wants us to imagine very slight movements in one of our fingers and the feeling we get during these movements. We feel these movements, and it is tempting to say that these movements tell us how our fingers are moving and so cause us to know, say, the position of our fingers. This might be considered a picture of the relationship between sensation and knowledge. Again, the picture might be one of a mechanical connection between sensations or the nerves in the finger and the brain. Thus we would seem to have an empirical basis for the language of sensation as the empiricist sees it—a direct connection between knowing and seeing. But as we will see, the logic or the use of these words is not found in such a picture—hence the picture leads us astray. Let us look at this text from section viii.

> "But after all, you must feel it, otherwise you wouldn't know (without looking) how your finger was moving." But "knowing" it only means being able to describe it.—I may be able to tell the direction from which a sound comes only because it affects one ear more strongly than the other, but I don't feel this in my ears; yet it has its effect: I *know* the direction from which the sound comes; for instance, I look in that direction.[9]

While it is true that I certainly feel a sensation in my finger, to say that I know how my finger is moving means that I can describe its movements. If someone asked, "In what direction is your finger moving?" it would be useless here to say simply "I have a feeling in my finger." This statement could mean a variety of things, but it certainly doesn't tell us what we know about the motion of the finger—direction, rate, etc. This example illustrates the logical or grammatical disconnect between the question "what do you know?" and the statement "I have a feeling." To the question of the direction of the motion of my finger a *description* of the motion would be an answer. Here again this shows us something about the concept *know*. The upshot is that *know* and *sense* are very different concepts and so have different uses. We cannot simply blindly connect them.

Just as the relationship between our "external" sensations, such as touch, and our ideas of these sensations can be confusing, so too, our "inner" sensations, such as our emotions, can cause similar difficulties when we come to our ideas or what we know of these feelings. As we noted previously when we discussed pain, it would not be correct to say "I know my pains" as if it is through a mental awareness that we experience pain. I do not know my pains—I simply have them. In a similar way, as Wittgenstein notes in section ix, it would be incorrect to say grief is experienced through observation or through a particular inner sense. Again, it would be difficult to make sense of someone saying "I am observing my grief"—except to mean simply that you are grieving. What use could we make of the phrase? Through what sense would we be observing our grief? Is the grief that you observe somehow altered when you are observing it? *Grief* clearly does not mean "something that I have observed in myself." I can see that someone is in mourning—but how would I see it myself? As with pain, grief is something that is felt, talked about, expressed, or observed in the behavior of others.

Again, in general, the problem is thinking that there is a reference for our psychological vocabulary, when really there are different language games and circumstances, different contexts that delineate our psychological language. There is no single, overriding logical structure to our psychological language. Rather, the logic of these concepts is more involved. If I wanted to explain fear to someone I might act it out—but this would be difficult for hope or belief. Thus our attempt to cover the logic of our psychological terms with a blanket category such as "mental state" is bound to cause confusion. Here we can say that just as we must pay attention to the language of our sensation, so too we must understand the language of our emotions. Our emotions as we experience them are not something "inner" to which we are trying to reach with our ideas or faculties of knowing. Rather, we feel our emotions and our concepts of our emotions and our sensations belong to a variety of language games and contexts. They cannot simply be reduced to the concept "mental state."

Section x focuses on the idea of belief. However, belief seems to be discussed in a way that seems to be inconsistent with the previous sections on psychology, sensation, and so forth. But as we will see the inconsistency is only apparent because Wittgenstein is still discussing the logic of psychological concepts.

The topic of the section is "Moore's paradox," which Wittgenstein thought was very important and overlooked.[10] This topic actually requires a deeper and far more extensive discussion that would take us beyond the bounds of the present volume. This idea is the subject of Wittgenstein's *On Certainty*, which occupied him for the last year and a half of his life. What we will do here is to discuss a rough sketch of the general problem generated by Moore's paradox and point the reader toward Wittgenstein's general solution.

Moore's paradox is that someone can say "I suppose or speculate that something is the case, but I don't believe it," but I cannot *assert* that something is the case and I don't believe it. Both sentences seem to be about the same thing, but the first sentence is okay and the second sentence makes no sense. In other words, we can imagine that the earth is round and that someone doesn't believe it. Or we can frame the sentence as a hypothesis "Let us just say: The earth is round but I don't believe it." This makes sense. But now take the same sentence as an assertion that someone makes—"The earth is round, but I don't believe it." This makes no sense. The person would be declaring something to be a fact, something that he knows to be true, and in the same sentence declaring that he can't accept it as true. Moore wanted to outlaw this on psychological grounds—but for Wittgenstein the assertion violates the logic of assertion.

A letter Wittgenstein wrote to Moore in 1944 explains his position succinctly:

It seems to me that the most important point was the absurdity of the assertion, "There is a fire in the room and I don't believe there is." To call this, as I think you did, "an absurdity for *psychological* reasons seems to me wrong or *highly* misleading. (If I ask someone, "Is there a fire in the next room?" and he answers "I believe there is," I can't say: "Don't be irrelevant. I asked you about the fire, not about your state of mind!") But what I wanted to say is this. Pointing out that "absurdity" which is in fact something *similar* to a contradiction, though it isn't one, is so important that I *hope you'll publish* your paper. By the way, don't be shocked at my saying it is something "similar" to a contradiction. This means roughly: it plays a similar role in logic. You have said something about the *logic* of assertion. Viz.: It makes sense to say "Let us suppose: p is the case and I don't believe that p is the case," whereas it makes *no* sense to assert "P is the case and I don't believe that p is the case." This *assertion* has to be ruled out and is ruled out by "common sense," just as a contradiction is. And this just shows that logic isn't as simple as logicians think it is. In particular: that contradiction isn't the *unique* thing people think it is. It isn't the *only* logically inadmissible form and it is, under certain circumstances, admissible.[11]

In other words, logically speaking if a statement leads to a contradiction, then that statement is ruled out. If I say, "I have a square circle," we say that this statement is illogical and makes no sense because a square circle is a contradiction in terms. That the person does not have any such thing is not decided empirically—there is nothing to look for. But we could imagine a child asking, "Is there such a thing as a square circle?" In this context the phrase, in a way, makes sense. I know what the child means, and I can answer his question. We would explain to the child there is no such thing. An oxymoron is a contradiction put to literary use: "That was the loudest silence I have heard. As usual, the chairman's silence speaks volumes." Or on a movie set we might say, "That house is not a house—it only a façade." But in most cases if a person said, "I just bought a house but it's not a house," it would be difficult to know how to reply. Generally we would have to conclude the person is not making any sense. We would clearly have to rule out such statements if made in a factual context. "I just gave you a half pound of turkey, but it's not turkey." "Here is your book that is not a book." "I gave you your antibiotic but it is not an antibiotic." If these statements are admissible then any statement is admissible—nothing would make sense. We would have to move to Wonderland ("Nobody is in the drawing room."—"Good. Tell him I'll be in shortly."). But clearly contradiction does not only have a formal logical status.

Moore points out a similar absurdity. The assertion "x is the case, but I don't believe it," has to be ruled out. It says, "I claim that x is a fact, but can't accept it." But to claim x is a fact rests on an established language of facts and claims. To make sense of the idea of a claim or an assertion presupposes certain circumstances—in general, it presupposes a body of knowledge. This is something that often escapes notice. Think of telling someone about a play in a baseball game: "The last out was a classic 6-4-3 double play." If you know nothing of baseball terminology then that would be opaque. Even if you know nothing about baseball you might describe the scene thus: "Well, one guy threw the ball to the other guy who threw it to some other guy while these two guys were running." But even that description presupposes a lot of language. Let us say you had never seen any games of any sort. Then perhaps you could only say: "There seems to have been a lot of activity just now." But even that presupposes at the very least the whole idea of making a report or telling what has gone on, and there is a great deal that is presupposed in even that simple language game.

In other words, making a claim makes sense in certain circumstances and presupposes a certain body of knowledge that must be accepted on the part of the person making the claim. We cannot simultaneously make a claim and reject that background knowledge. In our present case doing so would make the word *belief* meaningless.

> When you say "Suppose I believe . . ." you are presupposing the whole grammar of the word "to believe," the ordinary use of which you are the master.—You are not supposing some state of affairs which, so to speak, a picture presents unambiguously to you, so that you can tack on to this hypothetical use some assertive use other than the ordinary one.—You would not know at all what you are supposing here (i.e., what, for example, would follow from such a supposition), if you were not already familiar with the use of believe.[12]

Let us say someone says, "Suppose I believe the earth has existed only since yesterday." So the sentence is a hypothetical, yet it seems to be saying something important about belief—that it makes sense to say that you believe something that is manifestly false. It looks as if there is this assertion "the earth has existed only since yesterday" and that "belief is perhaps a psychological state that is appended by the individual to the assertion." But this misunderstands both *belief* and *assertion*. We cannot just haphazardly connect words without considering their use—this assumes that they have a meaning apart from their use, and I hope we are sufficiently disabused of this notion by now.

In what context would the statement "the earth has existed only since yesterday" be considered an assertion—that is, a statement of fact? Surely, it is simply nonsense. Certainly this statement presents a picture to us. I can imagine all sorts of things in connection with it—although they would have to be quite fantastic—memories of the past have been falsely implanted in everybody and all the buildings and so forth did not take years to build but were created in an instant and so on. But what actual use would this statement have? How would I insist on this, or begin to try to prove it, offer evidence for it—as I would any other assertion? Hence calling this sentence an assertion would be misleading at best.

But now this statement, since it is ruled out as an assertion, looks like a perfect candidate for belief. Isn't it the case that we can believe something outlandish or nonsensical, something for which there isn't a shred of evidence? Yes certainly, but that is not the point at issue.

We are not concerned here with what it is permissible to believe but with the logic of *belief* and *assertion* itself. We cannot use belief to turn a statement into an assertion, when logically we don't have an assertion. Belief will not turn "Blimey truggles the wipples had" into a good English sentence. When a sentence such as "the earth has existed only since yesterday" is shown not to be an assertion—what sense can we make out of "I still believe that it is"? Can my "belief" here somehow turn the statement into an assertion? Can we say something like, "Well, for me it is an assertion"? But as we have seen, we can't privately define *assertion*.

Belief does not mean a psychological act but presupposes the grammar of belief. To say I believe in a certain statement cannot alter the meaning of the statement, any more than it can change the fact. What you accept or don't accept is up to you—but this cannot alter logic. To attempt to see belief in this way changes the language of belief in such a way that negates the ordinary use of *belief*.

Let us return to our original predicament. Someone asserts that "p is the case and I don't believe that p is the case." Why does this assertion have to be ruled out? In what way is it similar to a contradiction? On the surface it seems that Moore is correct, and we would have to say this is absurd on psychological grounds. We can't say on one hand that I am certain x is clearly a fact that I am convinced of—I am asserting it to be true—but on the other hand that I can't accept it. But Wittgenstein wants to say the absurdity is a logical one, and a fundamental one at that.

If we allowed the above assertion, then *assertion* as well as *belief* and *certainty* would lose their senses. To call a statement an assertion means we have to be able to use it as an assertion. That is, a wide range of conditions and circumstances has to be obtained in order for a statement to make sense as an assertion. We cannot pluck a statement out of the air, call it an assertion simply because it may have the form of an assertion and say I believe it or I don't believe it—I doubt it or not, etc. Here the conditions and circumstances for belief, doubt, etc., would be lacking.

Hence we must find a use for the statement "I assert p is the case, but I don't believe p is the case." Clearly, this is not the assertion that p is this case. If this is a statement about belief, then in what sense is it one? The only sense it might have is something like "I don't believe a particular fact that I have just asserted." But how can we make sense of the phrase "don't believe" in this context? To assert a fact means accepting a series of background conditions and circumstances. Again, a fact cannot be asserted in a vacuum. *Assertion, fact,* and so on, have sense within particular language games. But "I don't believe what I have asserted" can only mean rejecting the very background conditions that give the assertion sense. Just as we just can't assert a statement in a vacuum, neither can we disbelieve or doubt a statement in a vacuum. To doubt or disbelieve a statement means rejecting that which supports a statement as well. In other words, to doubt the statement "the earth has existed for millions of years" would mean removing it from all the circumstance that give the words their meaning. In order to make sense of *doubt*, here I would have to abstract the statement from its normal language game and declare the statement's ordinary employment essentially meaningless. I would have to surround the statement with a variety of conditions: we are all insane or deluded—our memories have been implanted, dinosaur fossils are fakes, all geological evidence to the contrary is wrong, and so on.

Although it may not be apparent, there is a strong connection between the previous material on psychology and this section on Moore's paradox. As we can see here, *belief* cannot be construed to mean simply a mental state. As with *grief* or *hope* or *pain*, this can be seen through the grammar of the word—the logic of the concept. Clearly any assertion about the psychological presupposes the grammar of assertion—that is, the series of conditions and circumstances regarding any assertion and our psychological language. Deviating from the stricture that meaning is found in the use of the word can lead us into absurdities.

Section xi is quite lengthy and a good deal of it is a (somewhat) uncharacteristically sustained effort on the idea of seeing something as something. Hence it is often known as the "seeing-as" discussion. Certainly, the idea of a "visual impression" figures prominently in this section, and very quickly Wittgenstein focuses on the various ambiguities involved in the concept of "a visual impression." One of the most perplexing problems occurs when we consider the fact that something may be seen in a variety of ways. For example: what is it about a stop sign that makes me see it as a signal to stop? Is this really something to do with my visual impression of the stop sign? Does a person who knows nothing about traffic signs have a different visual impression? If so, how would we tell? When I look at a page written in Arabic script it means nothing to me, while someone who speaks Arabic finds the writing full of significance. Some people look at modern art and are astounded and see something deep and meaningful, while others just scratch their heads and see only childish doodles. Are both groups seeing something different? What would that be? Again, if I don't see the beauty in a modern sculpture, am I lacking something in my perceiving faculties?

As usual, Wittgenstein does not outline the source of his difficulty, but much of this section is apparently a response to reading the works of Gestalt psychologists—particularly Wolfgang Kohler, and perhaps Kurt Koffka. Gestalt thinkers were eager to counter what we might call sense-data theories of perception in which a visual perception is constructed out of more discrete bits of perception. For Gestalt thinkers, visual perceptions come to us as organized wholes. They were much exercised by the "ambiguous" figures like the "duck-rabbit," illustrations of the interplay of figure and ground such as the "double cross," and so on that play such a prominent part in this section of the *Investigations*. Gestalt theorists were anxious to counter mechanical theories of sense perception that held that sensations traveled along hardwired neural pathways and were built up into visual impressions by the brain. They used these so-called ambiguous figures to demonstrate their objection to the sense-data idea. Say we see a red book lying on a black table. "Traditional" psychology says that we only see color, so the book obscures part of the table. Since the part of the table the book is actually resting on is out of our view, we then do not actually have a visual experience of what we say we see. To make sense out of "I see the book on the table," the traditional empiricist psychologists have to resort to, e.g., habit or learning to fill in the perceptual gap here. But the Gestalt thinkers are eager to explain the truth of the statement, "I see the book on the table" in terms of visual experience—in terms of our perceptual faculties.

Gestalt holds that the piecemeal explanation offered by empiricist or sense-data psychologists is incorrect. Rather, as we noted, for the Gestalt thinker, the visual experience is organized as a whole from the beginning. The Gestalt theorist maintains that there exists an "isomorphism" between visual impressions and brain processes because he is anxious to explain visual experience solely in terms of the sensory apparatus of the observer. There are, they thought, structures in the brain that correspond to the organization of visual experience. To show this the Gestalt psychologists developed a number of ingenious experiments—generally involving optical illusions, many of which are probably familiar to the reader. For example, if we take two parallel lines on a page one above the other, most people have no problem seeing that they are parallel. But if the top line is intersected by a series of short lines inclined to the right and the bottom line is intersected by lines inclined in the opposite direction, invariably people will say that the lines are not parallel. The Gestalt theorist claims that since this response is automatic or spontaneous it is not the result of habit or learning. Visual experience is subject to the "structural dynamics" of the sensory process. Just as the interplay of physical forces produce a soap bubble as a whole entity—not something constructed out of pieces, so too our visual experience is constructed whole and entire out of the interplay of "forces" in our sensory apparatus. Certainly, it is hard to deny that our visual experience contains certain "spontaneous groupings" that can easily be said not to be learned. We seem to naturally search out patterns and groups in what we see. Does anyone learn to see random configurations of stars as constellations or shapes and figures in clouds or similar patterns in nature—the delta at the mouth of a river, or the *s* curve in a road or a path? The Gestalt theorists argue that seeing these phenomena occur spontaneously or naturally and are due to the dynamics of our sensory apparatus.

But we must note a series of (by now) familiar philosophical concerns emanating from what Gestalt proposes. Let us say it is the case that our visual perception is organized in exactly the way we experience it thanks to the aforementioned isomorphic structures in the sensory apparatus. Our sensory apparatus mediates then what we experience—what we experience is determined by how we experience it. In a sense, for Gestalt, all seeing is seeing-as.

Now this idea of course has a very modern ring. Even though the Gestalt thinker is at odds with the sense-data theory of perception, most of us will recognize a relationship between the Gestalt idea and the idea that color is created when light strikes the retina or sound is created when vibrating air molecules strike the eardrum. In other words, both the Gestalt theorist and the sense-data theorist agree that our experience is at least partly the creation of our sensory apparatus. The Gestalt idea, of course, sounds somewhat Kantian: we know phenomena, which are partly a creation of the perceiver. And scientists have long become used to the idea that the observation of a system distorts the system. The observer leaves his imprint on what he observes.

But we must realize that as with sense-data theory, the Gestalt theory is all-encompassing as far as our sensory apparatus is concerned. All of what we observe is "filtered" through our perceiving faculties. Hence we can only speculate about the relationship of what we experience to the "external world." The Gestalt theorist would have to agree with Kant that there is part of our experience—the "external world" source of our experience—that remains "noumenal" or unknowable. We must take it on faith that our experience equals reality. The result of this idea is then a skepticism regarding the existence of an external world.

We can push this even further to a statement of solipsism. For how can I know that what I experience is the same as what everyone else experiences? We assume that everyone's sensory apparatus is the same, but these "isomorphic structures" have so far proved elusive. Hence it is possible that my world is unique to me.

As we have seen, Wittgenstein has previously gone to great lengths to undermine ideas such as these. In that Gestalt is antiempiricism in psychology, I think there is some common ground between Gestalt and Wittgenstein, but Gestalt falls into many of the same errors that plague empiricism.

Wittgenstein notices a great deal of conceptual confusion in Gestalt ideas. Again, Wittgenstein is clear that he is not carrying on a psychological investigation but a logical one. First we have to consider the concepts *see, seeing-as,* and *visual impressions.* As we saw above Gestalt wants to collapse any distinctions between these concepts. *Seeing* means having a "visual impression," which has to do with the structural dynamics of our sensory apparatus; hence *seeing* is a complex operation that might be understood better as *seeing-as.* Seeing is never "direct" or immediate. Opening your eyes is not like raising the shade on a window to reveal the world—what is seen is always mediated through the sensory apparatus.

We must first attend to the grammar of these expressions; in doing so we will also see the importance of language when considering experiences of this type. In general, for Wittgenstein, it is a mistake to try to understand the concept of *seeing* in purely visual or psychological terms. If this sounds so strange that it is putting up a roadblock to continuing, think of the meaning of the phrase "I see your point." Certainly this statement means nothing visual. The tendency might be to think that it means something psychological. But again, if taken quite seriously the visual model or psychological model for the meaning of this statement is hard to apply here. When you say, "I see your point," you did not "see" or intuit something in the other person's mind. But did you "see" something in your own mind? I hope we have seen enough at this point so that we see that this strategy is useless. What exactly did you see, and if you saw anything at all, how would it be relevant to what the other person meant? Surely when he was making his point he was not referring to anything going on inside you. This phrase, of course, means something like—"I agree" or "yes that follows." Again, interpreting *seeing* here along visual lines only leads to confusion.

Wittgenstein begins the "seeing-as" analysis by introducing and discussing certain ambiguous figures of the type favored by Gestalt thinkers. Again, these are figures that do not change on the page but change for the observer. For example, a drawing of a cube may at one time appear to project out of the page or recede into it; a step may be drawn so that it appears to be concave or convex. On page 165e Wittgenstein introduces the so-called "duck-rabbit." Turned one way it looks like a duck. But turned so that the "duck's" bill is facing up the bill looks like the ears of a rabbit, and so the picture may be seen as a rabbit or a duck depending on the orientation of the observer. Although it may not be obvious at first, there is quite a tangle of concepts here.

If someone looks at the "duck-rabbit" he may not notice the dual nature of the picture. He may simply say that he sees a picture of a rabbit. It is important to note that the verification of what he sees is part of a language game, and so we have necessarily entered the realm of grammar. If the person does not notice the dual aspect of the picture, he would not say he has "seen it as" a rabbit. He simply says, "It's a rabbit," and when we ask him what he sees, he explains his perception by pointing to rabbits or pictures of rabbits or he describes them. When someone picks up his fork at dinner it would make little sense for him to say, "I am now seeing this as a fork." Notice, though, if we see the dual aspect of the duck-rabbit and someone else does not and simply says "it's a rabbit," we might say of that person, "Now he is seeing it as a rabbit."

> I am shewn a picture-rabbit and asked what it is; I say "It's a rabbit." Not "Now it's a rabbit." I am reporting my perception.—I am shewn the duck-rabbit and asked what it is; I *may* say "It's a duck-rabbit." But I may also react to the question quite differently.—The answer that it is a duck-rabbit is again the report of a perception; the answer "Now it's a rabbit" is not. Had I replied "It's a rabbit" the ambiguity would have escaped me, and I should have been reporting my perception.[13]

Clearly there are different grammars for a direct perception versus what Wittgenstein calls noticing an aspect or the change of an aspect.

Again the point here is that we must guard against a purely visual understanding of the meaning of all of our language regarding this experience. If we fail to notice the different language games involved here—some sensory, some psychological, some logical, then we may be tempted to try to load all these concepts onto the back of one language game: "visual impression." This is approximately the gist of the Gestalt theorists' understanding of seeing. The Gestalt thinker wants to explain *seeing* in terms of sensory apparatus, hence what is seen has to be explained by some connection to or something happening to our visual impressions, but Wittgenstein wants to show that this is apt to cause confusions.

Let us look at some texts concerning this idea on page p. 167e.

I suddenly see the solution of a puzzle-picture. Before there were branches there; now there is a human shape. My visual impression has changed and now I recognize that it has not only shape and color but also a quite particular "organization."— My visual impression has changed;—what was it like before and what is it like now?—If I represent it by an exact copy—and isn't that a good representation of it?—no change is shewn.[14]

In other words, if we look at the concept of visual impression for a moment we might see that the above experience as a confirmation of the Gestalt theory. The puzzle-picture that Wittgenstein is alluding to is probably of a type we might be familiar with from children's magazines. Amidst the drawing of, in this case a tree, the artist "hides" a series of other pictures by mingling them with the parts of a tree. A branch is subtly altered so that if you pay attention to it you see a baseball bat—or where the branches become very fine there is a human hand, etc. Thus where there was once color and shape there is now a particular organization that gives rise to a figure. In many ways this is similar to seeing constellations in random grouping of stars. The patterns appear to the observer spontaneously.

But why must this be due to some alteration in my visual impression? Let us assume that "visual impression" means what is literally before my eyes. Certainly it seems natural to say that when I notice something new in what I am looking at then my visual impression is new as well. But we should be wary of locating this change in a spontaneous mechanical manipulation of the sensory apparatus. If my visual impression in that sense has changed, I should be able to demonstrate or show it. What is "before my eyes" should have altered. But the best way of showing this change would be before and after pictures—but of course in this case both pictures would be the same.

The temptation here, in order to maintain the theory, would be to say that the picture we are looking at is not the visual impression, but the visual impression is something "inner"—within the observer. But here, Wittgenstein wants to point out, we have taken a very wrong turn.

And above all do *not* say "After all my visual impression isn't the drawing; it is *this*—which I can't shew to anyone."—Of course it is not the drawing, but neither is it anything of the same category which I carry within myself. The concept of the "inner picture" is misleading, for this concept uses the "*outer* picture" as a model; and yet the uses of the words for these concepts are no more like one another than the uses of "numeral" and "number." (And if one chose to call numbers "ideal numerals," one might produce a similar confusion.)[15]

Let us say a visual experience is an inner picture in the manner suggested above—perhaps we can imagine it to be a picture made by my imagination that duplicates the scene I am looking at. So the inner picture is like a mental copy of what I see. It has the same borders and dimensions as what I am seeing—the same arrangement of shapes and colors—it is as if I took a photograph of the scene with my mind. But can we give the same sense to "inner picture" as we do the "outer" one—the one we hang on the wall? Our language certainly allows us to create this idea of the "inner picture." But what can I do with it? I can show the outer picture, take it down from the wall, reframe it, retouch it, sell it, give it away, throw it away, paint over it, put it in another room, and so on. None of this applies to the "inner" picture. Who can I even show it to? I can only make a drawing of it and now it is no longer inner, but outer. Thus we try to talk about a visual impression as an "inner picture," but we are using "outer picture" as a model and the grammars of the two concepts are very different. The circumstances in which the concept "outer picture" works do not obtain with "inner picture."

> If you put the "organization" of a visual impression on a level with colours and shapes, you are proceeding from the idea of the visual impression as an inner object. Of course this makes this object into a chimera; a queerly shifting construction. For the similarity to a picture is now impaired. If I know the schematic cube has various aspects and I want to find out what someone sees, I can get him to make a model of what he sees in addition to a copy, or to point to such a model; even though he has no idea of my purpose in demanding two accounts. But when we have a changing aspect the case is altered. Now the only possible expression of our experience is what before perhaps seemed, or even was, a useless specification when once we had the copy. And this by itself wrecks the comparison of "organization" with colour and shape in visual impressions.[16]

Clearly colors and shapes in a "visual impression" or what you see can be pointed to and described just as they could in any picture or scene. *Organization*—the kind alluded to by Gestalt; that is, the spontaneous grouping in the visual field as the result of the structural dynamics, cannot be treated in the same way. It is not a part of what I see but supposedly a necessary part of how I see it—a necessary part of the visual field. If I arrange a series of dots on a page to form a cross, I can say, "These dots form a cross." This description would be a quite ordinary part of many different language games—guessing shapes, connect the dots, perhaps used as a type of diagram, and so on. But that these dots are seen as a cross due to a certain structure in my sensory apparatus is a psychological hypothesis. There is no logical necessity in saying my visual impression has a particular organization in addition to colors and shape. It makes sense to say the drawing has a pattern or organization. But to insist that this is a feature of my visual impression turns the visual impression into an inner object that has no use—its part in any language game of *seeing* is hard to see.

If we have a picture that can be seen in various ways we can get someone to copy the picture as is and then draw the aspect that he sees. He can draw the duck-rabbit as it is and then draw it in order to show that he sees the rabbit aspect. But if we have a cube drawn on a page in which the aspects change back and forth—it sometimes appears to recede into the page, sometimes projects out—then the person can only in essence make two copies if I ask him to copy the picture and draw what he sees. The picture must be looked at to see the aspects change. But what we have drawn on the page or copied is restricted to colors and shapes. "Organization"—other than the arrangement of color and shape in what we have drawn—does not appear or enter into the process, yet the process is complete. Hence we cannot see organization as an element equal to colors and shapes in the visual field. "Organization" as used by the Gestalt theorist is redundant—it does not appear in any description of the visual field. I can describe the colors and shapes in what I see and their arrangement, but beyond this how can I describe *organization*? What role does it play in the language game? Again it is difficult to give a meaning to organization as an integral part of the concept "visual impression." What is important in understanding "visual experience" is the language game we play with these words. The meaning of the word *cross* is sufficient to *see* an arrangement of dots as a cross.

In the next few pages—168e.–173e.[17]—Wittgenstein continues to examine the concepts of *seeing* and *seeing-as*. He takes a number of examples and continues to focus on the various interrelationships between the concepts of *seeing, perception, seeing-as*, and so on. The general idea is showing that these various concepts and the relationships among concepts cannot be reduced to a single formula.

As we noted we also must be aware of the role that language plays in many of these experiences. Objects can play various roles in language games, and these roles can become quite complex. For example, a triangle drawn in a book may serve many different roles, depending on the context or use. It can be an arrow, a pointer, a mountain, and so on (cf. p. 171e).[18] Children may take a large box and use it to play "house." For them, in a sense, the box disappears, and for all practical purposes it is a house.

> This may look like an odd experience. But how is it possible to *see* an object according to an *interpretation?*—The question represents it as a queer fact; as if something were being forced into a form it did not really fit. But no squeezing or forcing took place here.[19]

This experience can seem odd if we try to fit it into a visual mold or if we try to account for it through our sensory apparatus. But it may be that we are not dealing with something purely visual. When children see the box as a house, what does this mean—are we talking about a sensory experience? Generally this would not fall under the category of a hallucination. Rather, the children pretend the box is a house by treating it as a house—surrounding it with similar circumstances and conditions, this is the door, these are the rooms, this is the address, these are the people who live there, and so on. There is no need to try to force this experience into a visual mold. Hence to see something according to an interpretation is quite a usual experience, as long as we see that the difference between this experience and a purely visual experience is conceptual. We are simply making a distinction within the family of cases related to the use of *see.*

Here, though, we seem to have hit on something with larger repercussions and an important relationship to some earlier material in the *Investigations.* Consider the following text on p. 173e.

> Here it occurs to me that in conversations on aesthetic matters we use the words: "You have to see it like *this,* this is how it is meant"; "When you see it like *this,* you see where it goes wrong"; "You have to hear this bar as an introduction"; "You must hear it in this key"; "You must phrase it like *this*" (which can refer to hearing as well as to playing).[20]

This is interesting because it is one of the few times Wittgenstein mentions aesthetics in the *Investigations.* As we noted earlier, Wittgenstein makes a similar statement in part I when he connects understanding a sentence to understanding a theme in music. There he wanted to say that expressing the meaning of a musical phrase means giving that expression a language—e.g., a musical passage may be explained to someone by telling him the passage has to be heard, for example, as an "argument" between the strings and the winds—they are both fighting for dominance—or something of that sort. Clearly, a sentence may have similar patterns of inflection or emphasis—words are often chosen for their color or liveliness, and so on. This adds to the meaning of the sentence in the sense of its significance. Clearly if I say the word "hey" to someone in an even tone of voice, I may just be saying hello. But if I shout it, then things have changed—I might be telling the person to beware of some danger, etc. The important point is that communicating is seen here as something that requires the mastery of certain techniques that vary over a range of circumstances. Hence it seems Wittgenstein wants to talk about meaning or significance in aesthetics in a related way. There is perhaps a relationship between *seeing-as* and understanding a musical phrase and understanding the meaning of a sentence.

Apparently Wittgenstein sees a similar relationship within the family of concepts of *seeing*. Seeing something as something often requires a particular interpretation or a mastery of certain concepts. *Seeing-as* is a particular concept of experience—similar to the experience associated with understanding a piece of music.

> "Now he's seeing it like *this*," "now like *that*" would only be said of someone *capable* of making certain applications of the figure quite freely. The substratum of this experience is the mastery of a technique. But how queer for this to be the logical condition of someone's having such-and-such *experience*! After all you don't say that only "has toothache" if one is capable of doing such-and-such.—From this it follows that we cannot be dealing with the same concept of experience here. It is a different though related concept. It is only if someone *can do*, has learnt, is the master of, such-and-such that it makes sense to say he has had *this* experience. And if this sounds crazy you need to reflect that the *concept* of seeing is modified here.[21]

In other words, rather than understanding "visual experience" as something purely sensory and all visual concepts as a part of this mold, I think Wittgenstein wants to say that *seeing-as* has a language—it is part of a language game and a form of life—like grief or hope, as we saw in the discussion in part I. To understand this experience we need to pay attention to its language. However, Wittgenstein is not trying to completely characterize this experience. Rather, he is attempting to pass on the tools that we need to understand it.

It is also of note that Wittgenstein wants to include an understanding of aesthetic experience along these lines. Again, as we saw in part I, I think he is trying to indicate that we should steer clear of the psychological as an explanation of aesthetic experience. The aesthetic must be understood on conceptual grounds as well. A sensory or psychological theory is not required to explain how and why we phrase a piece of music in a particular way. Rather, we must take into account the technique involved—the language that is used.

> Think of the expression "I heard a plaintive melody." And now the question is: "Does he hear the *plaint*?"And if I reply: "No, he doesn't hear it, he merely has a sense of it"—where does that get us? One cannot mention a sense-organ for this "sense." Some would like to reply here "Of course I hear it!"—Others: "I don't really *hear* it." We can, however, establish differences of concept here.[22]

Clearly we can hear a sad or plaintive melody, and we can certainly hear the melody. But does it make sense to distinguish the sadness as something that is heard or sensed apart from the melody? Is there something separate here that we can identify as the sadness? Again the problem is that the melody is something musical, while if we want to "separate out" the sadness as something existing separately this can appear to be a certain psychological component to the music or a hearing or understanding of the music. The melody then almost becomes unimportant because the emotional aspect of the music is now something psychological—perhaps imposed on the music from within the listener or an "aura" accompanying the music requiring some sort of as yet unnamed sensory faculty. Interpreting music, then, would be not related to music but to psychology.

But what would this extra sense be? What is it that you are experiencing apart from the way the melody is played or heard? Wittgenstein relates this to the idea of experiencing the meaning of a word. As we have noted, words can be charged with meaning, and we may have certain experiences while hearing them or saying them. We might learn a new language and notice that the words do not have the ring of familiarity to them as yet. Or if we set up a code with someone and say that when we say the word *Tuesday* we really mean *Wednesday*. I might feel very unnatural when I'm saying this, and I might feel that *Tuesday* has not yet taken on its "new" meaning. All these feelings are undeniable, but it is not the psychology but the use that dictates meaning.

> But the question now remains why, in connexion with this *game* of experiencing a word, we also speak of "the meaning" and of "meaning it."—This is a different kind of question. It is the phenomenon which is characteristic of this language-game that in *this* situation we use this expression: we say we have pronounced the word with *this* meaning and take this expression over from the other language game. Call it a dream. It does not change anything.[23]

Pronouncing a word with a particular feeling does not "make" it "mean" anything. This expression is "on loan" from the other language game, and we can establish a difference in this family of cases. So too with "hear" in the above text. In each case we want to say we can "hear" the plaint. But if we want to interpret this as something heard or sensed apart from the melody we are using "hear" in the sense of hearing a sound, but the language necessary to make sense of this is lacking. But correcting this situation is not simply a matter of inventing new words, but rather requires a conceptual distinction. Just as meaning is not something inner or something that accompanies a word, so too the plaint of a melody is not something separable from the melody. Such an idea could make sense only with, say, psychological theorizing behind it, but this is entirely unfounded. We would have to locate a hitherto unknown sense—and this is unnecessary once the conceptual distinction is made.

The case with seeing-as and Gestalt is similar. The hypothesis that there are structures in the brain that account for certain features of visual experience comes from, in part, trying to understand *seeing* and the experience of seeing in a purely visual way. This idea ignores the conceptual dimension. Not every case of seeing something in a particular way needs to be explained by appealing to our sensory apparatus or perceptions. Certain types of seeing—when children *see* a box as a house—require the mastery of certain techniques—a certain language game. There are a wide variety of meanings of *to see*, and it is a mistake to think this can only be explained by reference to an inner psychological process. It is not necessary to look at something accompanying visual experience to understand the meaning of "visual experience." Once we turn away from this picture the mental cramp created by trying to force our concepts into this one mold is relieved.

Seeing-as represents the final substantial section of the *Investigations*. As with the rest of the work we have not highlighted each and every discussion in this long and difficult section, which probably should have its own book-length treatment. Hopefully, from what has been said the reader can sift through the end of this section and the last few pages of the work.

NOTES

1. PI 148e., PI, Prentice Hall ed., 174e.
2. PI 148e., PI, Prentice Hall ed., 175e.
3. PI 151e., PI, Prentice Hall ed., 177e.

4. PI 152e., PI, Prentice Hall ed., 178e.

5. PI 153e., PI, Prentice Hall ed., 179e.

6. PI 155e., PI, Prentice Hall ed., 181e.

7. PI 157e., PI, Prentice Hall ed., 184e.

8. PI, Prentice Hall ed., 185e.

9. PI 158e., PI, Prentice Hall ed., 185e.

10. Ludwig Wittgenstein, *Culture and Value*, 76e.

11. Quoted in Garth Hallet, *A Companion to Wittgenstein's "Philosophical Investigations"* (Ithaca: Cornell University Press, 1977) 656.

12. PI 164e., PI, Prentice Hall ed., 192e.

13. PI 167e., PI, Prentice Hall ed., 195e.

14. PI 167e., PI, Prentice Hall ed., 196e.

15. PI 167e., PI, Prentice Hall ed., 196e.

16. PI 168e., PI, Prentice Hall ed., 196e.

17. PI, Prentice Hall ed., 196–202e.

18. PI, Prentice Hall ed., 200e.

19. PI 171e., PI, Prentice Hall ed., 200e.

20. PI 173e., PI, Prentice Hall ed., 202e.

21. PI 178e., PI, Prentice Hall ed., 208–209e.

22. PI 178-9e., PI, Prentice Hall ed., 209e.

23. PI 184e., PI, Prentice Hall ed., 216e.

What Does It All Mean?

At this point I would like to examine the question of whether there is any overall meaning to the *Investigations*. As we noted in the beginning there is a temptation to look at the book as a collection of discussions on various topics with no thread tying them together. But Wittgenstein does say in his preface that although he was unable to do so, he was trying to weld his results together into "a whole"—a book that had a "natural order." This suggests that Wittgenstein may have had a theme or purpose that was guiding his work and the creation of the *Investigations*.

Clearly Wittgenstein never directly specifies a theme for his work. But with a little bit of patience and a more detailed look at Wittgenstein's life and work as a whole, I think a theme becomes evident.

First we must remember that although it may seem as if the *Tractatus* and the *Investigations* represent two distinct philosophical periods, there is a great deal of continuity to Wittgenstein's work. Wittgenstein says that his new thoughts, the *Investigations*, "could be seen in the right light only by contrast with and against the background of my old way of thinking," the *Tractatus*, and we spent the first part of our present study elucidating the relationship between the two works. Wittgenstein talks about some "grave errors" that he made in the *Tractatus*, primarily relating to logical atomism and the picture theory of meaning. Overall, however, the topics in the two books are strikingly consistent: meaning, the nature of the proposition, sense, logic, mathematics, and so on. It is also important to see that Wittgenstein's conception of the nature and purpose of philosophy remains equally consistent throughout the two works. As we noted above on p. x Wittgenstein writes in the *Tractatus* that the correct method in philosophy is to say only what can be said (what makes sense), and whenever someone tried to say anything metaphysical we would demonstrate that he had failed to give meaning to certain signs in his propositions. Wittgenstein sees philosophy in much the same way in the *Investigations*:

> We must do away with all *explanation*, and description alone must take its place. And this description gets its light, that is to say its purpose, from the philosophical problems. These are, of course, not empirical problems; they are solved, rather, by looking into the workings of our language, and that in such a way as to make us recognize those workings: *in despite of* an urge to misunderstand them.[1]

It is also important to note that Wittgenstein said that the point of the *Tractatus* was ethical.

> The book's point is an ethical one. . . . My work consists of two parts: the one presented here plus all that I have not written. And it is precisely this second part that is the important one. My book draws the limits to the sphere of the ethical from the inside as it were, and I am convinced that this is the ONLY rigorous way of drawing those limits.[2]

This remark might seem puzzling at first, but if we take a closer look at Wittgenstein's influences and return to some pertinent elements of his biography, this idea will become clear. We will see that for Wittgenstein a logical or philosophical investigation is also in many respects an ethical one and that this idea is central to Wittgenstein's conception of philosophy in the *Tractatus* and that this theme carries over into the *Investigations*. If we look at the work of many of Wittgenstein's early influences a philosophical pattern emerges that actually has a long pedigree: morality and logic go hand in hand. It is only through a rigorous application of logic to our thought, in Wittgenstein's case our language, that we will clearly see the path to a moral life. Our thinking and therefore our choices go wrong when it becomes clouded with nonsense. Wittgenstein, following in the footsteps of his influences, wanted definitively to show how to remove that nonsense. To understand this philosophical pattern and its relationship to Wittgenstein's work, let's begin with Wittgenstein's own account of whose work influenced him most.

In his work *Culture and Value*, Wittgenstein lists his most important influences: Boltzmann, Hertz, Schopenhauer, Frege, Russell, Kraus, Loos, Weininger, Spengler, and Sraffa.[3] With the exception of Piero Sraffa, a Cambridge economist, and Oswald Spengler, whose book *The Decline of the West* appeared in 1918, Wittgenstein read or knew all of the above authors prior to studying at Cambridge in 1911. (Wittgenstein read Russell's *Principles of Mathematics* in 1911 and afterwards went to the University of Jena to discuss ideas on logic and mathematics with Frege. On Frege's advice he went to study with Russell in Cambridge.) Eight out of the ten thinkers were German or Viennese and three were important intellectual fixtures in Vienna while Wittgenstein was growing up: Karl Kraus, Adolf Loos, and Otto Weininger. Wittgenstein maintained an interest in these three thinkers in particular well beyond his youth.   Like many of his contemporaries, Wittgenstein was an avid reader of Kraus's journal *Die Fackel* (The Torch) even having it forwarded to him while he was living in seclusion in Norway in 1913–1914. He met the architect Adolf Loos, a member of Kraus's circle of expressionist writers and artists, and after World War I worked with Loos's student, Paul Engelmann, on building a house for his sister. The architectural style is clearly influenced by Loos's teachings.[4] Wittgenstein maintained a lifelong interest in the work of the Viennese psychologist Otto Weininger, whose book, *Sex and Character*, became a huge bestseller after Weininger's suicide in 1903. It would be beyond the scope of this book to sort out all of Wittgenstein's early influences, but the persistence of these three make them worth special consideration. In what follows we will examine what these thinkers had to say and show how they influenced Wittgenstein.

Karl Kraus (1874–1936) became famous during his lifetime as a critic, poet, dramatist, performance artist, and satirist. His speaking engagements and performances were always in front of sold-out crowds. His books were bestsellers, and people stood in line waiting for the most recent issue of *Die Fackel*, which he practically single-handedly wrote and edited. Kraus's fame was all the more extraordinary given that the media almost never mentioned his name. Kraus was nominated for the Nobel Prize in Literature—not a word in the papers. When his friend, the prominent poet Peter Altenberg, died, Kraus delivered the eulogy—Altenberg's obituary never appeared in the press. This so-called silent treatment was a response to Kraus's persistent diatribe against corruption and decadence in Viennese society, a general moral failing he blamed largely on the media and its perversion of language. From what we have seen of Wittgenstein's thought, it is obvious that the importance of language is an idea that would certainly resonate with him. Language was something holy for Kraus—he often spoke of himself as someone possessed by language and spoke of language and syntax in theological or religious terms. Language was not merely the vehicle for thought or symbolic of thought but intimately wound up with thought. "Language is the mother of thought, not its handmaiden."[5] Wittgenstein notes the same relationship in the *Tractatus*: "A thought is a proposition with sense."[6] For Kraus language was more than just the means to express the truth—it was the guardian of truth, and as such language revealed the character and integrity of the language user. "Something I cannot get over: that a whole line can be written by half a man."[7] Kraus was famous for the deft use of the aphorism (of course, Wittgenstein favored this style of writing), and this remark might seem very cryptic. But, for Kraus, because of the inherent ambiguity of language, saying what you mean, saying it clearly, and especially telling the truth was difficult and required enormous effort and commitment on the part of the individual. The task required a person of character and integrity—a "whole" man. A person lacking the essential intellectual and moral rigor—a half a person—would not be up to the challenge. Hence morality in the individual and the proper use of language supported each other. The struggle to say something clearly was also a moral struggle.

Kraus regarded any misuse of language as an attack on morality and the basic dignity of humanity. He traced many of the evils that plagued society, such as poverty and crime, to the corruption of language. Kraus blamed the disaster of World War I, the horror of the Nazis, and Hitler's rise to power on the corruption of language by the press. Kraus thought that in a purified German language evil could not be spoken.[8]

These statements may seem strange or perhaps overblown. But they will seem less so if we take a step back and examine some previous philosophical insights on the cause of our general moral failings. Certainly since the origin of philosophical inquiry, philosophers have tried to explain the nature of morality and assess the cause of our lack of morality, while offering remedies for this situation. Many thinkers have pointed out that one reason for our moral faults is the lack of clarity in our moral ideas. If we are confused about our moral ideas, the less likely it will be that we will think clearly in a moral situation and make the right choice. Socrates and Plato were certainly of the opinion that the proper definition of our moral ideas would result in the correct moral choices. The idea was that if we clearly understand how to distinguish what is good for us from what is bad, we would naturally want to choose what is beneficial since no one would intentionally seek what was harmful. So in Book I of Plato's *Republic*, Socrates and some friends are discussing the virtue of Justice. One member of the group, Polemarchus, defines Justice as helping friends and harming enemies. Socrates points out the contradiction with this definition. Doing something right, like being just, requires skill. So like being a skilled doctor or navigator or shepherd, being just means knowing how to do something well. Knowing how to do something well means providing benefit, not harm. A doctor that continually made his patients sicker is not a skilled doctor. So whatever Justice is, if it is a skill, it must be like all other skills and provide benefit, not harm. Thus, there is something wrong with Polemarchus's definition that Justice means benefitting friends and harming enemies, and so, according to Socrates, we cannot achieve Justice by following his idea. Now of course we might point out some problems with what Socrates says here and indeed much of the rest of *Republic* revolves around sorting out this argument, but that need not concern us here. What we do want to notice is that Socrates' (Plato's) method of attacking the problem is logical—focusing on the meaning of *Justice*; it is not, for example, empirical or historical. Socrates does not argue something like: look at all the people who have followed Polemarchus's idea and see how it didn't work out. Rather, he shows that Polemarchus is fundamentally confused because his idea contains a contradiction.

For our purposes the important point in the above discussion is the connection between logic and morality. We can trace this connection throughout the history of philosophy, but when we talk about the most significant philosophical precursor to Kraus's and Wittgenstein's time that connected logic and morality, we must talk about Immanuel Kant (1724–1804). For Kant, logic played a crucial role in distinguishing which of our principles were truly moral. According to Kant, those actions that are done simply because they are good and for no other reason have true moral worth. To use Kant's example, the shopkeeper who reasons that he is not going to cheat his customers because it is bad for business is obviously more concerned with making money than morality. Presumably, if he could cheat his customers and not lose them and thereby make even more, he would do so. His guiding principle is not a moral one—his guiding principle is making money. Assuming we want to act morally, the question is how can we know which principles to adopt? Which principles will lead without doubt to actions that are done for the good alone—actions of true moral worth? Although there are numerous interpretations and controversies surrounding Kant, a very fruitful way of understanding what he means is to note that his approach to the problem is logical. To distinguish which of our principles is moral, the *type* of statement we use in framing our principles is very important.[9] For Kant, when he talks about morality there are two basic types of statements: categorical and hypothetical. Categorical statements are meant to be universal and necessary, holding good always and everywhere, like statements of a law of nature. For example, one atom of sodium and one atom of chlorine, NaCl, always and everywhere produce a molecule of salt. Hypothetical statements are of the "if-then" variety and are not universal and necessary but are conditional statements, involving consequences and circumstances. "If the car is the right price, then I will buy it." So my actions here depend on other things—things beyond my control—being the case. Kant is clear that moral principles must be of the categorical variety, and if our principles can be stated hypothetically, in terms of "if-then," it cannot be considered a moral principle.[10]

This is certainly a difficult idea and of course whatever one says about Kant is open to reinterpretation. But Kant is clear that a principle can only be considered moral if it is universal and necessary, i.e., categorical, and therefore adopted without regard to consequences or circumstances. Since only a categorical principle—Kant calls it the categorical imperative—is independent of all conditions, it is therefore completely of our own choosing and therefore completely free. For Kant, and many philosophers would agree, without freedom morality makes no sense. If we are not acting freely then we cannot be held accountable for our actions. A person cannot be blamed for what they do while they are "brainwashed" or someone is holding a gun to his head. However, Kant argues, that when we are thinking hypothetically, that is, basing our actions on certain external circumstances or consequences, then we are not acting freely—our actions are being determined by those external conditions. We will perform certain actions only if certain conditions apply. Hence the aforementioned shopkeeper's principle, for Kant, is not a moral one since it is conditional. His statements have taken the form of "if-then": "If it pays, then I will do what is right." Kant argues that if we try to frame moral principles conditionally then we are not freely governing our own actions. Rather, our actions are governed by external conditions and circumstances. Therefore, we have unwittingly deprived ourselves of the freedom to choose: the principle that guides our actions states that we will act in a certain way only if certain external conditions are present. Thus something other than us is determining what we do or don't do, and we have eliminated the possibility of moral responsibility.

So to figure out if a principle is a moral one you have to apply a logical litmus test: act only on those statements that can be treated as a universal law of nature. To be a truly moral guide your principle must be unconditional.

Kant's moral philosophy is much more complex, but the above is a workable sketch for our purposes. Although Kant in his ethical writings takes exception to past schools of thought, we note that Kant has much in common with the ideas of Socrates and Plato discussed above. First, Kant agrees that there is a connection between logic and morality. Just as Socrates wanted to logically examine moral definitions to see which definitions were the correct guides to our behavior, so too Kant's theory applies logic to determine which principles are moral: only those statements that conform to the categorical imperative can be moral. There is a subtle shift in emphasis, however. Socrates and friends were interested in examining moral ideas: the virtue of "truth," for example. Kant is examining moral statements, e.g., "should I always tell the truth?"

The shift from idea to statement is significant. It is much easier to think of an idea as an abstraction, as an individual entity—in Platonic terms as the form or pattern for a group of things. A statement or proposition involves at least a subject and a predicate and is therefore much more easily seen as necessarily connected to language as a whole. And indeed philosophers after Kant, certainly in the German-speaking world, such as Schopenhauer and Nietzsche, began to focus on the nature of language and its connection to reason and morality. The Viennese writer, critic, and philosopher Fritz Mauthner (1849–1923), whose *Critique of Language* appeared in 1901, made this connection explicit: word and idea, reason and language, were identical.[11]

So we see an ongoing philosophical trend that is becoming prevalent in the German-speaking world just as Kraus is embarking on his moral mission. The philosophical focus is shifting from Idea to Word, and thought is seen to be intertwined with language. Thanks to the influence of Kant, logic is seen as an essential ingredient to moral thought and because of the identification of thought and language, the logical analysis of language is becoming central to moral philosophy. Seen in this light, Kraus's insistence that evil could be parsed out of the German language makes much more sense. The Socratic method was aimed at critiquing moral ideas through the use of logic in order to morally enlighten the individual and thereby society. Kraus thought that purifying language would achieve the same results. Although it will need more amplification in what follows, Wittgenstein is of the same opinion.

A few examples from his work should help us understand Kraus's connection between purifying language and achieving a moral society. When he talks of purifying language Kraus included focusing on the elements of language, like proper grammar and syntax. Incorrect grammar, punctuation, etc., is an indication of sloppy thinking, and sloppy thinking, especially on important topics, just won't do—it sets us on the path to failure. But Kraus was also talking about what today we would call "spin": twisting language to mask the truth. Kraus saw this as a pernicious disease that infected the media of his time, and he thought it was primarily responsible for the worst that his times had to endure. For example, Kraus was convinced that the media's spinning of certain events assured the Nazis' rise to power. Kraus opposed Hitler and the Nazis from the start of their prominence in 1923 and just as forcefully opposed the media's tacit collaboration with the Nazis. In *Die Fackel* Kraus pointed out numerous examples of this collaboration. The press, probably out of fear of reprisals, would solemnly assure its readers that no Jews were being harmed in Germany while the Nazis were in power. The media referred to the burgeoning concentration camps as benevolent "protective custody" and forced labor and other tortures as beneficial exercise or a benign kind of office work. Kraus proclaimed loudly that this was nothing more than spin and that the journalists were thereby simply lying. Telling the simple truth would have gone a long way to averting a catastrophe.

Kraus's weapon was satire. He would cull from the newspapers examples of the media's spinning the events of the day and show how blatantly ridiculous it was when put into its proper context. Often the Nazis would arrest a Jewish businessman and send him to a concentration camp in order to confiscate his property. In the *Fackel* Kraus would print verbatim the description of this event given by the press e.g., "a temporary curtailment of liberty with an educational aim," "comparable to a boarding school." Kraus would point out that in many cases the person in "protective custody" would wind up dead amid rumors of beatings and torture. Despite bruises and broken bones the papers would report things like the cause of death was "primarily losing the will to live." Death from a fall from a three-story window was blamed on the carelessness of the prisoner who had the misfortune of losing consciousness near an open window.[12]

For Kraus this perversion of language had nothing but a detrimental effect on society. It's worse than simply telling a lie. It's taking something that should be seen as abhorrent and cloaking it in language that makes it appear acceptable. The result is not only a loss of integrity but also a devaluation of society. I think we can say that for Socrates you are what you think—you are a product of your ideas. For Kraus you are your language—you are defined by what you read and say. The façade the media so carefully constructed perverted the language and thereby the society. The façade becomes a part of our foundations and then becomes reality—society tolerates, becomes immune to, and then finally approves of the evils within it. It should be remembered that Hitler was voted into power. Considering the above ideas it may not seem so farfetched for Kraus to hold that purifying language by eliminating the spin would also eliminate evil. However, it should be noted that the Nazis proved to be immune to Kraus's satire—apparently Hitler's "Minister of Propaganda," Joseph Goebbels, owned a complete collection of *Die Fackel*.

So hopefully we can see how it is possible that a critique of language can be intended to produce a moral result. Kraus's idea is that by guarding against the tendency to twist language out of its natural habitat the truth can be protected and allowed to be seen. Wittgenstein was certainly a follower of Kraus and showed the same passion for precision in language in all of his work. When we examine the *Tractatus* in more detail, we will see how he worked to uncover the logical foundations of language and how this is related to ethics. We have seen that Wittgenstein shows in the *Investigations* how we can avoid philosophical error by restoring language to its original context. Certainly these ideas show the influence of Kraus. In what follows we will see Wittgenstein's other major influences making many of these same connections among logic, language, and morality. Finally we will see Wittgenstein making the same connections in the *Tractatus* and the *Investigations*.

A member of Kraus's circle who had an appreciable influence on Wittgenstein was the architect and designer Adolf Loos (1870–1933). Wittgenstein greatly admired Loos, certainly as an architect, but more so as a critic of contemporary culture. Loos and Wittgenstein actually met and apparently Loos was impressed with their intellectual similarities. We noted that after World War I Wittgenstein worked with Paul Engelmann on designing and building a house for Wittgenstein's sister Margaret. According to Engelmann, he ended up assisting Wittgenstein, who took control of the project. As we noted, the design of the house clearly follows Loos's ideas. Loos's architectural ideas certainly had an influence on Wittgenstein, but the most important connection between the two was philosophical. Kraus inspired Wittgenstein with his deep respect for the purity of language and the central importance of language in our lives. Kraus wanted to demolish his contemporaries that perverted language and thereby hid the truth. In the same way Loos searched for purity in architecture, arguing that culture was decaying because his contemporaries preferred facades and masks that hid the truth and prevented social progress. Loos argued that the positive effect on society gained by Kraus's purifying of language would be complemented by his own insistence on clarity and precision in architecture and design. Clearly we can see why these ideas would have had an impact on Wittgenstein, who thought that the problems of philosophy could be solved through clarity and precision in language.

As with Kraus, a few examples should help to clarify Loos's connection between precision in architecture and the moral improvement of society. Loos was considered the enfant terrible of Viennese culture, always at the forefront of the avant-garde. His architecture sharply contrasted with the ornate style of the era, which Loos despised and thought of as a waste. His buildings were stark and simple and were meant to be functional, precise, and logical. The construction of one of Loos's projects generally met with public outcry and scorn. For example, a building which today is known simply as Looshouse went up across from the entrance to the Imperial Palace in 1911, and Emperor Franz Joseph was so appalled by the edifice that he had the entrance closed—he refused to use it. For Loos, architecture had a moral purpose. One of Loos's most influential writings was an article titled "Ornament and Crime," which became something of a manifesto for modern architects, designers, and artists. Loos argued that culture can only flourish when ornamentation is removed from objects of everyday use. He points out that when we go to a museum and look at objects from the past we see, for example, intricately carved ornate furniture, jewel encrusted goblets of precious metals, elaborate tapestries, and so on. Why did these survive to the present day, whereas we hardly ever find a workbench, a kitchen table, or a footstool? For Loos the reason is that the ornate objects were never used—they were and still are regarded as art objects and this gives us a skewed picture of culture and value. The ornamental objects give us little clue regarding the life of the people of the time period, and so it's even a greater mistake to try to connect with the past by copying the ornamented style of the period. Loos saw this tendency as the major flaw with the architecture prevalent in Vienna during his time. Architects tried to give their work the appearance of a style from the past—Baroque, Renaissance, whatever—thinking they were preserving or reviving the glory of a past age and thereby enriching contemporary culture. Loos argued, as we saw above, that the ornament of the past probably had very little to do with how the people of the past actually lived and is unlikely indicative what they valued. For example, we might admire a lavishly ornamented goblet from the court of Charlemagne and build up a fairy-tale image of a time replete with chivalry, castles, knights in shining armor, and all the rest. But the reality was far different. The life of the average peasant—probably over 90 percent of the population—was, as Erasmus put it, "short, nasty, and brutish." There was no sanitation or plumbing. Famine, plague, pestilence, and disease were quite common. Medicine amounted to superstition, applying leeches, and of course surgery, probably performed by the local barber, without anesthesia. The average person would probably have been happy to find out that life expectancy was twenty-something—less for women thanks to childbirth. I think the ornamented goblet would likely have been of little interest for most people—unless of course it was filled with something fermented.

But beyond that the ornament of the past is certainly not expressive of contemporary culture—it is at best a façade that hides or even falsifies the way things really are. The façade then prevents the development of contemporary culture. Modern materials, technological innovations, and craftsmanship are being squandered, adding useless layers of ornament to buildings, furniture, etc., ornament that contributes nothing to the object. Loos saw this waste as immoral on two levels. Precious resources and labor were being poured into things that had little value—ornament detracted from the usefulness of an object. Workers had to spend many hours producing ornamented objects but could not be in proportion to their work. Further, the ornament masked the truth because it told a pretty but false story about contemporary life, which at the time in Vienna, as we have seen, was plagued with nearly every sort of social ill—problems that were being hidden, not dealt with. Finally, the focus on ornament did not let modern culture develop—the focus on ornament kept people in what Loos compared to a primitive state. Aiming to poke some fun at his contemporaries in "Ornament and Crime," Loos claims that the only groups that need to express themselves through ornament are primitive tribesmen, or criminals in prison. The "Papuan" decorates himself with tattoos and ornaments every object because a lack of artistic and technological advancement affords them nothing better to beautify their environment and express social status. The criminal, for Loos, is a degenerate who wants to be a social outcast. The contemporary fad for ornament, Loos is arguing, is equally a case of arrested development. Although they lived in the midst of great achievements in the arts and technology, Loos's contemporaries fared little better than a so-called primitive culture. Even after being exposed to the artistic genius of the likes of Mozart, Beethoven, and Wagner, the Viennese would use the cutting edge of modern methods and materials to slap a stale, anachronistic façade on a building and then have the temerity to call it art. Having visited America and seen early examples of skyscrapers, Loos was incredibly impressed at what modern technology and materials could produce. Modern machinery and materials such as formed cement, steel, and glass could create living and working space for hundreds of people in one corner of a city block and eliminate the overcrowding that plagued Vienna. By focusing on creating the simple yet practical and useful instead of wasteful, superficial ornament, scant money and resources could be put to far better use, helping to eliminate poverty and improve living conditions, particularly for the average worker.

Many complained that architecture without ornament was dull and generally ugly. Loos argued just the opposite. He believed that the materials he worked with—various stones, metals, and woods—had their own natural beauty that should be brought to the surface and enhanced rather than covered with ornament. An ornamented object has value only as long as the fashion for the style of ornament exists. Once it goes out of fashion it must be (wastefully) replaced. However a well-made, useful, unadorned object can be profitably used until it wears out—sometimes for generations. It has value because it is precisely what it is—not pretending to be something other. It has a natural beauty and value. Again, the connection between logic and value is clear. If you want to design glassware, for example, as Loos did, think about what it is supposed to do and design it solely for that purpose. Then simply make it out of glass—a material that is beautiful in its own right. Now you have something that won't go out of fashion and so can be used and enjoyed for many years—something of true value. You can of course have glassware that is much more elaborate and expensive, but will your drink therefore taste any better? Unless you are adding to a collection, then whatever status or similar benefit you acquired by owning the item will evaporate once the next trend hits. For Loos true value can be found in precision and practicality.

In what follows we will see how these ideas are very much a part of Wittgenstein's thinking in the *Tractatus*, and we will also see how they continue to inform Wittgenstein's thinking in the *Investigations*. From what we have already seen in our various discussions of the *Investigations*, we know how much emphasis Wittgenstein placed on meaning and context. Philosophical error often arises because we take words out of their ordinary context and place them in a context not their own or invent a context for them. The result is that we assume we have given meaning to a word but we have only succeeded in creating confusion. Recall Wittgenstein's discussion of the idea that all words function as names. Wittgenstein points out that if we examine how words function in their proper context we see that while some words function as names, in the vast majority of cases words are meaningful through the use we make of them. To see the meaning of a word we have to examine how it functions in the role it ordinarily has. So when we try to explain all cases of meaning through naming an object we often create various philosophical difficulties. For example, when we insist that the word *thought* must name an object and that object is not readily apparent, philosophers tend to invent something that will suffice—usually some sort of psychological apparatus that proves very elusive and often creates as many difficulties as it purports to solve—Descartes' "mind stuff" is a classic example. As we have seen, Wittgenstein wants to circumvent these philosophical problems by "unasking" the question. As we have seen, Wittgenstein wants to show us that if we rid ourselves of the notion that there must be an object corresponding to the word *thought* many of these difficulties disappear. Once the word *thought* is returned to its proper context we can cease travelling down fruitless dark alleys, and we can see how this allows and aids the possibility of truth.

Although Loos was talking primarily about architecture, his point that ornament is essentially out of context and therefore ultimately has a detrimental effect on society has much in common with what Wittgenstein says about meaning. For Wittgenstein philosophical error can be avoided, and thereby our thinking on a host of important issues can be improved by keeping words from straying outside their proper context. The final thinker we will look at that had a powerful influence on Wittgenstein is Otto Weininger. Weininger examines many of the same relationships between logic and morality from a psychological point of view.

Wittgenstein maintained a lifelong interest in the work of the Viennese psychologist Otto Weininger (1880–1903). Wittgenstein certainly knew of his work as a young student in Vienna and mentions him in notes as late as 1950—Wittgenstein died in 1951. It seems that many Wittgenstein scholars have difficulty in coming to terms with Wittgenstein's admiration for Weininger—probably because most modern readers would hardly share Wittgenstein's enthusiasm, to put it mildly. In fact, I think most modern readers would find Weininger's principle opus, *Sex and Character*, somewhat bizarre. But if we look closely we will find ideas in Weininger's work that have much in common with Loos and Kraus and so we can understand why he influenced Wittgenstein's thinking.

First the bizarre part. Along the way we should keep in mind that the bulk of Weininger's book was submitted as a doctoral dissertation at the University of Vienna, and it passed. We should also keep in mind that Weininger's work exists in a sort of "halfway house" between science and speculative philosophy. Weininger was not a clinical psychologist in the modern sense. He was familiar with the clinical science of his day (he sent a copy of his work to Freud, who belittled it), but his tendency was to make use of whatever contemporary science supported his hypotheses, regardless of whether that science was credible. Basically he would co-opt a scientific theory if he thought it supported his ideas, but he apparently did no lab work or research of his own to confirm or deny a theory. Naturally, when the proper experiments were carried out, some of the science he depended on turned out to be wrong. Apparently, in many cases, this fact did not dampen the enthusiasm of his supporters.

Weininger's stated aim was to answer the "woman question." He also wanted to answer the "Jewish question," which he thought had a lot in common with the "woman question." The question under investigation was the public status of both groups: should they, along with the already enfranchised male citizen, be allowed to fully participate in society—vote, hold office, enter professions, and so on. It may seem strange today, but at the time it was a hotly debated issue. Many thought women should be restricted to the "traditional roles" of daughter, wife, and mother, and women voting or serving as doctors, engineers, or lawyers was unthinkable. The situation was the same for Jews. Although by the end of the 1860s Jews had been granted full political rights—they could vote, live wherever and marry whomever they wished, and enter any professions—there were many, mostly conservative, middle- or lower-class Germans that opposed this liberation and argued that it was having a detrimental effect on society. Of course, this largely anti-Semitic response to the question of full participation in society by Jews would find its fullest expression in National Socialism.

Weininger answered both questions with a resounding *no*—neither women nor Jews should have a place in public life, and he believed science and sound reasoning supported his claims. Trading on an idea he apparently stole from Freud, Weininger argued that everyone was bisexual on the cellular level and that a person's sexuality was predetermined by cellular makeup.[13] No one exists as either purely masculine or feminine. "Man" and "Woman" are only ideal types that act as two extremes on a scale used to identify the character or personality of each individual. For Weininger, the pure Man, if he existed, would be the ideal human being—perhaps not physically, but certainly morally. It is only Man that is capable of memory and therefore logic, and so only Man can attain truth, identity, and character.[14] Since pure Woman is primarily sexual, being physically predetermined for reproduction, she relies on fleeting feelings and passions and therefore does not develop memory, and so is excluded from logic and identity and therefore also excluded from truth and character. So Woman is physically determined to be illogical and amoral and therefore should be kept at home out of harm's way. Again these pure types don't exist in reality—everyone is a mixture of both, and Weininger contended that certain groups or races were naturally closer to one pole or the other. The Aryan or pure German was, not surprisingly, closer to the male, the Jews were closer to Woman. Weininger argued that the Aryans should benevolently "protect" women and the more "feminine" races: Jews, Africans, Asians, and so on.[15] I don't think Weininger had concentration camps in mind when he wrote this, but the Nazis did see ideas like these as a justification for claims of racial superiority and the need to "protect" racial purity.

I did say Weininger's ideas would sound truly bizarre to us today, but at the time Weininger's book was hugely popular, going through many editions and translations, attracting the attention of not only Kraus and Wittgenstein but also the likes of James Joyce and August Strindberg.[16] While there is no doubt that Wittgenstein read and was influenced by Weininger's work, there is no indication that he ever accepted Weininger's misogynist, racist, or anti-Semitic theories, and in fact I would argue that Wittgenstein would hold that this part of a Weininger's thought rests on a fundamental mistake, a discussion we will return to later. But for now we want to realize that what Wittgenstein did take away from Weininger can be seen as part of pattern we have seen in Wittgenstein's other influences that we have been discussing: Kraus and Loos. The fundamental idea that we have traced back to Socrates and, closer to the period we are considering, to Kant is the connection between logic and morality. The rigorous application of logic to our moral thinking produces excellence of character and in fact excellence of society and culture. For Kant the logical test of the categorical imperative—act only on those principles that can be treated as laws of nature—tells us which of our principles are moral. If we determine that it is wrong to, e.g., lie, then it is never permissible to do so under any circumstances—there are no reasons or circumstances that permit me to lie to someone. This means that no one else can be used as means to suit my own ends, and so I must respect the freedom and autonomy of others. Kant argues that a true utopia, what he calls The Kingdom of Ends, would be the result of everyone using the categorical imperative as a guide for their actions because then no one would use anyone else as a means to his or her ends. Kraus has a similar approach to language. By rigorously pursuing the logical or grammatical standards of language we can remove the "spin" or the false ways of representing the world, which allows the truth to appear. Kraus argued that bringing purity to language would make it impossible to speak evil, thus bringing integrity to the language user and eliminating evil from the society. Kant argued that making the maxims that guide our actions arbitrary, that is dependent on particular circumstances or results, was the source of our failure to do what is right. Kraus took it one step further and argued that since language was fundamental to our thinking, especially our moral thinking, it was treating language in an arbitrary fashion that was the cause of all our moral problems. Loos dealt with culture and society in a similar fashion. By searching for the logical functionality of an object of everyday use, ornament is avoided. Rather than being mired in an anachronistic façade that masks and falsifies the times we live in, we are free to become a modern people, face our challenges, and hopefully solve them. We see that like Kraus, Loos sees logic and precision as servants of culture, truth, and morality.

I think one of the chief reasons that Wittgenstein was attracted to Weininger is that Weininger's thinking on the relationship of logic to morality has much in common with what Loos and Kraus say on the topic. The ideal Man for Weininger is capable of great achievements in science, culture, and morality because Man possesses memory. Through memory we piece together our various scientific discoveries into grander and grander theories, and through memory the art of the present builds on the art of the past. But also through memory we piece together the events and actions of our lives into a seamless whole and thus create and acknowledge an identity. The stronger or clearer our identity, our sense of self, the more our moral responsibility is increased because we own up to our past actions, the good and the bad, and claim them for our own. We realize that what we have done has created who we are and that in denying what we have done we are denying our very selves, basically lying to ourselves. Only this sense of self makes repentance possible. Only by acknowledging what we have done wrong can we then begin to make it right. Identity, then, is fundamental to morality.

Apparently Weininger wanted to show that there is an equivalence between logical and personal identity, and he wanted to show that the equivalence of logic and ethics is a result of this relationship. His argument is convoluted and relies on a mixture of science, philosophy, psychology, and logic, all of which probably add up to a very large mistake. However, it goes something like the following.

Generally classical logicians, following Aristotle, consider the identity relation, the statement that "A," whatever "A" is, equals itself $(A = A)$, along with the law of the excluded middle and the principle of noncontradiction (discussed earlier, p. 48), to be a fundamental principle in logical reasoning. Weininger regarded the identity relation as the basis for the distinction between truth and error, as expressing the essence or fundamental principle of truth.[17] For Weininger the statement that any "A" is exactly "A" and nothing else can be seen as stating the paradigm of a self-evident or axiomatic statement. Or we might say that any absolute or fundamental truth says in essence the same as "A = A"; that is, the situation cannot be thought of as otherwise to any degree. For example, a scientific law is supposed to be universal and necessary—always the same or invariant under any circumstances. Any mathematical equation expresses that same invariance or identity relation: 2 + 2 always and everywhere equals exactly four—no more, no less. The same can be said for the rules of logic: If A = B, and B = C, then A must equal C always and everywhere, no matter what the circumstances and no matter what A, B, and C happen to be. (Wittgenstein holds in the *Tractatus* that all the propositions of logic are tautologies—always true regardless of the circumstances.[18]) Truth is always something exact or precise—a true statement represents things exactly as they are. We may certainly debate whether Weininger is correct here, and as we will see Wittgenstein eventually parts company with Weininger on this issue, but hopefully this is sufficient to explain what Weininger means when he says the identity relation is fundamental to truth. It is also important to note that Weininger is in agreement with most logicians by holding that the identity relation is fundamental to logic.

Weininger goes on to argue that logic and ethics are identical and that error is a moral failing. In other words, making a mistake, for example in developing a scientific theory, is not simply an intellectual failure but a moral failure as well. Any error in judgment represents a lapse in personal integrity. Weininger states that "Logic and ethics are fundamentally the same, they are no more than a duty to oneself."[19] These ideas are certainly difficult, but in sum Weininger is arguing that each person has a moral duty to pursue and achieve the truth, but first and foremost we must achieve the truth about ourselves. If we want to discover the truths of science, math, or philosophy, we must first develop the personal integrity that truth within these lofty pursuits requires. Weininger argues that personal integrity, or, more generally, being a moral agent requires a clear sense of self. Only a person with a clear sense of self, which requires us to own up to past actions, can accept moral responsibility. In other words, only those people that clearly acknowledge their past actions as their own have accepted moral responsibility for those actions. It is that clear sense of self that grants moral responsibility and so is the key to personal integrity. As we noted above, Weininger holds that logic is the key to all truth and therefore it is the key to the truth about ourselves. Discovering the truth about ourselves grants us that unambiguous sense of self that is the key to personal integrity, and personal integrity is fundamental to the pursuit of truth in all other fields.

We have already seen that many thinkers would agree that logical thinking is necessary to morality, but clearly Weininger is taking it a step further by specifically equating the two: being logical and being ethical are the same. The key to this relationship, for Weininger, is the idea of identity. Many thinkers, including Wittgenstein, would criticize Weininger for falling into the error of psychologism (discussed above, p. 81); that is, confusing logic with psychology or epistemology. But clearly Weininger sees no distinction between numerical or logical identity and personal identity and in fact, personal identity is ultimately dependent on logical identity. The statement of logical identity—"A" exactly equals "A" and nothing else or "1" equals precisely "1" and no other number—is the fundamental expression of truth. For Weininger, a person would express a clear sense of his or her identity in the same way: "I am uniquely I." When individuals achieve this sense of self they have recognized that they are ultimately independent of all others and all other circumstances in the sense that they acknowledge and accept moral responsibility for their actions. As we have seen, we cannot achieve this personal identity without logic, and without this personal identity we cannot be moral. So it is the identity relationship that is axiomatic for logical truth, and logical truth is the key to achieving personal identity. It is this personal identity that is the key to morality. Hence being logical and being moral are essentially the same.

So for Weininger anyone who is illogical; that is, cannot or does not precisely distinguish between "A" and "not-A," what is the case and what is not the case, easily lies, equivocates, evades personal responsibility, breaks promises, and so on. Such a person would rather deflect moral responsibility than accept it and therefore is incapable of building a strong identity and achieving personal integrity. For example, I think Weininger would agree with Kraus that the journalist who calls a concentration camp "protective custody" is morally wrong for letting something other than logic guide his conclusions and failing to describe something exactly as it is. The euphemism of "protective custody" is completely ambiguous, and it therefore hovers around the truth, existing in the "gray area" between "A" and "not-A." The concentration camp is certainly custody but hardly protective of the prisoner. The journalist is not governed by the exact truth and instead trades on this ambiguity and succeeds in hiding the truth. Logically, "spin" should be seen for what is: a lie. So for Weininger here the moral fault is indistinguishable from a logical fault. Ultimately the continual rigorous application of logic produces a moral character—a character governed by truth. For Weininger, when rigorously applied over a lifetime, logic produces a moral identity in the individual. The identity that you put together from your actions, actions that you own up to, will be morally pure. Even a cursory glance at Wittgenstein's biography shows a strong resonance with this idea.

Overall, I think we can see that in these three thinkers, Kraus, Loos, and Weininger, we find this common thread of the connection, in one form or another, between logic and ethics. Kraus sees it in language; Loos puts the idea to work in a critique of art, architecture, and culture, and Weininger sees this connection as fundamental to our very nature. I think if we briefly examine the *Tractatus* we will see that Wittgenstein was thinking along the same lines. I want to argue Wittgenstein was still of this opinion when he composed the *Investigations*.

In the beginning of our study we examined some of the main ideas of the *Tractatus* as they related to Wittgenstein's critique of these ideas in the *Investigations*. But here I want to try to understand what Wittgenstein means when he says the point of the book is ethical. To that end we should take a look at the *Tractatus* as a whole. In detail the *Tractatus* is justly famous for being an imposing work. However, I think it is possible to see the point of the work if we stick to its scaffolding or skeletal structure. The *Tractatus* is composed of seven major propositions placed in order, each indicated by a number 1-7. Each proposition so numbered acts as a sort of chapter heading that is further explicated by propositions labeled with that number followed by a decimal. So the proposition numbered 1 represents a fundamental statement that is further developed in propositions 1.1, 1.11, 1.12 and so on until we come to major statement number 2. Then the process begins again until we get to proposition 7, which ends the book. Let us look at the major propositions in order.

1. The world is all that is the case.
2. What is the case—a fact—is the existence of states of affairs.
3. A logical picture of facts is a thought.
4. A thought is a proposition with sense.
5. A proposition is a truth function of elementary propositions.
6. The general form of a truth function is $[p,\xi,N(\xi)]$. This is the general form of a proposition.
7. What we cannot speak about we must pass over in silence.

Obviously to get a complete understanding of the text a great deal about these propositions and the subpropositions must be explained, but as we said earlier, this task would take us far afield. For our purposes we are only looking for the general aim of the book. From the last proposition we get the idea that Wittgenstein wants to limit what can be said. Beyond what can be said we must simply say nothing, and Wittgenstein wants to make it clear that if we try to say something other than what can be said then we cannot make any sense. But what is it that can be said? The first six propositions give us the answer. The world is composed of facts. To think logically or rationally about these facts means constructing propositions with sense. Clearly, Wittgenstein wants to equate thoughts with propositions with sense, and here we should recall Kraus's idea that we think in a language. Thus it follows that nonsensical propositions are those propositions that do not represent any facts and therefore would not qualify as thoughts. But how do we recognize propositions with sense? Any proposition, and thus a proposition with sense, is a "truth function" of elementary propositions. To understand what this means we first start with the idea that an elementary proposition asserts the existence of states of affairs or facts. If we remember our discussion at the beginning of our study, this means the elementary propositions must refer to objects—the ultimate constituents of the world. If there are no objects to which the elementary propositions refer, then the elementary propositions would only have the appearance of sense. A proposition is logically constructed out of elementary propositions using the formula in proposition 6. The formula in proposition 6 is a reduction of all the operations of symbolic logic—"and," "or," "not," "implies," etc.—to one operation (sometimes called the Sheffer stroke). Again, the details of how that works need not concern us here. The important point is that a proposition with sense is a proposition that is logically constructed out of properly formulated or meaningful elementary propositions.

Thus what can be said has two essential components—logic and states of affairs or facts. Outside of this we are left nonsense, and our response to any question about what lies beyond the bounds of sense can only be silence.

Now what would qualify as something beyond the bounds of sense, or what Wittgenstein would call nonsense, and what is the point of staying silent about it? If we define nonsense as something outside the bounds of logic and the facts of nature, it is difficult to see what's so bad about it. A world without nonsense would be pretty boring indeed—we would have to throw out most if not all children's books, fantasy, science fiction, just about every movie ever made, Monty Python, the Marx Brothers, and most, if not all, of modern art and literature.

But if we just look at the seven propositions above, they are not so much about excluding nonsense as they are about the importance, method, and difficulty of making sense. Making sense is a challenge requiring the utmost care in the formulation of our propositions, which requires the utmost in logical perspicuity and the precise formulation of meaningful elementary propositions. Clearly this is no easy task. Making sense is a dedicated effort at finding truth and perfection, and if we remember that for Wittgenstein a thought is a proposition with sense, then this means this effort is aimed at the complete clarity of thought. It is here where we see the intersection of logic and ethics in the *Tractatus* and the influence of Kraus, Loos, and Weininger on Wittgenstein. Thought is not something abstract and impersonal but the thought of an individual. Lack of clarity in thought is lack of clarity for *someone*. By putting your propositions in order you are putting your thoughts in order, which means putting your facts in order, which means putting your world in order—with the end result being putting yourself in order. Making sense is not a mere philosophical exercise, and I don't think the *Tractatus* is just a philosophical treatise on abstract theoretical issues. Rather, as with Kraus, Loos, and Weininger, Wittgenstein is showing us that being logical is a moral duty to oneself.

However, we must be clear that Wittgenstein is not saying the "meaning of life" or questions of morality can be solved the way a scientific problem can be solved. Wittgenstein writes that "The sense of the world must lie outside the world."[20] Once we have said all that makes sense, stated all the facts, the problems of life are untouched.[21] For Wittgenstein, our philosophical questions are not factual questions. It may seem that this idea runs counter to much of the philosophical tradition which would equate philosophical truths and facts. For example, when Aristotle or Descartes offer proofs for the existence of God, they are certainly arguing that God's existence is just as factual as any scientific law or observation. However, when Wittgenstein is talking about the "meaning of life" or "the problems of life," he is focusing more on what we would identify as moral issues. ("It is clear, however, that ethics has nothing to do with punishment and reward in the usual sense of the terms."[22] "The world of the happy man is a different one from that of the unhappy man." [23] "Death is not an event in life: we do not live to experience death. . . . eternal life belongs to those who live in the present."[24] "[T]here is no guarantee of the temporal immortality of the human soul . . . "[25]) Clearly for Wittgenstein, when it comes to these issues we are not dealing with what he calls facts: the relationships between objects, and so these issues cannot be settled by factual methods such as experiments, analysis, or gathering evidence. Moral problems are not solved by figuring out what is going on in the world or what is the case. Moral problems are about how we relate to what is going on—what we believe, do, or say about what is the case. Morality is about how we see the facts and what they mean to us, and no fact can ever force a particular point of view or course of action. Although, say, a winter snowstorm is a fact, the skier may happily head to the slopes while the miserable golfer, dreaming of spring, rolls meaningless putts across his carpet. On a more serious note, let's say that we agree global warming is a fact. Certainly some people may be very concerned about the hazard this presents to the environment and so try to do all they can to reverse this trend by conserving energy, recycling, and so on. Some people, for a variety of reasons, may do little or only what they are required, and, unfortunately, there are those that may not care and do nothing at all. We can certainly recount a litany of facts regarding our moral or social problems: for example, we see reports daily on the numbers and whereabouts of the poor, starving, and homeless all over the world. But what is most important is not included in the facts; that is, what the facts mean to us and how we respond to the facts. Wittgenstein wants us to understand that the moral problem does not hinge on what is the case in the world, but how we see the world.

So the first step in attempting to solve our moral problems is making the above distinction: between those statements that are statements of facts and those statements that are not. We remember that in the *Tractatus* Wittgenstein equates statements of fact with statements or propositions with sense, while all other propositions are relegated to nonsense. We saw that one of Wittgenstein's goals was to show just how difficult making this distinction is, and now I hope we see how important this distinction is because it allows us to outline and highlight the sphere of the moral. That is, when we make the distinction between sense and nonsense with regard to particular statements, we are able to distinguish between which language counts as moral and which counts as factual. In other words, when we distinguish between sense and nonsense we can tell the difference between what can be solved by factual or scientific means and what cannot. So for example, let's say we have discovered the technology to solve the global warming crisis—that is a factual or scientific issue. However, whether we put that technology into practice is not solved factually or scientifically, but rather socially, politically, and morally.

Most likely, very few thinkers would object to what Wittgenstein has said so far. Ethics has always involved distinguishing between what is or what can be done and what ought to be done. What makes Wittgenstein different is that he wants to examine the typical philosophical response to our moral questions and show how that response is inadequate. In other words, a philosopher, we would assume, wants to offer a moral theory as a solution to our moral dilemmas, and there have been many such theories: the ethics of virtue, natural law, utilitarianism, deontology, and so on. Of course, with regard to any particular theory the point might be debatable, but Wittgenstein wants to say that they all suffer from a major flaw: they are trying to make sense out of nonsense. In more Wittgensteinian terms, they are trying to say the unsayable.

Again, most philosophical statements do not involve facts; only statements of facts have sense. As we have noted (p. 5 above) Wittgenstein states that the correct method in philosophy is that whenever anyone wanted to say anything other than a proposition of natural science, perhaps something metaphysical, then we should show the person that their words had no meaning.[26] Clearly most philosophical statements would, given these stipulations, qualify as nonsense, and certainly this would apply to most philosophical theories that deal with ethics. We can see that any of those theories that depend on things like Plato's "form of the good," the soul, the existence of God, and so on, would be considered nonsense. But in general, Wittgenstein wants to say, the whole enterprise is doomed from the start. The subject matter of ethics, as we have seen, is not about the facts, but about how we view the facts. So the subject matter of ethics is always going to be nonsense, for Wittgenstein. It is important to note that Wittgenstein does not exempt his own work when it comes to critiquing the legitimacy of a philosophical answer to our problems. In the next to last remark of the *Tractatus*, Wittgenstein says:

> My propositions serve as elucidations in the following way: anyone who understands me eventually recognizes them as nonsensical, when he has used them—as steps—to climb up beyond them. (He must, so to speak, throw away the ladder after he has climbed up it.)
>
> He must transcend these propositions, and then he will see the world aright.[27]

This last sentence is very important and represents a good summary of what we have been saying so far. The *Tractatus* shows us the difficult path we must take in order to make sense, in order to distinguish sense from nonsense. We must not only master the method for doing so but also then apply that method to particular cases—in other words, understand the circumstances in which we are making sense and those in which we are not. Clearly, for Wittgenstein, once we have reached this point we are only at the beginning. It is only when we get beyond the philosophizing, when we have successfully transcended it, that we can achieve our goal of *seeing the world aright*. Notice that Wittgenstein is not saying that the philosophical enterprise, as Wittgenstein has framed it, has no point; rather, it is not the end point. We must work through our difficulties, rigorously separating sense from nonsense so that we will then see things correctly.

Thus for Wittgenstein, ethics, or the question of value, the meaning of life, etc., is not about something factual or empirical, and so we cannot form meaningful propositions regarding these matters. Hence most writing on ethics would have to be classified as nonsense. The ethical life is not found in what you can say but is the result of distinguishing sense from nonsense—seeing the truth—seeing what is. Language disguises its logic, but through applying a rigorous symbolism to language that logic can be shown, and once we have this in hand distinguishing sense from nonsense becomes possible. Once you clear away the garbage it is possible for the truth to manifest itself and doing what is right now becomes clearer.

From this perspective the *Tractatus* is part of the philosophical trend that we have seen exemplified in Kraus, Loos, and Weininger. The focus is different for each thinker, language and media for Kraus, architecture for Loos, and psychology for Weininger, but the message is the same: logic is the gateway to morality. Wittgenstein, looking at the foundations of language and therefore thought, agrees. By clearing away the nonsense, the application of logic to our language makes truth and therefore ethics possible.

Admittedly, for a book on the *Investigations* we have come a long way through the *Tractatus*. But I wanted to explain these thematic elements and show how important they were to Wittgenstein and how much they were a part of the fabric of his long-term philosophical thinking. It is worth remembering that Wittgenstein was still commenting on Kraus three years before he died and Weininger in his last year.[28] I want to show now that although some elements of the *Tractatus* are criticized in the *Investigations*, the basic philosophical project remains the same. In the *Investigations* Wittgenstein is certainly trying to clear away particular philosophical difficulties, but there is more than that at stake. He still holds that bringing logical clarity to language ultimately brings moral clarity. Fixing bad philosophizing by bringing logical purity to our use of language has the same result that was announced at the end of the *Tractatus*: seeing the world aright.

Wittgenstein's first task was to clear up certain problems with the picture of language in the *Tractatus*. Besides abandoning the ontol-

WHAT DOES IT ALL MEAN?   179

ogy of logical atomism, the chief difference between the two works is that Wittgenstein no longer sees the notation of symbolic logic as providing the necessary perspicuity for revealing the logic of language. Instead, Wittgenstein elaborates a key insight of the *Tractatus*—our language is in logical order as it is.[29] What is needed to clarify language is to understand the use we make of it. (It is interesting that this too is an insight of the *Tractatus*.)[30] In the *Investigations*, Wittgenstein shows that ordinary grammar is the logic of language and once we see that the meaning of a word is the use we make of it, we see that any misunderstandings of the logic of language will reveal themselves when we try to apply them—try to make them work in the everyday circumstances of our lives. So in the *Investigations*, Wittgenstein still focuses on achieving logical clarity in language, but he no longer associates clarity with the extreme precision of symbolic logic. As he notes in the *Investigations*, the meaning of the request, "stand roughly here," is perfectly clear but hardly exact.[31]

Certainly in this detail Wittgenstein parts company not only with the *Tractatus* but also with some of his earlier influences, particularly Weininger. Weininger wanted to equate truth and ultimately morality with the extreme precision dictated by the logical law of identity: A = A. This type of thinking led him to a binary view of truth and morality: the good—Man– existed at one pole, while the bad—Woman—existed at the other. So truth and goodness can only be achieved by focusing on the "good" end of the spectrum and ruthlessly disregarding all the rest. Clearly in the *Investigations* Wittgenstein shows that this way of thinking about logic is mistaken, and so I would argue it follows that Wittgenstein came to the conclusion that aspects of Weininger's approach to truth and morality is equally mistaken. In many passages in the *Investigations*, Wittgenstein shows that he has advanced beyond the idea in the *Tractatus* that logic is limited to the precision dictated by the strict true/false either/or of symbolic logic, and that trying to force our thinking into this mold is a source of error. So, for example, at PI 352 Wittgenstein examines the case of someone considering the expansion of π. Invoking the law of the excluded middle, someone might claim that the series 777 must occur or must not occur in the expansion of π—there is no third possibility. In other words, as a Platonist might insist, what is contained in the expansion of π is already predetermined; we just don't know the particulars. This might appear to be trivially true at first, but Wittgenstein warns us that mathematically speaking so far we only have a picture, an idea, that something must be the case, which seems to be logically supported. It seems since there are only two choices—the three sevens are there or they are not—then the law of the excluded middle is telling us one case or the other MUST be true. Unfortunately, though, Wittgenstein argues that we have allowed a logical picture to dominate our thinking, tricking us into making a false assumption. We have made a mathematical statement, but we have no mathematical proof of our proposition, and so what appears to have been a case of knowing something for certain turns out to be of no use at all. Logic in this case has not told us much of anything here in the way that the statement "either it is raining or it is not" gives us no information about the weather. Since the decimal representation of π expands infinitely and does not repeat, the only way to settle the proposition would be empirically—by physically examining the expansion of π and seeing whether this sequence occurs. The point, for Wittgenstein, is that a picture forced itself on us driven by the assumption that applying a type of logical precision—either/or reasoning in this case—was sufficient to tell us what must be the case. We believe logic has provided us with a method for achieving certainty, for saying something factual, but actually no such thing has occurred. What is missing is the application of the picture—what was needed here was a mathematical proof of a mathematical proposition.

Wittgenstein goes on to say that we make many similar false assumptions about a host of philosophical issues, particularly mental states. For example, let's say someone proposes the theory that "hope" is a particular feeling and goes on to describe a sensation, perhaps some sort of tingling, they have when they hope something is the case. Now of course, as we have seen, Wittgenstein would argue that it would be a mistake to think that any particular sensation someone might have can suffice for the meaning of *hope*. In addition, however, our present discussion shows that it is useless for our fictional theorist to argue that logic dictates it must be one way or the other. "Either people experience this sensation as a feeling of hope or they do not—at least we have identified what we are looking for." In other words, our theorist believes logic has assured him that he is on a legitimate psychological quest. However, logic has done no such thing. Our "scientist" simply started with an incorrect assumption and used a logical idea to create a picture of a psychological investigation—a picture of clarity that does not exist. What looks like a sure path to the truth is simply a façade. We can see that Weininger has made a similar error by making a logical structure a precondition for the truth, trying to make reality conform to logic. Weininger begins with the assumption that all truth is logical, based on the law of identity, and constructs a psychological theory to fit this assumption. Logic appears to be the immutable scaffolding that supports all truth, and the Wittgenstein of the *Tractatus* agreed with this idea.[32] However, in the *Investigations* Wittgenstein shows that truth does indeed come from the logical clarity of language, but this is not a preordained logical structure or even derived from a set of logical laws. Rather, we must look and see how language is employed, to see its logic and test our ideas against that actual employment—not to try to make our language conform to a preconceived notion.

Despite this important difference with the *Tractatus* and the ideas that influenced it, I would argue that Wittgenstein still holds in the *Investigations* that clarity of language equates to moral clarity. That is, by engaging in the difficult work of clarifying our language, ridding ourselves of nonsense, bad philosophy in particular, we can also rid ourselves of many of the ethical problems that plague us. The misuse of language often hides many problems, and the bad philosophizing often makes us think we have solved problems that we haven't, or worse, sends us off on wild goose chases, looking for solutions down a road that leads nowhere.

In the *Investigations* Wittgenstein is still concerned with the moral problems that plague our society, but as with the *Tractatus* it takes a little analysis to uncover this theme. As we noted above (p. 98), Wittgenstein writes about the "darkness of this time" in the preface to the *Investigations*. Wittgenstein, of course, could have had many reasons for this allusion, some very personal. When we looked at Wittgenstein's biography we saw that the Vienna of Wittgenstein's youth was plagued with many social problems: anti-Semitism, racism, housing shortages, an impoverished lower class, and an epidemic of suicide among the young that claimed three of Wittgenstein's brothers, to name a few. In addition, Wittgenstein served in World War I, actually seeing combat and ending up as a prisoner of war. By all accounts WWI was a tragedy of epic proportions. Modern warfare saw the introduction of modern technology: machine guns, artillery, aerial bombings and combat, and chemical weapons, which resulted in over ten million killed and twenty million wounded, with seven million being permanently disabled. WWI had its share of genocide, civilian casualties, mistreatment of POWs, and the like. Afterwards, the map of Europe was redrawn with the previously vast Austro-Hungarian Empire reduced to the small state of Austria. The sanctions imposed on the vanquished Central Powers caused runaway inflation and great economic hardships. Obviously many people, Wittgenstein included, lost family and dear friends during the war. It is also the case that the aftermath of WWI was one of the reasons the Nazi movement had such success in Germany and Austria. The Nazis were able to fan the flames of anti-Semitism by blaming the Jews, many of whom were vocal pacifists, for Germany's defeat in WWI, and claiming that Jews with "international" business connections were profiting from the reparations that Germany had to pay. After Hitler was elected Chancellor of Germany in 1933 the state began seizing the property of Jews and other political enemies and then deporting them to concentration camps for torture and forced labor. By 1942 many of the concentration camps became death camps, built for the purpose of exterminating the Jews and other so-called "undesirable races." Only those with wealth, connections, or some sort of notoriety could hope to escape. After the unification of Austria and Germany in 1938, Wittgenstein's family, being of Jewish descent, were classified as Jews under the Nuremberg laws and faced the possibility of the concentration camps. Wittgenstein's surviving brother Paul fled to Switzerland, while two of his sisters were arrested trying to flee using forged passports. Eventually, after a long series of negotiations in which Wittgenstein took part and the payment of what amounts to a huge bribe, the Wittgenstein's were reclassified as Aryans and allowed to remain in Vienna. Wittgenstein wanted no part of Nazi Germany. After Austria became part of Germany, he renounced his German citizenship and became a British subject.[33]

Clearly Wittgenstein had more than a passing acquaintance with the "darkness of this time." However, the darkness Wittgenstein speaks of should, of course, be seen in philosophical, not just personal, terms. There is ample evidence Wittgenstein saw the moral crises alluded to above as symptomatic of a general intellectual malaise in the society at large, and just as the *Tractatus* can be seen as part of a philosophical trend that uses the precision of logic to address moral problems, the *Investigations* likewise is intended to dispel intellectual darkness as an antidote to the moral darkness of the age.

To begin to see that this is so we should note that Wittgenstein writes in his preface of the poverty of his work and the unlikely event that it will cause any enlightenment. Here Wittgenstein might be taken as merely attributing the difficulties of the *Investigations* to his inadequacies as a writer and a thinker. However, there is also a sense here that the audience is at least partly to blame. Wittgenstein writes that one of the chief reasons for publishing the *Investigations* is that even his own students had failed to understand him and, in his words, "mangled" his work. Time and again in his letters and in the recollections of friends and students, Wittgenstein complains about the general callousness, usually coupled with a lack of intellectual insight, of people in modern times. He was generally depressed by the superficiality and lack of intellectual rigor, particularly in those that should know better. Wittgenstein once remarked that people would be better served intellectually by reading detective magazines instead of *Mind*, the philosophy journal of Cambridge. One of his students, Norman Malcolm, writes:

> Most commonly his thoughts were somber. He was constantly depressed, I think, by the impossibility of arriving at understanding in philosophy. But he was worried perhaps even more deeply by the stupidity and heartlessness that present themselves daily in the world in forms that command respect. Of the things that came to his attention in the normal passage of events hardly any gave him pleasure and many produced in him an emotion that was not far from grief. Often as we walked together he would stop and exclaim "Oh, my God!" looking at me almost piteously, as if imploring a divine intervention in human events.[34]

In this context it is important to recall (see above, p. 34) Wittgenstein lists Oswald Spengler as a major influence. In his *The Decline of the West*, Spengler identified the late-nineteenth and early twentieth centuries as a period of what he calls "Civilization"; that is, the twilight of a "Culture." "Civilization" is controlled by money, industry, and the media, with the populace described as soulless, materialistic masses that have lost interest in the strength and spirit of the ideas that created their culture. The end result will be a period of social upheaval and wars waged by the new "Caesars" who seek the power to control the earth, leaving the aforementioned masses in a primitive state, uncomprehending, uncaring, and compliant.[35] This picture is certainly depressing and pessimistic, but we saw that Wittgenstein (and many others) in the first half of the twentieth century had ample personal confirmation of Spengler's predictions for the West. It is certainly likely that Wittgenstein saw his personal experiences from the horrors of war to the stupidity and heartlessness he saw around him as evidence of the truth of Spengler's beliefs. In any case we can certainly see sufficient reason for Wittgenstein to describe his times as dark, and this fact was certainly on his mind as he composed the *Investigations*.

No doubt Wittgenstein's personal outlook on this was pessimistic, but can we read the *Investigations* as Wittgenstein's attempt to address these issues? If we look at the topics Wittgenstein continually circles in the *Investigations*, it becomes evident that he has become concerned with specific ideas and theories regarding human nature. He is continually discussing thinking, hoping, feeling, pain, sensation, and of course that most human of institutions: language and its proper understanding in a social context. Almost all of part II is dedicated to psychological theories. In examining Wittgenstein's treatment of these issues we have seen him constantly reminding us that our thirst for generality and our craving for scientific explanation make us susceptible to misleading pictures about human nature—particularly with regard to human psychology. Using a number of examples (see the discussion of reading p. 66ff. above), Wittgenstein shows that when we try to understand the psychological we often want to explain it in concrete language, usually as some sort of process, and in our times psychologists and philosophers have adopted empirical, mechanical, and behaviorist—to name a few—models of the human mind and the human person, almost without question. We have seen that Wittgenstein was familiar with a number of thinkers that held these views. It is also the case that many of these same thinkers tried to find physical, mechanical, or scientific explanations for art, culture, attraction, and emotion. Freud was criticized by Kraus and others for trying to explain artistic genius in terms of a neurosis. Weininger tied to prove that attraction, ger der, and character were in part determined on a cellular level. William James thought that emotion was a reaction to an internal physical event. In other words, he thought, for example, we are sorry because we cry. That is, the mental state of feeling sorry first requires the physical experience of crying, or we feel afraid because we are first trembling after a car accident.[36] The upshot is that many of those characteristics that mark our humanity are in this manner reduced to mathematical formulas, physical states, neurochemistry, and the like. Putting scientific issues aside for the moment, we can see that explaining Leonardo da Vinci's masterpieces as the result of a mental illness, or great love as the product of cellular attraction, certainly decreases the value of said virtue. If the effect of these ideas is a trivializing of what is most human about us, it should not surprise us when a lack of regard for humanity follows right behind. We noted that Wittgenstein had plenty of evidence of this lack of humanity.

The important point is that our language shows what we think, what we value, and where we stand. Our concepts or things we say about human nature have moral consequences. Clearly, Wittgenstein is not offering us a theory of human nature in the *Investigations*. But he is in many instances taking great pains to try to show where our theorizing has provided us with detrimental views of what it means to be human. For example, Wittgenstein spends a great deal of time examining the idea that our psychological vocabulary refers to some sort of inner mental state or activity. As we noted, his "private language argument," discussed above on p. 87ff., and the "beetle in the box" discussion, p. 95 above, show that when we try to construe language as indicating some inner process then language cannot be meaningful. Therefore, we fail on two fronts. We don't have a working apparatus to accurately describe our psychology. And the insistence that we have a unique or privileged access to our own mental states essentially cuts us off from everyone else. In other words, the idea that words about "inner" states, like feelings, have meaning through referring to what is going on in the individual can make it seem as if only each individual can be sure of his or her own mental states. This raises concerns about "other minds" and creates skepticism about the so-called "inner states" of others. As we mentioned above (p. 98), the moral consequences of this position might not be obvious, but I think once we accept the notion that we can be sure only of our own minds and feelings and that the inner life of others is at least questionable, then likely it becomes much easier to disregard the others. It is difficult to see how we can maintain any empathy with other people when our language continually reinforces the notion that we may never know what they are truly thinking or feeling. I think from here it is a small step to the idea that "I know I have all the rights to which a person is entitled because I know I have thoughts, feelings, beliefs, and the like, but I'm not quite so sure about anyone else" or "I can verify that I am human but those others may be a different story." Certainly much of what we saw as the darkness of Wittgenstein's time resulted from what amounts to the denial of humanity to arbitrarily designated members of the society. One of the things Wittgenstein was working to prevent, as was Kraus, is having these concepts take up permanent residence in our language, which certainly could have a detrimental effect on our culture. Showing the public or social nature of our psychological language attempts to sidestep the solipsistic and skeptical tendencies engendered by the belief that our language is private, and so we hopefully avoid the moral consequences outlined above. In general, in the *Investigations* as in the *Tractatus*, Wittgenstein wants to show us how to remove the nonsense from our language so that we can see who we really are and put our world in order. Again, this is a demanding search for truth and perfection, the result of which is an ethical life.

NOTES

1. PI 109.
2. Quoted in Allan Janik and Stephen Toulmin, *Wittgenstein's Vienna*, 192.

3. Wittgenstein, *Culture and Value*, 19e.
4. Cf. Bernard Leitner, *The Wittgenstein House*, 25.
5. Karl Kraus, *Half-Truths & One-and-a-Half Truths*, ed. and trans. Harry Zohn (Chicago: University of Chicago Press, 1990), 64.
6. TLP 4.
7. Karl Kraus, *Half-Truths*, 49.
8. Cf. Erich Heller, *The Disinherited Mind* (New York: Harcourt, 1975), 235-260, and Karl Kraus, *No Compromise: Selected Writings of Karl Kraus*, ed. Frederick Ungar (New York: Frederick Ungar Publishing, 1977), 9.
9. Immanuel Kant, *Groundwork of the Metaphysics of Morals*, ed. Mary Gregor (Cambridge: Cambridge University Press, 1997), 25ff.
10. Kant, *Groundwork*, 47.
11. Cf. Janik and Toulmin, *Wittgenstein's Vienna*, 120ff.
12. Karl Kraus, *In These Great Times: A Karl Kraus Reader*, ed. Harry Zohn (Chicago: University of Chicago Press, 1990), 105ff.
13. Chandak Sengoopta, *Otto Weininger: Sex, Science, and Self in Imperial Vienna* (Chicago: University of Chicago Press, 2000), 15, 138-9.
14. Otto Weininger, *Sex and Character* (New York: Howard Fertig, 2003), 142-152.
15. Otto Weininger, *Sex and Character*, 338ff.
16. Sengoopta, *Otto Weininger*, 139ff.
17. Otto Weininger, *Sex and Character*, 155ff.; cf. Sengoopta, *Otto Weininger*, 54-61.
18. TLP 6.1—6.111.
19. Otto Weininger, *Sex and Character*, 159.
20. TLP 6.41.
21. TLP 6.52.
22. TLP 6.422.
23. TLP 6.43.
24. TLP 6.4311.
25. TLP 6.4312.
26. TLP 6.53.
27. TLP 6.54.
28. Wittgenstein, *Culture and Value*, 65, 84.
29. TLP 5.5563.
30. TLP 3.328.
31. PI 88.
32. TLP 4.023, 5.511, 6.124
33. Ray Monk, *Ludwig Wittgenstein*, 389ff.
34. Norman Malcolm, *Ludwig Wittgenstein: A Memoir*, 29-30.
35. Cf. Erich Heller, *The Disinherited Mind*, 182-3.
36. William James, *The Principles of Psychology*, vol. 2 (New York: Dover Publications, 1950), 449ff.

Selected Bibliography

Besides the books found in the endnotes, the following works will help the beginner delve deeper into Wittgenstein's thought.

Baker, G. P. and Hacker, P. M. S. *Skepticism, Rules, and Private Language*. Oxford: Basil Blackwell, 1984.

Hacker, P. M. S. *Insight and Illusion*. Oxford University Press, 1972.

————. *Wittgenstein: Connections and Controversies*. Oxford: Clarendon Press, 2001.

Kripke, Saul A. *Wittgenstein on Rules and Private Language*. Harvard University Press, 1982.

Malcolm, Norman. *Wittgenstein: Nothing Is Hidden*. Oxford: Basil Blackwell, 1986.

————. *Wittgenstein: A Religious Point of View?* edited by Peter Winch. Ithaca: Cornell University Press, 1994.

Pears, David. *The False Prison, Vol. II*. Oxford University Press, 1988.

Wittgenstein, Ludwig. *Blue and Brown Books*. New York: Harper, 1965.

————. *On Certainty*. Edited by G. E. M Anscombe and G. H. von Wright, translated by Denis Paul and G. E. M Anscombe. New York: Harper Torchbooks, 1972.

————. *Wittgenstein's Lectures on the Foundations of Mathematics*. Edited by Cora Diamond. Ithaca: Cornell University Press, 1976.

————. *Philosophical Grammar*. Edited by Rush Rhees, translated by Anthony Kenny. Berkeley: University of California Press, 1978.

————. *Notebooks 1914-1916*. Edited by G. H. von Wright and G. E. M Anscombe, translated by G. E. M Anscombe. University of Chicago Press, 1979.

————. *Wittgenstein's Lectures: Cambridge, 1932-1935*. Edited by Alice Ambrose. University of Chicago Press, 1979.

————. *Zettel*. Edited by G. H. von Wright and G. E. M Anscombe, translated by G. E. M. Anscombe. Oxford: Basil Blackwell, 1981.

———. *Wittgenstein's Lectures: Cambridge, 1930-1932.* edited by John King and Desmond Lee. University of Chicago Press, 1982.

———. *Remarks on the Philosophy of Psychology, Vol. I and II.* Edited by G. E. M Anscombe and G. H. von Wright, translated by G. E. M. Anscombe. University of Chicago Press, 1982.

———. *Last Writings on the Philosophy of Psychology, Vol. I.* Edited by G. H. von Wright and Heikki Nyman, translated by C. G. Luckhardt and Maximilian A. E. Aue. University of Chicago Press, 1982.

———. *Last Writings on the Philosophy of Psychology, Vol. I.* Edited by G. H. von Wright and Heikki Nyman, translated by C. G. Luckhardt and Maximilian A. E. Aue. Oxford: Blackwell, 1992.

———. *Philosophical Occasions 1912–1951.* Edited by James Klagge and Alfred Nordmann. Indianapolis: Hackett Publishing Co., 1993.

Index

About the Author

John Ross teaches in the liberal studies program at New York University. He lives in upstate New York with his wife, Nina, and their twins, Ian and Larissa.

Printed in Great Britain
by Amazon

48907872R00122